THE
COSMOGONICAL
CIPHER

The Function of Time, Myth, & Cosmic Harmony
on the Human Journey

MICHAEL E. CLEGG

The Cosmogonical Cipher: The Function of Time, Myth, and Cosmic Harmony on the Human Journey

Copyright © 2017 Michael E. Clegg

Myth, Logos, Time, History, Quantum Theory, Matrix, Duality, Cosmology

ISBN: 153983719X
ISBN-13:978-1539837190

ACKNOWLEDGMENTS

This book is dedicated to Beth, my wife of 36 years. Thank you for encouraging me and giving me the time and the push to complete it.

And to Tori Clegg for her editing assistance.

To my family who I hope will find a renewing and refreshing concept of our mystical, magical, and mysterious God.

Thank You …

Michael Clegg

CONTENTS

PREFACE

The Cosmogonical Cipher developed after several conferences that implanted seemingly antithetical concepts to current religious viewpoints. These pillars which appeared to uphold traditional faith were lacking cohesion with other principles. A cipher is a key or an algorithm for either encryption or decryption and involves a repeating process that always derives the same conclusion time and time again. If it fails, then entire aspects of the decryption will be missed.

Cipher, whose etymological meaning is zero, later came to mean the key to a message with the intent of making the message known, rather than locked away for all time. It was not hidden to prevent decryption but for the intent of discovering the message, and yet not the message itself but the journey of discovery.

This book restructures concepts that once delegitimized God. In searching through language and etymology, one finds a reformatting of divergent concepts. From this search, an amazing, mystical, and magical God emerges in shared relationship and union. A God who explains science rather than a God science cannot define. And finally, a God beautifully and perichoretically involved with the cosmos on all levels—from the mountains and oceans to the atom of light.

THE INCONGRUITY OF MYTH, HISTORY, LAW, & TIME

Incongruity

I ncongruity reflects the idea that something does not fit current preconceived notions. For example, if you saw your pastor in the local liquor store which is considered inconsistent with current religious concepts of the office; that is incongruent. Another example might be a very wealthy woman driving a Honda Civic instead of a Mercedes; that does not fit with her stature. While neither is wrong, both stray from preconceived norms of acceptable behavior resulting in judgment.

In Latin, it means not meeting together. Other synonyms include disparity, incompatibility, inharmonious, and discordant. Incongruence is a term I have applied to the lack of interaction of myth, history, law, and time which does not synchronize into a harmonious whole. Duality has caused an invisible split between each parameter and to find or restore unity one must deconstruct what religion has entombed around each of them.

Myth, history, law, and time do not say the same thing. They are not in agreement in their current conceived ideologies. History seems inconsistent with myth in that myth insists we believe outside of what history has declared as truth because our Western mind expects the myth to be literal. We tend to bind spiritual occurrences by locking them in time nullifying their significance. We, recognize biblical laws inconsistent with a benevolent Creator while we define verses such as Deuteronomy 25:11 which describes a woman grabbing the genitals of her husband's attacker and her ensuing punishment as the law of God and His intent. We have made myth, history, law, and time stand alone and this divergence has continued to pose division and discord on the human journey rather than supporting and revealing the mystery that resides in the thrill of discovery.

On the surface, myths are accepted and used by a people and culture on a basic level to maintain a history or flow of events telling that culture's unique story. Our Western mind first wrongly assumes they have no basis in truth, then, in an amazing act of mental gymnastics, wrongly assumes the stories and variances that arise from them are literal not realizing myth tells more so why instead of how. It is this current understanding of myth which causes an aversion to the Bible being perceived as a mythical book which is locked in literalness nullifying mythical aspects resulting in a dilution of the spiritual significance losing the mystical timelessness of our journey.

Language of Religion & Language of Myth

Bishop John Shelby Spong said, "Religion is primarily a search for security and not a search for truth (Spong 2005)." Men feel secure in their similarities but fearful in their diversities. Religion was thought to find its origins in magic being a collection of esoteric beliefs centered on the human desire to control and manipulate the physical realm. From religion through magic came science which was thought to contain the fulfilled desire of magic as nature appeared under the control of science. Said another way, science seemed to manipulate nature the way magic had only promised. Magic once stood as the origin of religion, philosophy, and science and from these myth, theology, and logic arose. This process may look like the following diagram.

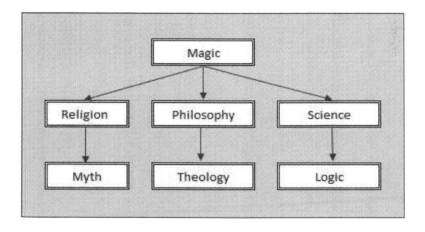

This ancient schematic of the flow of thought is discredited as the current stream of thought pits religion and philosophy against each other as ancient religion did not grow out of magic and myth but produced them. Religion seems to arise out of an innate desire to link with human origin, or more precisely, the origin of soul; while magic, in contemporary thought, seeks to relationally manipulate future outcomes. Religion looks to beginnings while magic seeks to alter perception. What if religion was the origin? What might that array look like?

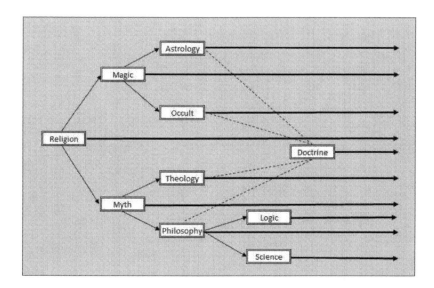

In this schematic, religion stands as the origin of the human thought processes as religion gives birth to myth and magic; not in opposition but in conjunction. Theology and philosophy are derived from myth after which comes doctrine from multiple branches. Religion stands as the headstone of human thought and from it comes mythic ideologies and magic from which flows philosophy as man sought concreteness versus an abstract explanation for what he was perceiving. As these processes matured they birthed other concepts which found home in theology and myth.

Myth does not thrive in contrast and argument while philosophy thrives on the debate. Religion mixes philosophical elements retaining an "authoritative link to a mythic context" while maintaining a historical thread through time (Ross 2002). It seems philosophy does not always link to a historical element and yet religion reaches through myth seeking an anchor in time locking to a historic event or tradition. Mythic thought and by default, religion, cannot be replaced by philosophy nor by science. In addition, philosophy tends to be descriptive, outward, and distant while religion is inward, superficial, and self-centered. Myth, on the other hand, is deep, flowing, and experiential. Philosophy seeks to find God, religion claims exclusivity to God, and myth unifies divinity and humanity. It is in this context that language was used to imply separation and division through religion and the initiation of laws.

In early civilizations, the experience of language was personal as words were spoken between individuals. A spoken word was always an encounter and as conversation develops, one experienced the person. One learned what the person was thinking or wished to do. They then became affected by what was said and must prepare a response. Conversation is a subjective experience in which two people interact and to hear a spoken word is to experience or relive the event described as perceived by the orator.

In ancient cultures, the Hebraic language recognized the power of words. The Hebrew word *dabar* represents far more than a unit of language as it carries a meaning conveying the idea of power released through the spoken word. Isaiah 55:11 is an amazing portrait of this concept by saying God's word will not return to Himself empty. As mankind learned to place thoughts on paper, words were then able to be seen. So instead of concepts and opinions entering through the ears they could now enter through the eyes. Words were now able to convey thoughts from the past to the present through writing but a primary element of language was lost and that was personal contact through the conversation.

In Greek cultures, the emphasis was on sight as their philosophers were the first to understand the new power of the written word. Plato did not just hear words, but he also saw them. He knew words as ideas (meaning to see), but lost the personal encounter. As the Greeks learned to not only hear words but also see them; they were the first to create an analytical culture which functioned to trace the missing elements as conversation was replaced with written words.

In contrast to the Greeks, the Hebrews did not develop analytical thinking because Israel was a nation of prophets not philosophers and these prophets listened to God while the Greek philosophers envisioned ideas and concepts. For the Greek philosopher, understanding came through the eye and for the Hebrew prophet, it came through the ear. The eye tends to see and dissect while the ear, on the other hand, hears and obeys. Now perhaps Job's exclamation becomes clearer in Job 42:5 when he says: "I have heard of you by the hearing of the ear, but now my eye sees you." Job was used to hearing God and obeying what God spoke to him but now he sees Him face to face as an image is produced. The hearing of the ear offered one mode of perception and the seeing of the eye offered another.

The Hebraic culture in emphasizing their Scriptures said God spoke and all came into existence. In the Hebrew faith, God is the subject and we are the object. In other words, we are the focus of God's intent or the target to whom or for whom God speaks. They wrote down what the voice of God had spoken to them but it seems they never felt they had succeeded in containing or owning the words of God. To them, their texts contained the words of the Story Teller and the story was their story which seems to be something we have lost today.

After hearing and seeing, yet another dimension enters the journey of man. For many centuries, the Hebrews listened to the words of God through their prophets but then the word came even closer to them when God moved and placed His Words, His Intent in flesh. Then in the fullness of time, using an eschatological term, mankind was permitted to envision the Word as an image; not as written words, nor hearing or implanted, but a living en-fleshed idea. The Message Bible phrases John 1:1-2 as, "From the very first day, we were there, taking it all in—we heard it with our own ears, saw it with our own eyes, verified it with our own hands. The Word of Life appeared right before our eyes; we saw it happen! And now we're telling you in most sober prose that what we witnessed was, incredibly, this: The infinite Life of God himself took shape before us (Peterson 1994)." Doctrine apprehends this to be one man but because of the enlivening power of myth, man is witness by sight, hearing, and experience the implantation of the Logos—the purposeful intent of the Creator.

Now, we are seeing the intersection of the Hebrew hearing culture and the Greek seeing culture. The Greek culture gave us exegesis, dissection, and etymology of words while the Hebrew culture taught us to hear with clarity building a picture with our heart based on experience. One was a nation of philosophers while the other was a nation of prophets. One had developed a culture of analysis and the other lived under the belief that God was telling them a story—their story. At this cross, we see the Christ in which the ear meets the eye in God's intent as His Plan becomes visibly alive and religion attempts to capture this phenomenon in a doctrine, a historical man locked in time instead of the enlivened myth involving all mankind that is timeless.

The Language of Religion and its Exclusivity

Charles Templeton's book, *Farewell to God: My Reasons for Rejecting the Christian Faith* is a work that details the author's derailing of his faith per the book's posted description. In reviewing this book, I found the following earth-shaking paragraph by an individual who, in responding to another reviewer, left no hope for mankind or for themselves in their comment. Here is the review as posted on Amazon.com in 2014.

> I wanted to respond to S***** W****** below who posted among other things this charitable loving Christian line, 'It is comforting for me to know that all atheists will spend their eternity in a lake brimming with fire and brimstone!' Splendid! After dealing with years of abuse in an abusive church I have been contemplating leaving my faith. This was one book on my list that I was considering reading. I am also planning to read some Christian apologetics before making my decision. Yet, when I looked and saw S***** gleefully gloating over human beings suffering eternal punishment as his sadistic 'I told you so' one-up-manship; I was reminded of why I left that place of pseudo love to begin with. Why should a loving God want such a hateful attitude in a perfect heaven? But I must thank you S*****, you have reminded me why I left church to begin with - threats, intimidation, and fear do not co-exist with love. Torturing people for eternity with no redemptive or corrective purpose does not coexist with mercy and justice. I hope you don't die and find out we are judged on our attitudes and not our religious system. I'll do well to have nothing to do with this false humility, compassion, and love again. Farewell Christianity - guess I don't need this book after all- S***** made the author's case (posted on Amazon.com as a review for the book *A Farewell to God: My Reasons for Rejecting the Christian Faith* by Charles Templeton).

This is a dramatic portrayal of the language of religion and its effects. In Bell's book *Love Wins*, he asks if one knows of any individual who has walked away from the Christian church and had to deal with the worry of their spirituality. Bell considers the idea that people may not be rejecting Jesus but excluding the Jesus presented by the church. They, more correctly, resisted the interpretations of this man who was locked in time. Bell also surmised Jesus would have likely rejected them too (Bell 2011, 8).

What is the purpose of language? Is it to express ideas? Is it to unite, to divide, or to share truths? Language, regardless of its purpose, will always identify the speaker. A friend was discussing a comment her husband made about returning soldiers suffering from PTSD. A soldier is trained in the art of war against an enemy whose language he does not understand; yet on the battlefield, there exists a universal language that does not need translation. Among all men there are three utterances that do not need interpretation, they are the cry, the laugh, and the shout for help. These verbal responses are essentially identical for mankind and when a man hears himself in these vocalizations, he then identifies with humanity.

Many religions have a unique language as the mode of transmitting understanding and truths; Hebrew for Judaism, Arabic for Islam, Sanskrit for Hinduism, and so on and within these languages the various religions obtain their defining characteristics. The vocalizations of language must be understood by someone before communication can begin and this is also true in religion. There must be more than one person to communicate, in other words, one person alone cannot be religious. Religion forces outward communication highlighting diversity whereas communion or fellowship celebrates similarities and if diversities arise, they are not the primary focus.

The root word "religion" is traced to the Latin *religare* (*re*: back, *ligare*: to bind) making the term associated with being bound or being held back. It means "to place an obligation on (Online Etymology Dictionary 2013)" but from what perspective? Is it bondage to a God in covenant or bound to rules and rituals established by those who have supposedly arrived at truth before others? Is there any difference? Is the religious person bound by choice or by commitment to the tenets of a particular faith system? One's religion becomes one's way of life and how one lives considering a particular set of commitments provide a strong directional force and often the result is pain, fear, and isolation when a different path is selected.

When consideration is given to languages and the Bible the account most often recalled is the Tower of Babel in Genesis chapter eleven. Verse one of that chapter says the whole earth had the same language and vocabulary and utilizing the power of unity they purposed to build a tower to God's throne. The Bible indicates in Genesis 11:5 God "came down" alluding to a distant God or division between God and man and noting that due to their unifying efforts nothing would be impossible for them so He confused their speech to put an end to their plans of invading His throne. As is true with Bible study, one must consider the time period and the current understanding of cosmology which believed the heavens were held in place above the earth by the mountains, so to their minds their task was actually obtainable.

There are similar accounts of the Tower of Babel in other ancient texts such as the Book of Jubilees, Josephus' Antiquities of the Jews, Third Apocalypse of Baruch, Qur'an, and Kabbalah, of the peoples that existed during this period of time and is often used to explain the power of a single language and why we do not have a single language today. The ancient views of the purpose of the tower seem to indicate it was to avert another destruction by flood as a judgment from God. In other words, it was a place of safety to bypass or escape God's judgment symbolizing an attitude of the power of humanity. Was God threatened by the power of the people? The Bible also seems to suggest a teleportation of sorts occurring in verse 8 which indicates God scattered the people from that area to over the face of the earth. It is interesting to note a verse before the Genesis 11 account of the tower and confounding the languages found in Genesis 10:5 implying Noah's sons migrated after the flood and bore children whose language was unique to each group and not the same as stated in Genesis 11. This is also indicated in Acts two as each heard in the language of birth.

Once saved always saved, speaking in tongues, trinity, communion, Passover, sin, and hundreds of others are words or phrases defining or used to define certain attributes of Christianity. Just as Christianity has its own language so does each of the other religions but we are not versed in them because they are not our native language. What is Christianity and how is it defined? A follower of Jesus? Being Christ-like? Believe the Bible? When one seeks a definition for Christianity they are assaulted with various creeds and definitions and each of them are based on certain methods of biblical interpretation. These factors make the language of Christianity very difficult to comprehend. Many just accept its varied tenets and love God in the only way they know how and know they will go to heaven when they die. Is that all or is that simply what we have made it? Have we defined religion as following a set of denominational rules and rituals many of which are not in the Bible anyway but are simply tradition; all the while most followers cannot prove or disprove them anyway? The language of Christianity, and other religions for that matter, is so vague and seemingly loveless especially to those who express differences in belief. Most religions are man's attempts at describing a God that is too awesome to be known by laws, rules, and statements of faith. It is these limitations which place a box around God and the followers of the particular tenets do not step out of the box nor expect God to veer from His course. Timothy Keller states the case very well when he says, "Each religion informs its followers that they have the truth and this naturally leads them to feel superior to those with differing beliefs. Also, a religion tells its followers they are saved and connected to God by devotedly performing that truth. This moves them to separate from those who are less devoted and pure in life (Keller, T. 2008, 4)."

Kathy LaPan takes a different approach as she says "If any religion is true, it must be exclusive. The exclusiveness of Christianity provides evidence that Christianity is true" (LaPan 2006). This statement is the same as saying the ocean is water so it must be wet. If LaPan's statement is valid then certain verses should be rewritten to fit this presumed universal truth proving the exclusiveness of Christianity. John 3:16 should now say "For God so loved Christians that He gave His only begotten Son." It is this perception of Christianity that dulls our understanding of His love and hampers compassion. Most religions marry law and tradition rather than a viable experience with a real living touchable God. Once rules and rituals are established the freedom for God to move is restricted. If God moves outside the rules it is perceived it cannot be God. The question asked in many religious settings is, "Where do you go to church?" What if we asked, "How do you know God." Or "What is God saying to you?" It is the usual boxed answer that hinders realization of God. It has been intimated religion has led to untold strife, division, and conflict and it may be the greatest enemy of peace in the world. Christianity continues to insist they have the truth and if other religions hold to the same idea, the world will never know peace. A frightfully true assumption, but the Bible exclusively says Jesus is the only way to know God, or does it?

The Bible—A Mythical Book

The Bible is not a single book but a collection of sixty-six books so designated by two church councils and two papal decrees (Pope Damascus in 382 AD, Council of Hippo in 393 AD, Council of Carthage in 347 AD, and Pope St Innocent I in 405 AD who closed the cannon) and is a Greek word *ta biblia* simply meaning "the scrolls" or "the books." It was penned by 40 different authors including fishermen, kings, shepherds, farmers, scribes, poets, priests, and prophets in different languages over a period of some 1,500 years to different groups who spoke different languages in different generations all supposedly excluding cultural diversity. It is accepted as divinely inspired but penned by men and is both God's word to man and man's word about God. The Bible although inspired contains contradictions that give different perspectives of how men in various situations perceived God in different times under different situations. These contradictions demonstrate a different aspect of God's dealings with man and reveal man's understanding of God's plan in time and in varied situations. The contradictions are not error, but are man's interpretation based on current knowledge at that time for a particular people.

Christianity claims the Bible is the inerrant Word of God and the truth of God given to man through anointed men as they were moved by the Holy Spirit. One writer stresses the above statement is not what Christians really believe but what those same Christians must state as truth leaving no room for discussion. Most Christians hold to the infallibility of the Bible and as the Bible implies, Jesus is the only way to God; then according to logic there can be no other religious path that leads to God. Is this what the Bible states? Does Colossians chapters one and two intend to convey the Bible is the image of the invisible God, for in the Bible all the fullness of God was pleased to dwell and through the Bible God was pleased to reconcile all things unto Himself? Or, does Hebrews chapter one indicate it was the Bible in which God speaks to us in the last days. Their writings are the reflection of God's glory and the exact imprint of God's very being. The Logos in John's Prologue did not become the Bible but was the Son of God. Christianity denies any other path to God because allowing the possibility of another path would seemingly reject the power and greatness of God, but is that true?

Paul's account in Acts 17 seems to indicate otherwise. While in Greece he sees the people at the Acropolis who are very religious and their demonstration of worship is very outward. The Greek word used here is *deisidaimonesteros* which contains a good and bad term usually translated religious or superstitious, however, the base words imply dread of devils. Jonathan Mitchell says the worship exhibited here was animism meaning the belief that disembodied spirits inhabit other living beings and inanimate objects (Mitchell 2014). These people were not Christians in the modern sense of the term but a culture who worshiped demons or idols and note what Paul says to them. He told them the One you are worshiping without knowing—is the One I am going to proclaim to you. He did not tell them they were worshiping satan or they needed to say the name of Jesus. What we have seen is not that God was insufficient to reach these people but was more than able to make His presence known in any situation. He is boundless and not limited by man in anyway including Christianity or Islam or any other religion. Peter was very clear when he proclaims "In truth I perceive that God shows no partiality. But in every nation whoever fears Him and works righteousness is accepted by Him" (Acts 10:34-35). This is precisely what the people in Athens were doing when Paul saw their inscription "to the unknown god."

Ephesians 1:7-10 declares God gathered into one all things in Christ. It is not all have to touch Christ but Christ has touched all. As God was in Christ reconciling the world, He touched all and not that all must touch Him. (2 Cor. 5:19, Eph. 1:10). That is what is meant when Paul says, "Nor is there salvation in any other, for there is no other name under heaven given among men by which we must be saved (Acts 4:12)." This is not an exclusive text but a very strong inclusive one as God brought all into the One. God was exclusive in His Son and inclusive as all were placed in Him.

Look at Jonathan Mitchell's translation of Acts 4:12 and note where you hear exclusion.

> And thus, the rescue and deliverance – the restoration to health and wholeness, the safety and salvation, and the return to our original state and condition – is in absolutely no other person! For neither is there a different name under the sky (or: heaven) that has been given, and now exists as a gift, among mankind (or: in the midst of humanity) within which it continues binding and necessary for us to be saved (restored to health and wholeness; delivered and kept safe; returned to our original state and condition) (Mitchell 2014)!

The exclusion is in the Christ not Christianity as the only one salvation comes but He was so inclusive that it is only through Him that all men, all nations, all ethnic groups, were gathered in the One and He was the One. In John 14:6 Jesus said to him, "I am the way, the truth, and the life. No one comes to the Father except through Me" would be an exclusive statement, except God gathered all into the One and He was the One. All that God did he did in Christ—

His Logos and what was done then effected all demonstrating God's inclusiveness through the exclusive son; but who or what is this Logos?

According to Brian McLaren, there are several issues with our usage of the Bible in daily guiding human morality and rightly so because the date of writings is several hundreds of years old depicting a different time, a different society, and a different view of the world. One problem, according to McLaren, is fundamentalism establishes the Bible as a divinely dictated science textbook because mechanical details of the universe and the physical aspects of man are mentioned. Another issue is the human ethical component when the Bible is taken as a book of rules and yet it simply does not offer clear cut paths for many of our current issues such as abortion, capitalism, communism, mental health, autism, racism and many other "isms" that have arisen to the forefront of society in our time. It does not nor cannot address such wide topics as genetic engineering, space travel, and various aspects of warfare (nuclear, biological) and now cyber warfare. The Bible, for the most part, is read and recited every Sunday morning as a legal covenantal document in that the Christian church considers itself to be its keeper and interpreter. McLaren says "lawyers in the court room quote articles, sections, and paragraphs to win their case and we do the same with the Bible citing testament, book, chapter, and verse. We tend to approach the Bible as universal law rather than a book of poems, prophecies, histories, fables, parables, letters, quarrels, and meditations. The Bible gives a basic guiding principle and not a strict list of do's and don'ts for modern society (McLaren 2010, loc. 1241)."

N. T. Wright explains "The biblical writers use the language of mythology, not because they believe the myths concerned were literally true, but because this is the only available and appropriate lens through which to see the full significance of certain events (Wright 1980, xxii)." Wright goes on to say one often uses words that have migrated away from their etymological meaning through cultural shifts. An example is our phrase regarding the rising of the sun though we know scientifically it is an optical illusion due to our position on the earth but is used as a descriptor out of familiarity rather than scientific fact. It is in this way myth may have actually rewritten history. Caird notes the accounts of the death of Jesus depict a wide range of events and offer subtle views by the storyteller (Caird 1980, 213-214). His point is made when considering the time immediately preceding the crucifixion as the events of the storytellers do not agree. Mark 15 indicates a curtain is torn from top to bottom while in Matthew an earthquake occurs yet in Luke an eclipse is noted. Is the tearing of the curtain an actual event which occurred simultaneously in two different locations or is it solely a metaphorical description offered by a contemporary witness? Mark describes Jesus' death viewed by the centurion confessing him to be God—and for him perhaps the curtain split allowing him entrance as perceived by Mark. In Matthew, it is described differently also using mythical language as he links it with an earthquake and Luke with an eclipse. All are figurative statements as seen through the lens of the author who was seeing/perceiving through culture, personal beliefs, and social input. It is interesting to note however, the three effects seen and described in mythical language effect the spiritual (curtain of the Holy of Holies), the physical (the earthquake), and cosmic (eclipse) realms immediately place a metaphysical aspect on those portrayals.

The Bible is more a mythical book than a literal book. Does this make its contents false? No. It simply demonstrates the intense desire of man to unite with his beginnings in God however he may be described. The creation myths of Genesis chapter one and chapter two express the belief that all things, for their existence, depend on the creative acts of God as his word being the intent of creation. The doctrine extracted from literalness is made very rigid while the mythical story maintains fluidity. A myth more often tells why and not how. While truth is unchangeable, the myth flows because it is filled with the nuance of multiple layers of understanding and then retelling, as man seeks to comprehend the mysterious God.

How is the Bible mythical? Consider the Behemoth and the Leviathan. The Behemoth in Job 40 is a beast "whose strength is in its loins and its force is in the navel of his belly (Job 40:16)" and "who can drink up a river (Job 40:23)" and is "chief of the ways of God (Job 40:19)." Even though they exhibit raw power, yet to the author of Job they are fully tamed by their Creator. The Leviathan in Job 41 is a water creature with a nose and has a double coat of armor and whose snorting throws fire of light and flames stream from its mouth. It also pours smoke from its nostrils and "nothing on earth is its equal—a creature without fear (Job 41:33 NIV)." If this paragraph were read from any book but the Bible, it would be understood as a myth, as a story portraying truth with no literal meaning whatsoever nor would researchers try to find an ancient creature now extinct to fit the description.

Another doctrine that misapplied myth was the Incarnation. The traditional stance of the doctrine maintains the Incarnation was in one man while the fluidity of myth recounts the story in all men. The truth arising from myth then, is the expression of unity of the human and the divine. Doctrine attempts to portray truth through myth yet the effect of doctrine more often fractures the symbols and parables to fit a specific purpose forming a belief.

If the Bible is opened as a mythical book of man's journey rather than a literal view of his history then depths begin to unfold detailing a richer story of God's visitation and if allowed to be our own, morphs into our personal journey of discovery of the mystery. Man is not journeying to go from point A to point B; but in realizing the journey is the destination, man communes with a mysterious and mystical God.

Why does religion tend to pursue literalness in their sacred writings? The Bible is formed from the Hebrew and Greek mind, but does the Bible join the two minds as is currently suggested by Western religious views? The Greeks gave us the science of history and the Hebrews gave us historical religion. Put another way, the Greeks pursued a logical flow of linear time while the Hebrews introduced the idea of a cyclical process of fall, redemption, restoration. William Barrett said, "the distinction [between Hebrew and Greek thought] arises from the difference between doing and knowing. The Hebrew is concerned with practice, the Greek with knowledge. Right conduct is the ultimate concern of the Hebrew, right thinking that of the Greek. Duty and strictness of conscience are the paramount things in life for the Hebrew; for the Greek, the spontaneous and luminous play of the intelligence (Knowles 2013)." The Greeks learned in order to comprehend and the Hebrews learned in order to revere contemplating the mystery. What about modern man? The modern man learns in order to influence combining logic and experience to better himself. The Greeks viewed the world and events through concrete logic— mentally figuring things out and how they work while the Hebrews viewed world events through abstract experience—what they saw, heard, felt, and tasted fully dependent on experience and observations without the need to logically understand them. In Hebraic concepts theory and reason takes a backseat to beauty which inspires reverence as they see signs of God's continued action in history.

Another major variation of the two minds is the concept of things. For example, the Greek mind would describe a pencil as a yellow object about eight inches long while the Hebrew mind would associate the description with its function such as a pencil is an instrument to write words. The Hebrew description uses a verb signifying action while the Greek description is an adjective. In one description, the emphasis is on the object itself focusing on what the eyes perceive (yellow, eight inches long) while in the other it is focused on the person or its function in relation to the person (I write, I chronicle thoughts). This is also seen in the Greek description of God saying God is love while the Hebrew mind conceives God loves me.

When we bring the usual scientific approach of our western mind to the study of Scripture without consideration of the structural mental source, our outcomes are exegetical distortions rather than the intent of the writer. Abraham Heschel, a Jewish philosopher, said "to try to distill the Bible, which bursting with life, drama, and tension, to a series of principles would be like trying to reduce a living person to a diagram (Heschel 1999, 20)." That is our result as we have thought we could understand the incomprehensible God in concrete terms. To the Jewish mind, the understanding of God is not attained seeking to clarify some timeless divine attribute of a sovereign God or looking to ideas of goodness and perfection; "but rather by sensing the living acts of His concern to His dynamic attentiveness to man (Heschel 1999, 21)." The Jewish focus is not on the general goodness of God per se, but His intervention in man's affairs on a one-on-one basis proving His intention to direct and influence the lives of men as seen in individual instances effecting humanity. God is not known in the abstract but in the specific situations into which He has inserted Himself—the divine intrusion. One comes to know God "by what He has revealed Himself to be and not what one has theorized Him to be (Knowles 2013)." This is the difference of myth and religion as myth tells the story of the effect on man while religion tends to define how it happened and how man should respond. Now, enter the power and abilities of myth as myth enjoys the interaction and expounds it.

Time and Creation

The descriptive idea of God asserting himself in creation is found in the *Sefer Yetzirah*, the Jewish Kabbalah text also called the *Book of Creation*, which says the Creator—or Former is simple meaning singular and contains no plurality as there can be no plurality if there is not more than one. It goes on to paint an awesome picture of creation in which God must carve out a place, creating empty space, to begin the formation of creation (Kaplan 1997, 13-77). *The Book of Creation* further says God engraved out of empty space the plan He held his mind. It was out of this undifferentiated essence that a space had to be engraved or carved out and not written. The difference being an engraving removes material by pressure or stress while writing adds material. According to the *Sefer Yetzirah*, God first created the name Elohim. It seems the Hebraic intent is not plurality but unity speaking not to number but function. The process, as stated in the *Sefer Yetzirah*, is caused by the Breath of God (*Ruach*) as it emanates from His mouth giving vocalization or forcing the physical manifestation of His mental image. The Ruach of God initiates the process whereby God engraves or carves His mind. As a glass blower, which by his breath, puts pressure on the molten glass forcing form and function in the glass; God engraves

(Hebrew—*chakak*) or pronounces His mind and the force or pressure of the Ruach produces or carves (Hebrew—*chatzav*) the expression of His intent making it visible to the eyes.

Our Bible attempts to explain a Hebraic concept to an English audience who perceives creation as an event that happened in time and once upon a time. However, the Hebraic concept details a creation that is a continual process and not a completed act in history long ago. Because it is a process we are not bystanders but participants in the drama of God's intent once held in His mind but now forced outward and visible by His breath as he speaks his intent. A Jewish prayer in the *Shacharit* called the *Yotzer Or*, says that God re-creates the universe daily, and the identical prayer at the evening reminds us that the evening falls at his word and in wisdom he opens the gates (constellations) and his understanding causes a change in times and seasons, ordering the stars in their orbits in the heavens. In the Hebraic concept, we are parts of the creative Divine act and the ongoing creative process. What does the creative process mean? When God spoke, engraved, or pronounced his mind by saying "Let there be..." he established the creative act as a response to words or simply communication. Therefore, every act of communication in our becoming the Christ is an act of creation as we dance in the Divine nature in ways we do not yet realize.

Lynn Hayes said, "duality is the work of religion for there is no dualism in truth (Hayes 2012, conference at Lake DeGray)". Both Greek and Hebrew concepts entertain some form of dualism. Like the Gnostics, Greek dualism sees two worlds, one visible and physical and the other invisible and spiritual; and man stands between these worlds perceiving he is related to both. On the other hand, Hebrew duality is not cosmological but theological in that perceived dualism exists between the Creator and the created.

Efficacy of Myth

"A myth is an image in terms of which we try to make sense of the world."
Allan Watts, British Philosopher

Religion tends to proclaim myths are fact starved accounts reflecting the fears and frustrations of humanity; or more precisely, realities experienced which could not be comprehended and put into words. Is the prime purpose of language solely to convey truths and express ideas or is there a deeper action occurring when words are spoken? But first, consider the difference between words and language? Language is an identifier; for example, when a speaker relays information in their native tongue, you immediately know something about the speaker's heritage. Language must be comprehended before communication can commence. Religion often forces divergent communication whereas mythical language tends to celebrate communion, relationship, and restoration with divinity.

Language is composed of words and in Ancient Near Eastern cultures words were not only sounds caused by a grouping of letters, but when articulated, they possessed independent existence acting upon the hearer revealing the intent of the speaker. The experience of language was personal as words spoken were an encounter as conversation allows one entrance into the mind of the speaker causing an effect on the hearer. To hear and comprehend words forming language was to experience the event being described.

Words are fragments of a story and are meaningless unless they are ordered and structured becoming a sentence which is a form of language that conveys meaning and depth. Language functions to enliven a story rather than just convey facts or details that can be mundane and meaningless. When words are spoken with purpose and order they cause the hearer to experience the event. The purpose of language then, is to take an experience or event and propel its purpose through the ages of time to become a cosmic event for all humanity. Words and sentences simply are there to list the facts but language which includes the human expression interprets those facts and causes a conscious awakening that moves the event from a story of one to a myth of all on the human journey. At this level of the power of language, the shared experience has caused an impact on humanity and remains viable for all times afterward. Words were more than a unit of language or a string of ideas expressed in conversation but carried thought (potential energy) to actualization (kinetic energy) as the Hebrew word debar conveys. Isaiah expressed this idea as God said His words will not return to him empty and void but will accomplish their purpose for which they were sent. It is with this understanding of words and language that we now consider the intent of myth in realizing it is not a negative application lacking depth and truth but a powerful use of language to convey the heart of man's experiences.

Myths are accepted by a culture as a means of documentation as they, on the surface, maintain a flow of history telling the story of the journey as it is assumed to be a retelling from a linear historical standpoint. It is when a variance from history is noted, the myth becomes perceived as false and becomes the musings of a mind distanced from reality. We must understand myths examine why rather than how of an account and are told through the lens of culture, history, belief, and ideas imaged in the language of the storyteller.

As one explores this concept in our Bible, realizing it is a mythical book not telling us how but attempting to convey why, then we can see a very enlivened journey of man rather than a literal view of history. We are invited into depths of a richer story of God's intrusion in humanity and once we realize it is personal; we then see ourselves in the drama of the cosmos, a journey of discovery and mystery from an amazing Creator-Father.

Is history recorded accurately and fairly without contradictions? One must realize history is truth to the narrator, the one telling the story, and if we are under the impression that the story is conveyed without personal influences then we may be in for an abrupt cosmic surprise. A record of any event is only infallible if it is realized it is solely based on the record keeper's interpretation of the event infused with personal perception, cultural embellishments, and tradition. Man has long told his story through myth when not concerned with the actual flow of history but rather why the event occurred and its implant into humanity. So, does myth deconstruct history or does it reinterpret it? It is neither, for myth is not primarily a historical account but a metaphorical one in that it adds layers and concepts linked to one's established perceptions. Then is myth doctrine? No, in that doctrine is the simplification of myth and this occurs when the myth is being retold and the hearer says, "I believe." A myth is an experience not a belief. R. J. Stewart says, "the declaration or recounting of a myth is, at its deepest and most powerful level, a reverberation of the event which it describes. Thus, myths are not allegories but resonances or reflections of actualities, of occurrences or manifestations at the heart of being (Stewart 1989, 6)." What does that mean? He is saying each time a myth is recounted or retold, the truth of the event is re-lived and again affects the hearer as it comes through the filters of the myth-teller.

Could it be the Old Testament is not meant to convey a linear history of events but more a story of a people evolving as they come to understand their God and His interactions with them interpreted

31

through their unique perspective? As for the New Testament, could it be more an impetus, a starting point for humanity to perceive divinity? Alvin Boyd Kuhn said, "as real as history seems to be, it is less true than myth, as myth presents the true narrative of the human experience rather than a chronological replay of events (Kuhn 2014, 25)." Myths contain the interpretation of the experience rather than a linear transcript of the events. In other words, a myth is an interpretation of truth while history is a translation of facts. Language plays an immense role in the recording of history. What is the difference between interpretation and translation? An interpretation is from words spoken in the moment—a conversation interspersed with real time perception and experiences, feelings, and enlivened by the interpreter; while a translation is from a written document which is more often cold, detached, and for the most part lifeless.

It is true that humanity is the only creation of God that lives through history. It is man that defines his life based on history as he constructs a linear timeline from his first breath to his last to seemingly give humankind definition and purpose. Why is this dangerous? It seems to cause him to focus on what happened in the past retaining it to compare rather than why it happened veiling the potential of living now. The present moment conveyed in myth can never be historical. History attempts to bury the myth by transforming it into a literal occurrence in time. A myth is not defined by whether it is true but whether it functioned to relay a story while linking humanity with divinity, a story of divine intrusion with cosmological effects. The present moment is not static but dynamic and characterized by constant change, activity, and progress being not a moment in time but rather a timeless moment; a moment when time is not marked. Markus Cicero, a Roman Philosopher proclaimed, "History is the witness that testifies to the passing of time; it illuminates reality, vitalizes memory, provides guidance in daily life, and brings us tidings of antiquity (Cicero 106-43 BC)."

John Walton indicates the biblical account in the Old Testament was not necessarily written to all people of the earth, but more so to Israel. Consequently, when we read the Bible realizing it was not written in English but addressed to another culture before us, we must not only translate the language but the culture as well (Walton 2009, 7-13). The idea of translation involves extracting the ideas from their native context and transporting them into our own world and present time; and rather than translating the culture which cannot be done, we must enter that world by re-entering the conversation. While it is true the Israelites held many concepts and perspectives common with the rest of the ancient world; it is not altogether true Israel was fully influenced by that world. It must also be entertained they were an influence because that was their world. Myth, according to Walton includes the idea the Bible must be understood as a piece of ancient mythology. He goes on to say that we should accept Genesis one as ancient cosmology and cease trying to translate it into modern cosmology (Walton 2009, 12).

Myth: Defined and Discovered

The mythos is a recurrent narrative theme of all civilizations linking divinity and humanity usually through supernatural events whose main purpose is to repair the perceived breach between the two. Even though the accounts vary, the central theme is union with God however He is known or imagined. Is the purpose of myth to recount history? Not necessarily, as myth is not intended to portray the historical or mechanical flow of an event but more so the event's purpose as it touches humanity. The historical account is influenced by the story teller's culture, oral tradition, and geography. The purpose of the story reveals deep truths of God's interaction with man and yet embedded in the story teller's account.

Myth, in the Western mind although erroneous, is thought to be an illogical made up fantasy; and yet the Bible is a collection of myths relating a mystical reality as accounts of God's interactions with man and man's interpretation of those interactions. When men extract doctrine from myth then the account is literalized and must be recounted the same way or it is not true. The extraction of doctrine makes the encounter rigid and locked or entombed in time while the mythical concept is fluid flowing and bending with humanity yet retaining truth. When doctrine is used to retell the mythical story, it fractures the symbols and parables to fit a distinct purpose fortifying a doctrine as fact over truth.

The Bible, in telling its story, utilizes mystical terms conveying spiritual realities not understood nor apparent to the senses or intelligence as a mode of relating God's interaction via man's interpretation. It is not a book of do's and don'ts from which to build doctrines but a book of possibilities and potentialities. Joseph Campbell introduced three main functions of myth. First, myth is vitalizing to all and causes a sense of awe to the mystery of being. Awe is face to face with the author of reality comprehending you are not alone but are connected to all. It is that moment you realize there are not two. Second, myth offers a cosmological image of the universe that supports the awe before the mystery of Presence and the Presence of mystery. This image presents a God that extends to all civilizations and not just a Christian God. The awe issuing from myth carries you from anticipation to realization of presence. Third, myth guides the individual by enlightening his psyche, his source of thought, feelings, and the inner place where beliefs, hopes, and dreams are kept. It is in this way our beliefs and our hopes yield to knowledge as awe issues from myth (Campbell 2001, 2-5).

Myth: Purpose & Power

Is the sole purpose of myth to factually convey the historical record? Myth is used to recall an event and often uses descriptions outside natural laws through supernatural cause and effect to detail the event. In doing so, myth adds levels and concepts flowing through one's established perceptions grounded again from culture, oral tradition, and geography. When the Bible is opened as a mythical book of man's journey rather than a literal book in events of history then depths begin to unfold and a richer story of God's visitation is provided and if made our own, will develop into our personal journey of discovery and mystery. The power of myth survives all cultures through the perichoretic variances in each culture. As one's culture may see their mythical power resident in birth and another in the power of death, yet both builds an orchestrated image of Source greater than themselves in seeking relationship. It is seen in the Orphic Myth of the cosmological egg that divided into heaven and earth who then copulated giving birth to time. Also evident in the grief of the mother goddess who laments her daughter taken to dwell in death for a few months as the sun was held captive as the winter season came and the vegetation died. Development continues as virgin birth of a savior and the death of the savior to pardon and regenerate. Are the symphonies of mankind the same? No, but all contain a core, a central trail of similarity speaking the same thing. What is that core principle of truth resident in myth? The organic driving force in myth is the mysterious ratio, the harmony of creation personified as the Source of the cosmos who embodies man in all civilizations and in all times as there always seems to be an Incarnation, a Crucifixion, and a Resurrection and other movements of the Cosmic Structure as His prolation continues to uphold all things.

I think a beautiful example of the power of myth is seen in the actions of a prism which is a rectilinear solid that alters light, but in what way? It disperses the light into its components making them visible. It is an excellent tool, in my opinion, to explain myth but first a question; is the dispersion of the light beam an illusion? Is it distortion? It is neither, for something to be illusive or distortive it must be masked from view and intentionally hidden from perception marring the correct view. The prism simply clears the view as it is the same light entering and exiting the prism but the action of the prism on the light allows multifacets of the light to become visible. The effect of the prism on the light is not distortion masking the light but dispersion emphasizing it. The prism enhanced what was inherent in the light beam by adding another dimension exhibiting the power of myth which disperses the Light of Truth in the myth revealing many dimensions further unveiling other hidden structures telling our story. But as time encapsulated myth, it also bound the parameters or the many dimensions of myth in time also. For example, in Christianity we see the Incarnation, Crucifixion, and Resurrection as a historical event and cannot fathom it occurring in the present moment simply because we have locked it up in one man in history never seeing it is us also.

What is Myth?

Myths are believed by a people or culture and are used to maintain a history or a flow of events that tell a unique story. The Bible was penned by men who brought a diverse understanding about God. Even though discrepancies and errors exist such as the account of

David numbering Israel where it was Satan in 1 Chronicles 21 and God in 2 Samuel 24. The father of Joseph is stated as Jacob in Matthew 1 and Heli in Luke 3. Jesus says he and his Father are one in John 10 and the Father is greater in John 14. Another mythical example is seen in the serpent in Genesis which was cursed to crawl on its belly and eat the dust of the earth. Does a snake eat dust? Metaphorically and mythically yes, as the serpent devours man causing him to thwart his intended purpose as a battle between the ears. These contradictions only serve to demonstrate a different perspective of how man in various situations perceived God in different times. They are not error because to the author, they depict a definite process of God and his interaction with man, or rather the author's translation of the interaction from his exclusive perspective; and if we did not hear or see the account firsthand, we cannot say the interpretation is error because it was through the lens of another. Perception is a mental function and therefore imposes a limit on truth as it can only see through what is received by the body's senses. Perception basically deals in facts which tends to be cold and impersonal while truth is an expression of reality coming from the psyche who has experienced the wonder and awe of God. Truth tends to alter or correct perception and is the state of all things according to the decrees of God.

Myth is initiated through experience with a deep seated spiritual truth and may follow a great focal figure such as Jesus, Muhammad, or Buddha, and may include other participants in the experience such as Krishna, Abraham, or Paul. A very important aspect of myth is its ability to endure over a period of ages appearing timeless. For example, what makes the incarnation and crucifixion mythical? An account of the divine incarnating into humanity is not solely historical truth being an event that happened about 2000 years ago such as the crucifixion; but its function is in the continued and ongoing story of divine incarnation. While Christianity sees it as a tragic death of the son of God it is symbolic of the interaction of God and the world and therefore properly termed a myth.

The enduring aspect of myth is often typified in cosmology as cultures comprehend the cosmos to be a stage of God's interaction with man. Cosmology is the study of the origin and development of the universe and simultaneously coming to understand humanity's role in the cosmological cycle as man becomes fully functional and expressed as the intent of God. This is accomplished by allowing the story to develop and understand it has always developed in all cultures of mankind. Amazing views come into sight as each layer is built upon and seeing the entire portrait rather than destroying each previous culture's understanding and labeling it as error simply because it varies from one's own current spiritual worldview. In viewing the universe, we gaze upon a magnificent tapestry of the journey of man. The Zodiac and its view through ancient religions is a picture of God showing himself to man and man's interpretation of the show. In the prevalent cosmological view, science has fostered the concept that has reduced the role of mankind to that of a spectator. Richard Smoley insists our worldview of the universe has displaced our position in it and thus diminished the role of man. Out of our own achievements, "we have constructed a cosmos in which we are irrelevant and out of touch with creation (Smoley 2002, 99)."

In Ptolemaic cosmology, the earth was the center of the understood universe and all the luminaries worked to provide fulfillment for the earth of which we were the crown of creation. Modern science has since changed that perception and correctly so indicating the earth runs its course around the sun just like all other celestial bodies in our solar system making the universe seem mechanical and in-human. In the former view, there was mystery as everything served the earth while in the latter Copernican cosmology the universe became intelligent, rational, and logical to the human mind and the magic and mystery waned — along with a decreased perception of man's purpose in the universe. The starry heavens have always declared God's glory and they do it without error, night after night, year after year, century after century, and their words have abounded to all ages and will continue to do so. This awareness should not make us small and insignificant, but assures us we are in the palm of his hand and have the best seats in the house. The stars do not declare humanity's end or impending judgment but the unending purpose of God to bring about His plan in the glory of His creation.

The Distraction or Distinction of History

"History is indeed little more than the register of crimes,
follies, and misfortunes of mankind."
Edward Gibbon, English Historian

History seems to be solely a chronology of significant events as determined by the narrator. Is history always a true unbiased account of the events or is it influenced by the recorder? The loudest voice gets to be the story teller of history and the narration is impinged with the narrator's personal influences through his perceptions. The historical record is only infallible if the record keeper's images of the event are true without sway from his personal perceptions. It is like a football referee who sees a play at his particular angle and throws a flag based on what he perceived about the play. The replay of the events slowed down in time reveals the action so the senses can reprocess it and often the play call by the referee is overturned resulting in a reversal of one historical event and sets in motion a completely new path for the outcome of the game to unfold. Therefore, the events in history are an account being facts based on perception which is input via the human senses and may not necessarily be the truth of the event.

Man tells his story [his-tory] in myth, but is the underlying intention of myth to deconstruct history? Myth tends to utilize supernatural cause and effect to detail the full scope of the natural event. Said another way, myth adds levels and concepts linked to one's established perceptions. Dogma and doctrine are the simplification of myth and appears as myth is retold becoming doctrine when the hearer responds, "I believe." Charles Hedrick says the idea of history is created by the historian as they collect and interpret random events of the past. Hedrick says, "the causes, outcomes, and significance of events in theological histories are tied to the belief systems and theology of the historians doing the writing (Hedrick 1999, 4)" and due to such conditions objectivity in evaluating the events is usually lost. A mythicist is not necessarily concerned with the literal interpretation of the historical event as much as what caused the story of the event to be passed down through time and its impact on those it involved.

The Old and New Testaments are not intended to be a historical record of events but is the story of a people evolving and it conveys their understanding of God and of His interaction with humanity as they interpreted it through their unique perspective. Is history the recording of facts objectively and chronologically or is history an attempt to preserve significant truths in meaningful or memorable ways without regard to objectivity? Was the New Testament supposed to be a chronology of historical events? Not necessarily, but it functioned as an impetus, a starting point, for humanity to see the Divine in themselves and coming to the realization all men have the divine seed. Most civilizations develop myths to placate what they do not understand or cannot explain. When Jesus did not turn out to be the Messiah the Jews wished for, they turned his messiah-ship inward stating it was not of this world but a secret kingdom yet to come by placing it in time. This allowed a reason for the Jews not being immediately released from Roman oppression according to the Jewish timetable by offering a "yet to come" agenda. The Jewish nation rejected the Jesus of History who not only did not save the Jews but was also coming to save the Gentiles too, a fully inclusive act in that historic period of time. John Dominic Crossan said, "my point once again, is not that those ancient people told literal stories and we are now smart enough to take them symbolically, but that they told them symbolically and we are now dumb enough to take them literally (Crossan 1996, 79)." Even though Gnosticism was known to be tolerant of varied concepts and practices, the literal view at that time was to accept a man called Jesus who became a representative of God rather that the Gnostic view which was to be more aware of the process and experience the awareness personally in becoming the Christ. In the path of history as religion has dictated, the Christian faith has required a false concept of faith and blind assurance in what happened (history) rather than learning from direct experience the Divine in all men. Religion took history which was simply a spiritual path for learning our origin and replaced it with a rigid structure of do's and don'ts and called it God's Law.

What is time? Is it just numbers on a clock? Does time occupy space? Time has been defined as the unrestricted continual process of existence marking events in the past, present, and future regarded as a unit. Time is a non-spatial (does not occupy space) continuum (flow or progression) in which events occur in irreversible succession from the past through the present to the future. Time is divided into seconds, minutes, hours, days, months, and years and are parts of time; while past, present, and future are forms of time.

Genesis chapter one is noted as marking the initiation of time. Creation is considered an event beginning time and an event which was completed in the act of time beginning. But is this the sense of Hebraic thought? The truer sense is "When God began creating...." Creation is not a completed fact but rather a process—not paired with time. When creation is a continuous process then we are allowed input in the creative process also. So, we are parts of the creative act as well as its process being contributors to the event. What is the meaning of the process of creation for us? The Hebraic account in Genesis said God spoke "Let there be light and there was light" marking the act of creation being initiated by speech, by words, by communication which is fully exemplified in Psalm 33:9 saying "Because he spoke and they existed; he commanded and it was established (http://www.biblehub.com/aramaic-plain-english/psalms/33.htm)" indicating it is the spoken word that brings existence.

There is a translation of history that exits without regard to time. This record of truth resides within each of us and is bound to the Logos, the intent of the Creator, in all men revealing nothing was ever lost or diminished. This record is not a translation of a written text as a law; but is an interpretation of the myth incorporating the movements of the Logos which mimics God's intent; and one example of that intent is the incarnation expressed in all ancient civilizations. History attempts to bury myth by transforming the Incarnation into a literal occurrence in time and in one man, Jesus. History is recorded in the context of time while myth is not limited by time. In other words, it cannot be proven until it is universally manifested at which point no proof is necessary. Myth is not defined by whether it is or was true but whether it functioned to convey a story serving a link between worlds or realms such as between spirit and flesh, between past and present, or the crucifixion linking God and man. As time is ineffective in myth so too is law. A law's purpose is to govern by control and a myth rises above seeking control or being controlled. History can define a period in time such as the Golden Age, Silver Age, or Bronze Age in Greek Mythology and like the Age of Taurus or the Age of Aquarius of astrological periods. These periods do not limit history but simply describe or define a brief amount of time in history. The former are not mythical periods because they did not link the spirit to another realm unlike the astrological periods which are bridges that serve to erase duality and maintain the layers as astrology functions as a powerful myth.

Man, being unable to comprehend or wanting to understand what the heavens are now declaring, established rules or laws to link the world's histories as they understood them. I think law was a major initiator in religion forcing judgment and separation. Myth seems to endure while religion must continually fold and divide itself to accommodate faith. Myth can answer the difficult questions if we let it while religion cannot and deters the search for truth by proclaiming "just believe." Mark Eaton asked what if history is simply the story of us comprehending the mystery (Mark Eaton, e-mail message to author, July 14, 2014)? Hebraic history is based on sight or observation through imagery as a basis of interpretation. It also adds to the story another aspect by asking why it affects me. Hebraic history includes the effects on a specific people while Greek history is more informal and transparent being more concerned with the cosmic ideal. The Hebraic idea birthed the declaring heavens while the Greek ideology gave us "ye are gods" noting one is to us and the other is about us. I do think history is our story translating the mystery as is evidenced by the abundance of religious laws and out of our lack of interpreting the myth we became satisfied with methods rather than experiences. The mystery and awe of the cosmos is not history but myth as it cannot be ascertained through instinct and logic but must be perceived by the senses and experienced as myth which is loaded with layers of freeing truth of the Creator and the created.

I had previously defined the present moment as a point in time but I don't think that is accurate now. In mathematics, a point does not take up space, has no volume, nor surface area on a number line; therefore, a moment is not or cannot be defined by time nor placed in time. Marquis Hunt says, "we are God's moment and His location and if that moment is not bringing you joy then there must be a re-assessment, a repentance, a change of mind, to see the moment correctly (Hunt 2014)." In a line of time, the moment is not the past or the future. I think I had to arrive at the concept that the present moment is eternal and not defined or constricted by history or time to realize that the past and the future are resolved in the present moment. Is time relative to the present moment? Not really, but we have let time (including history) both define and determine the moment. When time is removed, the Logos is seen and experienced and the mystery is unveiled.

How does one recall history? Does one not say, "Remember that time when...." or we give a specific date and time when the event occurred. Did creation occur in time or did creation begin time? Revelations 10:6 declares that time shall be no more according to the KJV while other versions translate as delay. Is creation an ongoing process? The universe is still expanding and limitless; why is that? Perhaps God is still creating and the act of creation was not a historical event but a continuous moment. Creation takes place every day because God's word proclaiming "Let there be" has not returned to Him. God has not retracted His command to "Let there be…" and never will. If the moment never ends as God intended then creation, evolution, incarnation, eschatology, and history are all one and the same moment but time has determined how we define and limit them. In the moment, there is no time nor limits, therefore no history or future. As in the football analogy, there is never a need for a slow-motion replay because there never was a bad call. When this moment is eternalized then time shall be no more and duality will have ceased.

I've noticed as understanding comes the historical translation of those events is more often radically altered or a new cosmic explanation is brought to the forefront. In other words, things change from being about one man to being about humankind. The *chronos* gives way to *kairos* yielding a fuller and richer potentiality being a move from static to dynamic and unlimited possibilities. Time seems to progress in rhythm. Our consciousness or awareness of time seems to occupy space similar to the concept of a song. A melody when it is played, is begun in a moment in time. In a few moments, the beginning is now in the past while the end of the song is yet to come. The song is a unifier or bridge that serves to connect the past and future. In a similar progression of analysis, before and after are temporal terms but are represented in opposite ways. General concepts place time on a line at a point called "now." Then we have the future before us and the past stretches behind us. Ancient Hebraic thought sees a somewhat opposite concept as living men who are on a journey from birth to death also represent humanity whose journey is pressing ceaselessly forward. The generations of the past are our progenitors who existed before us and we follow them in which case the past is our foretime. The future generation then, will be our descendants, or those who come after us. They belong to the after age, our posterity. Thus, the notion of time of before and after have somewhat opposite ideas based on whether we have in mind physical-astronomical time or psychological-historical time: the future lies before us but comes after us.

There are two main viewpoints of time and both stem from religious concepts. The cyclical worldview is represented by Hinduism and the linear concept is from Judaism. Hinduism being born out of reason, sees the universe in a cyclic process. It sees winter, spring, summer, fall, and the rising of the sun in the east and its setting in the west as other scenarios in nature pointing to a repeating of events. When considering these aspects, it is natural to assume a man is born, he lives, he dies, he's reborn, he lives, and he dies, and this process of reincarnation is termed the transmigration of the soul. In this view, the material body, the house of the real you is considered to be an evil prison. In contrast, the linear view offered a form of history that had a beginning and proceeded or advanced in a straight line toward a definite goal. The Islamic and Judeo-Christian concept says time is linear beginning with an act of creation by God. The general Christian view is that time will end with the end of the world. The Greeks see time as being numeric, chronological, and quantitative in the Greek word chronos and the right opportune moment and qualitative in the word kairos. The Hebrew Kabbalah views time as a paradox—an illusion. Both the future and the past are recognized to be a simultaneous present.

When law is perceived as the fracture of time then fulfillment is discerned correctly realizing nothing is left to fulfill. History is thought of being static and dead based on translating facts while myth is dynamic and living and based on interpreting the union of God and man. Myth negates duality disintegrating the timeline to an eternal now.

- II -

DUALISM THROUGH THE LENS OF PERCEPTION

We see the world not as it is, but as we are!
The Talmud

History & Principle of Duality

T raditional dualism is the concept of philosophy stating reality is the outcome of two principles which cannot be reduced to an ultimate first cause. In other words, which one of the principles exhibited influence over the other. The history of Western religions indicates philosophical dualism goes back to Platonism and developed as the idea of an opposition between spirit and matter. Applied to man, this concept gives rise to the notion that the nature of man was composed of a lower part (body) and a higher part (soul) which resulted in a contempt for the physical body or this material world and a grand expectation in an afterlife. In contrast, moral dualism insists there is an irreducible battle between good and evil in which the higher deity intervenes and saves the world from the power of the evil or lower god who holds the world imprisoned for a specified time allowed by the higher god.

Dualism was placed in our philosophical processes mainly through Plato who emphasized the separation of the immortal soul and the mortal physical body. Augustine brought this principle into the religious world by defining the soul as the ruler of the body, independent of it, and out-lives it. But earlier still, Babylonian Zoroastrianism implied there were two deities who were co-eternal and in constant battle. Dualistic streams entered Judaic thought around 1000 B.C. when the Jewish nation, exiled in Babylon, was part of the Persian empire. Judean literature then incorporated God's adversary the satan. The conquering of Persia by Alexander the Great transported the dualistic principle from Asia, through the Middle East, and on to the Hellenistic empire of Greece and Rome entering the Christian New Testament and other early Christian writings. Man, now has a God to worship and a devil to resist.

Dualistic ideologies are present in man even as a child. A baby must learn what is part of him and what is outside of him. From infancy, the idea of separation is ingrained in him as he is constantly bombarded with pairs, with contrasts, with choices, and all these things force a decision of judgment. Did God impart this mindset or was it learned from conditions that were present? The body, in determining temperate comfort, the mind's interpretation of pain, and the fear of the dark when the lights go out, is constantly processing contrasts and making judgments as to how they affect the person. Were ideas of contrast present at creation or did man bring the concept perhaps in part to deal with the origin of evil?

Dualism divided the world into opposing forces and set mankind in the seat of decision choosing whom to obey, who is stronger, and who is right or wrong, the kairos point.

Dualism essentially consists of ongoing contrasts utilized in explaining concepts which precipitate in judgment. Can one produce a substance or object that causes darkness? Darkness is the absence of light. A flashlight has the capacity to produce light but when it is not operational then no light is produced and darkness ensues. Incidentally, there is no object that produces darkness without first acting on the source of light. We have terms such as polarities and pairs that are not true to the dualistic concept such as a positive and negative. In a battery, the positive and negative charges are required for the battery to function dissipating its charge; yet both can be defined without the other. Judgment is incorporated because we assume positive is always the good of the two but when the doctor says your test is positive for a specific disease such as cancer that is not good. Yet a positive pregnancy test is usually good news. A pair is not opposites but simply parts that make up a whole.

Religious Dualism

Duality is the work of religion; there is no division in truth.
Lynn Hayes, 2012 Conference

Another parameter of dualism says that all life can be separated into the secular and sacred. Does this not sound like the contrasts that occur between Law and Grace? The Law is the portrait of duality in that from it issues cause and effect, credit and debit; while grace, which is nothing to compare, is non-duality and oneness. Dualism separates human beings into hierarchical planes which says a Christian who wants to be a missionary is in a different plane (reward status) than a person who wants to star in a rock band. It causes mankind to look at men and place each one in a certain order of worth making one more important or vital than another thereby closer to God. This division of two competing groups has caused man, religion, the church, and other institutions to label or pass judgment on each other. It forces one to gauge, to place an interpretative value, or to measure worth. Dietrich Bonhoeffer says: "Thinking in terms of two realms understands the paired concepts worldly-Christian, natural-supernatural, profane-sacred, rational-revelational, as ultimate static opposites that designates certain given entities that are mutually exclusive. This thinking fails to recognize the original unity of these opposites in the Christ-reality (Green 2013, 602)." His thoughts are their restoration in Christ principle and in their repair, one can then participate in the physical and spiritual world simultaneously. The Gospel is missing many dimensions when it is preached only in hopes of an afterlife, when it stresses earth is heaven's waiting room and death is a portal to the afterlife and God's lap. The Gospel is multifaceted and a journey of discovery and was never intended to define a breach but portrays what is, revealing there is nothing to repair.

Christian Anthropological Dualism is a view which proposes all men are composed of two distinct and separate substances or forces one being temporal and bad, and the other eternal and good. The Christian religion calls them body and soul and in this dichotomy, one tends to exert itself over the other; one as master and the other succumbs as slave. In this vein of thought the body is corrupt and decaying while the soul is eternal and cannot die. It also exerts the idea that the body must be cleaned up in some way whether it is mastered by the spirit or is corrected in hell fire but either way, a correction is inevitable. This is the standard Christian view of the composition of man which sees one part as redeemable and the other part lost, the ultimate separation and the price for unrepentant sin.

Christian Metaphysical Dualism is a view that establishes heaven is the goal while earth is not worthy of renewal. It strives to place all things in the heavens now, in the place of light, while the earth, which is the shadow of heaven, is consumed by darkness and is not fit to be saved. It characterizes the things of the world as ungodly and should not be enjoyed as one's heart and purpose is to strive for the heavenly home. This dichotomy deals with reality and its definition placing what is real in the spiritual realm and the visible physical realm is an illusion. This view also places faith in a corner and it becomes private, not for outward show, and not a valid necessity for living. It also pushes God outside and makes Him an ethereal otherworldly untouchable power who is to holy to care and unconcerned with the affairs of his creation.

A somewhat antithetical view is Wholism which places the singularity of being in each person as reality and life. Anthropological Christian theology is a part of Christian theology that is concerned with the genesis, nature, and future of humanity especially as contrasted with the nature of God. In this idea, man, although seemingly composed of parts (body & soul), is not separated and therefore functions as a collective whole (Wong 2002, 1, 10). It sees the whole man created good and redeemed. In the metaphysical aspect of reality, it identifies only one reality and that is the present moment. It recognizes the division of heaven and earth but it does not say one triumphs over the other. Heaven and earth are one cohesive whole in purpose rather than a fragment of reality. As I was editing this chapter, I was watching Super Soul Sunday with Oprah Winfrey and William Paul Young. They were discussing out of what stresses he wrote *The Shack* and were also discussing his new book and the concepts we have developed about God to fit our paradigm. Young was discussing his restoration when he said, "The movement toward wholeness is when the way of our being matches the truth of our being (Young 2017)." We become an expression of wholeness when duality ceases and our path matches our truth. There is no proverbial fork in the road nor spoon when matter succumbs to mind.

The Tree of Duality: Refocusing the Creation Story

What is done out of love always takes place beyond good and evil.
Nietzsche

When considering the Genesis creation story, we tend to focus on what happened after the Tree of Knowledge of Good and Evil rather than trying to get a glimpse of what it was like before "the fall." One major aspect that is removed was the concept that creation was inherently good. God pronounced it good—no mistakes and if creation was comprehensively good then all parts of creation including persons were good. All places, all things, all ideas, were good. According to the Genesis narrative, the fall plunges all this good into vanity and now it becomes not good. Dualism has restructured the good creation into a creation in need of fixing—in need of redemption. Was redemption a saving mechanism from hell or a saving of man's ideas, dreams, perceptions, and his soul from a perceived hell? Through dualism, man became lost and in need of salvation.

Matthew 18:11 says the "Son of Man has come to save that which was lost." The Greek word for lost is *apollumi* and is rendered destroyed, useless or ruined. It is assumed lost to mean location but this word implies nothing about lost as losing a home in heaven but indicates a loss in function. When something is rendered useless it is another way of saying it is unable to function as intended. So, the lost mankind that the Son of Man came to "save" was not a loss in location but a loss in function, an inability to function in the fullness of God's intent; God then demonstrates this intent in the Christ who is the implied destiny or future of every man. Romans 8:20 says creation was placed in vanity and whereas lost was the inability to function; vanity was a state of unending defeat and loss of potential as man became dysfunctional perceiving hopelessness. Dualism makes implication that hope is a process of learning as man was placed in this position of need, a process of restoration to what once was, to a return home.

Dualistic concepts have caused us to fail to see beauty in creation. We don't comprehend the beauty of God in the stars and we have forgotten the beauty of life experienced in the birth of our children. We have lost the freedom to enjoy the arts and music in lieu of a forced religious attempt to be holy. It also causes us to see our different personalities as something to overcome rather than embrace; painting the self as bad and sinister. C S Lewis said, "either the world has gone wrong but still maintains a memory of what it once was or there are two worlds each influenced by independent powers one good and the other evil and we are in the middle of the battlefield of an endless war (Barrs 2009)." Duality diminishes God's influence over all creation and portrays a small Christ who has failed to exert a cosmic influence leaving man's path to one of correction and restoration causing a need to return rather than enjoying the mystery of the journey.

Is not the Tree of Life experienced when we understand nothing can separate us from the love of God? Love (union, without contrast) is the fruit of the Tree of Life just as fear (separation, duality, judgment) is the fruit of the Tree of Knowledge. They ate of the tree and then their eyes were opened being a conscious act and not one of sight for they knew they were naked and then they saw their nakedness. The fruit of the Tree of Knowledge was, I believe, a realized fear manifesting from a perceived separation from God. Could they have eaten the trees in the wrong order? In the concept of mathematical multiplication, if you have nothing and multiply it by any number you still have nothing such as seen in the solutions of "0 X 1" and "0 X 99." In order for something to be multiplied you must have some of it already; it must be immediately present such as seen in the solutions of "1 X 1" or "1 X 99." In Genesis 3:16 we are told "I will greatly multiply your sorrow and your conception." Sorrow must have been present to be multiplied. Also, if life was a promise of the Tree of Life and they were removed from it then they apparently did not have it to begin with. Were sorrow and death present in the Eden of God along with other things we have not associated as being in the presence of God?

Martin Buber, an Austrian Jewish philosopher, says the Tree of Knowledge of Good and Evil (*tov va'ra*) actually means any duality. Genesis 2:7 utilizes the word "formed" (*vayitzer*) which means impulse. Therefore, man was created with two impulses one good (*yetzer tov*) and the other evil (*yetzer ra*). The good being moral conscience and the other a selfishness without benevolence. Yezter ra was not an entity to force one to do evil but an internal voice that focused on selfish fulfillment (Kepnes 2004). This later became the understanding of satan in Judaism as satan was the inner self that pursued division from God.

In the realm of religious duality, we have created a God to be feared, who is vengeful, and who punishes forever. We then assume we have the obligation to be like Him and we exact these same responses on our fellowman. We have built this warrior God who defends us while destroying others who are what? Unloved? Undeserving? We make Him big enough to handle the things we do not understand and use His sovereignty as an excuse. As we have not understood who we really are, we have allowed the teachings of Jesus to be our focus and worshiping him as a being we cannot become rather than understanding his teachings point to Father and realize He is us in the intent of a great God; a portrait of who we really are in the mind and purpose of the Progenitor of all creation.

Illusion of Separation

Sometimes people do not want to hear the truth because they don't want their illusions destroyed.
Friedrich Nietzsche

We know the story in Genesis with Adam and Eve and when we tell it we do not bat an eye as we say God removed them from the garden so they could not get back to the Tree of Life. I first concluded God did not forsake Jesus to understand that there never was a separation. Jesus proclaims Psalm 22 and perceives forsakenness and later in the Psalm he realizes he was never left alone in verse 25.

The eye-opening event Adam and Eve experienced suggests a new development in their maturity and it also began their concept of separation. They were one flesh but now they saw themselves as separate from each other and from their Creator. It also hints at their separation from creation in that they were tillers (co-workers) of the garden and they became subject to the produce of the garden (thrones and thistles shall it bring forth and returning to the ground from which you were taken).

In Colossians 1, Paul is talking about all mankind being reconciled in the Christ and in verse 21 he clarifies the reason this message must be clear. He says you were "alienated and enemies in your mind..." and he goes on to say because of this perception (this image) you acted out what you believed to be true (Col. 1.19-22, Eph. 4.17-24). Your perception of distance from God caused you to perceive separation and based on that concept you built a God up there rather than God within.

The word "alienate" in Colossians 1:21 is the Greek word *apallotrioo* which means to shut out from fellowship or intimacy. It also carries the meaning of being separated from one's origin because of belonging to another (JMNT). The word for enemy is *echthros* and means opposing God in the mind. This person who has perceived himself distanced from God does not realize this opposition has never been declared by God as truth, meaning it is only perceived—only an illusion in the mind of the man who has accepted it.

Ephesians 4:17-19 expresses the concept of darkness. How can understanding be darkened when understanding is a mental act not a sensual one using the eyes which interpret light and dark? This verse also indicates the estrangement is perceived because alienation is present due to ignorance and ignorance is present because of blindness of the heart not meaning the eyes nor the beating organ. These verses indicate a perception that is perceived from the senses and acknowledge it is a flawed perception.

These verses seem to indicate the idea of separation came from the perception of evil as lack of functionality and its power to cause a division. The parameters of evil are not solely locked up in a devil with or without horns or even whether an evil entity exists but it also encompasses hostility, hatred, and violence and these are all antithetical to love. In virtually every culture and basis of religion, evil is typified as a universal presence of a power that can bring sorrow, calamity, distresses, and misfortune. Evil seems to be a distinct occurrence in the human world as animals know nothing of it and at the same time there is not a religion, culture, or race of people that considers evil to be impotent. Mankind seems to be the primary progenitors of evil in that man sets the definition and perpetuates it. Most religions tend to imply that evil is necessary for man to know good. Then, satan is necessary for us to know God. Dualism portrays the world as a battlefield for the universal struggle of good and evil with good triumphant in the future. In this cosmic scenario, God is good and the devil bad and God is going to win some day. The constant stream of battles are the popular reasons for unpleasantness in life and act as proof of the distant of God from man as sin envelopes evil over good. In redefining our concept of God, we begin to see the life that God gave to us does not depend on man measuring good and evil, pleasure and pain, love and fear, or comparing God and satan. It is evident God is not concerned with these dualistic principles as they seem to detract from God rather than help us gain an understanding of Him.

Cause and Effect

We tend to merge the natural law of cause and effect with God's chastisement. The concept of cause and effect is a biblical concept known as sowing and reaping (Galatians 6:7). Mankind, when going through a period of trouble and forgetting what got him in the predicament exclaims "God is sure chastening me today" when in reality they are reaping what they have sown, or more simply put, enduring the consequences of previous actions.

The law of cause and effect states that every material effect must have an antecedent cause. As the idea of this law matured its meaning has also been refined. In 1781 Immanuel Kant said, "everything that happens presupposes a previous condition (Kant 1781)." In 1934, W. T. Stace, a professor at Princeton commented, "everything which has a beginning has a cause, and that in the same circumstances the same things invariably happen (Stace 1934, 6)." In 1977 at the Goddard Institute for Space Studies at NASA, Robert Jastrow added a much fuller comment still. He expressed, "the Universe, and everything that has happened in it since the beginning of time, are a grand effect without a known cause...the Universe, and man himself, originated in a moment when time began (Jastrow 1977, 21)." In the law of First Cause, God alone is the initiator while cause and effect occur outside of God's initiation being influenced by the multifaceted dynamics of human choice.

In Robert Clark's article entitled "The Christ Mind," he suggests cause and effect are not two different things as an effect is the manifestation of the cause and are intricately linked. The cause first occurs in the mind ("Let there be...") which is the birthplace of ideas and thoughts (Clark n.d. 42). Everything that exists does so because of a thought (cause) that initiated the effect being the physical demonstration of the thought. God imagined us (cause) and the living soul is the effect. In God, we are the glorious manifestation of His cause, His thought-out desire which is His intent becoming flesh. We enjoy the effect multidimensionally as experience and expression.

Where are we then? We begin looking for God in a mindset of already being separated by His hand. We are told we are sinners in the sight of God, He is angry with us, and has cast us from His presence. But we quote Psalms 139:7-8 "Where can I go from Your Spirit? Or where can I flee from Your presence? If I ascend into heaven, you are there; If I make my bed in hell, behold, You are there." One who accepts the illusion of separation is in their own hell and in this position, sees every problem as a punishment from God and the forecast for the world is impending doom now with a date of any day the planets align, the stock market crashes, or of the next blood moon.

This is an idea of the depth of the ideology that man is lost from His Creator. Acts 17:26 details the flow of blood through all mankind as coming from "one blood" (Paul, Acts 17:26). Paul goes on to say that in this God that you are not sure who He is, rests our causative movement and purpose and he closes with we are all the offspring of this very God as the birth of His cause, His intent, and His thought manifested. And then it perhaps makes sense that we have been looking in the wrong place for God. He is not out there but in us. Discover God rather than trying to believe in Him. The Tree of Knowledge has lost its power and its consequences are being brought to an end as the fruit of the Tree of Life becomes ripe.

What if we really studied the concept of first cause where would we end up? In our viewing the outcomes of cause, we allow our perception to alter the real outcome and see God as the instrument of our pain, our sickness, and even death of our loved ones. It is not God responding out of anger or hurt but a self-imposed effect, a consequence based on our own actions and interpretation of the cause. Man's view of the law of cause and effect has maligned the righteous inferences of God in creation into something that is even worse than a human father would do to his own children.

Duality and Our World View

A world view, according to James Sire, is not a matter of the mind or the thoughts we hold as truth but it is a matter of spiritual orientation. Our world view is rooted in the origin of our understanding of God and His dealings with man. It is a matter of one's heart after the concepts of God's wisdom, purpose, and other parameters have met and formed an image of God. Our world view is situated inside ourselves and it is from this single chamber of origination that our thoughts and actions proceed. Sire sums up the idea of one's world view as "a commitment, a fundamental orientation of the heart that can be expressed as a story or in a set of presuppositions (assumptions that may be true, partially true, or false) which we hold (consciously or subconsciously) about the basic constitution of reality, and that provides the foundation on which we live and move and have our being (Sire 2009, 20-21)" as he copies Paul from Acts 17:28.

We peer at this physical world through our dualistic lens and we see good/bad, spirit/body, faith/reason and others, yet in our uncanny ability to see things in opposition, we determine which is better, which is greater than. If there is a better one, then there is a less than better one. Through these lens the outcome is a loss in the creative abilities of man given by God producing a disharmonic expression of the divine and human. We see diversity in ethnic groups, cultures, and communities as we continue to fracture mankind into pieces and parts. This mindset stalls our ability to live in freedom and withholds it from those who we perceive are different or wrong missing out on the awesome mystery of the Logos of God hidden for us.

Reality is the state of things as they exist without filters of the senses and the mind. It is reality whether it is observable or comprehensible and it includes everything that has existed, that exists, or that will exist. John Gavazonni's definition states when identifying reality, one must ask could it and does it exist within God who is absolute reality (Gavazonni 2012). Phrases such as "believe you receive" and "I am not saved unless I believe" were based on the direct aspect of man's ability to pull these proofs into reality. What gives truth its power? Certainly not my belief. But realization of truth brings a powerful influence into one's life but why is that? If truth is active and dynamic, and I believe it is, then my awareness of it does not empower it but accepting it allows it to work on my behalf. To believe is to make a judgment and often it is made based on facts and not truth. Truth does not need acceptance to make it so while belief does.

Our world view is the manifestation of our reality which consists of our assumptions solely based on perception. It is from these perceptions that fear arises. It is not a rational fear of reality but an irrational fear of the reality we have created. How do we unshackle our eyes to see what is real? Is it not by refocusing the lens, removing duality, and negating the senses? If we would peer closely into the mirror of Christ being the reflection of God's intent; then seeing reality, we would understand who we are and the ghost of what we perceived was real would shatter. There is only one reality; the present moment and this moment contains a myriad of potentialities of exploration, discovery, and revelation. We are not locked in time unless we perceive we are caused by our tendency to focus on the past, to fear the future, and failing to live in the moment of His presence. It is in the moment life is experienced as life is not a series of separate occurrences but a whole life experience discovering presence, wholeness, and relationship being the dance of divinity and humanity.

Perception, Illusion, & the Line of Sight

"If the doors of perception were cleansed
everything would appear to man as it is, Infinite.
For man has closed himself up,
till he sees all things thro' narrow chinks of his cavern."
(William Blake 1908)

Perception depends on one's world view and is integrated into that world view to define reality. Imagination is the ability to form an image and is needed to make sense of perceptions. Imagination is also the awareness of one's inner most thoughts and intentions. Its literal meaning is seeing within one's being. Perception effects the imagination—the seeing within—by forming concepts received through the senses. It is the birthing of these concepts from which one forms beliefs thereby constructing reality. As our perception of reality takes form, we can only see things that are not obstructed by something else causing distortion or distraction. How can we determine if our view is obstructed? Like natural sight, if I can draw a line from my eyes to the object without any deterrents then my line of sight is unobstructed. In dealing with our constructs of perception, if the image I see can be viewed without distortion then the constructed perception is valid; but who determines if distortion is present? This means that two people can have different perceptions depending upon where they are seeing the image from. In other words, the foundation for the object seen must be true before one can know the derived perception is also true.

Is man a tripartite being? Can he function in any one part separate from the others? In the Genesis account, God formed the flesh, infused life, and man became a living soul. The soul is not a part of man but is man. The soul ceases to exist if the heart stops beating, the flesh decays, and the spirit returns to God. The soul is the result or reaction of the union of flesh and spirit, in that it is the resulting life force of divinity and humanity. He was man before the breath and he simply became a breathing man functioning as a living soul. The ego seeks to dominate through competition while the spirit co-creates. The ego's primary focus is the final outcome while the spirit of man loves the process. Its functional purpose is to experience sensual reality or perceived reality and convince the soul of its authenticity. The ego incorporates perception which is data gathered by the senses but it is spirit which brings reality convincing the ego. The ego tends to depend on duality which judges reality while spirit clears the living soul to experience an eternal present moment.

Neo, in The Matrix, was awakened out of his false perception of reality and then realized his real strength (Wachowski 1999). I think we confuse our concept of the law because we have so confused our perception of God. God did not give the law to correct but to demonstrate the need for re-alignment. Religion took it to mean a realignment from bad to good making it behavior oriented, but was it? Or was the realignment supposed to be a mindset? I think the true precept of God is there and freely given but the filters that are used to interpret cause the obtained image to be out of focus. In our reasoning, we think God caused evil when it was just the effect or consequence of misapplied law arising from our understanding of God's requirements which we see through the lens of dualism.

The Eye

The light of the body is the eye,
if your eye be single (not two) your body will be full of light.

Matthew 6:22-23 KJV

Matthew 6:22-23, I believe, is saying metaphorically the source of light or the source of reality for man is his eye of understanding which must function properly. If you have double vision your understanding is out of focus. In saying the eye should be single is speaking of the ability of the eye to convey insight correctly with the image in perfect focus. The word for single is *haplous* and carries the meaning of clear, good, sound, and perfect all which speak of functionality. The eye of the mind when functioning properly is the illuminator, the source of light for the living soul. Verse 23 says "but if the eye be evil..." and here we see an awesome definition of evil and that is simply inability to function properly. The phrase "full of light" means the illuminator in the first part of this verse in conjunction with the fully functioning eye of the mind produces a clearly reflected image of truth and reality.

The eyes and the idea of sight are often used in scripture to convey perception. When we see something that is remarkable to the sight we say it was "eye catching" or an "eye opener." When a person is great at a certain task he is said to "have an eye for it." The eye is the organ of perception and perception involves more than what is seen with the natural eye and the eye has experienced a tremendous mystic history in folklore. When we understand a certain point, we say "Oh, I see that now." When we ignore a certain action of our children we are said "to have turned a blind eye." In biblical accounts sight is indicated by possessing knowledge and wisdom while evil is associated with sin and darkness as the inability to function properly.

Blindness is not only caused by a physical problem with the eyes but it can also be a problem with lighting and interpretation of what is seen. If there is insufficient light on the object it cannot be reflected therefore it cannot be seen with functioning eyesight for even a fully sighted person is blind in darkness. 2 Corinthians 4:4 deals with blindness of perception being sense derived. In Romans 11:8, God giving them over to a spirit of stupor so their eyes would not see was not a loss of sight but a loss of interpretation or understanding of what was seen. And finally, in John 9:1-44 the one blind from birth is a physical problem with the eyes experiencing a loss of function.

Some problems with sight can be reception, distraction, and perception. Reception is a normal seeing eye that is being blocked from seeing the object. When Peter was called out of the boat in Matthew 14:28 he stepped out and started walking then he saw the waves, which blocked his sighting of the Christ. Another is distraction which is looking at more than one thing and can't see the intended object clearly. In John 6:9 when Andrew is faced with feeding five thousand he proclaimed, "but what are they among so many?" He was seeing thousands of men, women, and children through the five loaves and two fish. Perception is something wrong with the interpretation of what is seen. I see it but I don't believe it. In John 9 the man was born blind and Jesus spits on the ground, makes mud, and rubs it in his eyes. The Pharisees were uncertain of what they just witnessed with their eyes. They questioned him and the man told them you don't know nothing about him but I know he opened my eyes. What occupies your line of sight, occupies your heart.

Sometimes, in order to see the object, we may need to shift position realigning our mindset. We have allowed filters to block our line of sight to God. These filters, such as law and grace or good and evil, cause us to see a distorted image of God. It was the effect or birth of our perception coming through these filters which caused our blindness. In Mark 4:11-12, Jesus tells the disciples it has been given them to know the mystery of the Kingdom of God but to others it has not been given and he says in verse 12 that "seeing they may see and not perceive, and hearing they may hear and not understand; lest they should turn, and their sins be forgiven them." Here in these verses a desire to understand is required and if that is lacking, then perception is blinded. Perception is the process of apprehending or coming to understand through the senses a clear and correct image. It is the basic component in the formation of a concept. They were unable to form a concept deriving truth because of a lack of understanding.

I believe the reference in Matthew 6:22 regarding the single eye is a functional perception of reality or said another way; not seeing two images, not having double vison. The duality of the mind's eye is found in Paul exclaiming "and be not conformed to this world" or do not allow your mind to pattern reality based on perceptions of this world; "but be transformed by renewing your mind" which is the removal of double vision and seeing single. A true focus of the object producing a correct perception of the image. Two words are used here with subtle differences. I believe their variations lie in inward versus outward changes. Conform is the Greek word *sumorphos* meaning to fashion alike in the sense of equal purpose without regard to ability; while transform is the Greek word *morphos* being a physical alteration. The change occurs as we look in the mirror and we are changed from glory to glory or from an incorrect opinion to a correct opinion. We see and recognize the correct image and we are morphed—transformed into what we see—the word is the same as transfigure. Conform is undergoing a change to function properly or from dysfunctional to functional and the process is imaged in Philippians 3:20-21. 2 Cor 3:18 as transformed carries the idea of being changed into another form—

we are being afterward formed or formed after the image seen—His Logos being the picture in God's mind.

Man, naturally considers the events of his life to be the result of luck, chance, or even an accident; which is a state of mind missing a creative force to alter reality in the circumstances of life. However, we need to understand that we live our life out of consciousness which is a part of the spiritual capacity God has built into every man. This awareness has been called our sub-conscious mind, spirit, logos, or force; but regardless of what it may be called, it links our life either to the realm of potentiality or to the illusive world of duality created by and around us where this powerful creative force is absent or non-functioning.

Non-Duality

All separation, every kind of estrangement and alienation is false.
All is one.
Sri Nisargadatta Maharaj, (1897-1981) Indian Spiritualist

There is a vast amount of evidence indicating the world is steeped in contrasts: up and down, in and out, black and white, right and wrong, true and false, and the major one, life and death. Language continues to convey pairing of opposites to increase understanding but can we really learn by using comparisons? In the reality of God do opposites exist? In discussing non-duality, it must go beyond defining opposition. Non-duality is a translation of the Sanskrit word *advaita* which simply means destitute of duality and having no duplicate (Monier Williams Online Sanskrit Dictionary, 2008 Revision). It signifies unity and completeness and to full intimacy and love beyond words in the present moment experience. What does it mean to consider non-dualistic concepts? It points to a reset of the mental image of God and humanity. You are not a sinner saved by grace but a son of God, a relational part of the Creator of all things and you stand in union with Him—His intent visible. It may cause you to see you are not incomplete and broken as you were told you were and it may allow you to see yourself in the mirror of His mind being the amazing intent and purpose of a magical and mysterious God to be seen in every man.

Belief, Perception, & the Map of Reality

Things that do not require their opposites to express them do not constitute duality. If the entity exists independent of its opposite, then it is real. You have no need of an opposite to understand you therefore you are real. When you hold your baby in your arms you do not need to imagine an opposite to understand your child—you simply love. Now, in expressing that love your heart fills for the child and thoughts about him overtake your mind and you have a full perception of this moment. Then you suddenly imagine and see the time before the child existed and you feel empty as compared to now or you fear the loss of that child in the future stepping out of the present moment; that is dualism and is a perceived act based on false assumptions and is not real but is made up in your mind and acted upon in your emotions. What is real? "If real is what you can see, feel, smell, taste, and hear; then real is simply electrical signals interpreted by your brain (Wachowski 1999)" or is real what does not go away when you stop believing?

Personal beliefs play a dramatic role in how we view life and our interpretation of life is based on those beliefs. They provide a means through which we evaluate everything in our lives and in the lives of those around us. Our version of reality is the sum of our beliefs and our beliefs force us to see through them and interpret the world around us deriving our perception of reality. What you hold as truth whether it is truth or not is based on your perception. Through life experiences we collect and amass large amounts of information and in processing this data we form our system of beliefs building our worldview. It is because our belief system is built on our evaluation and interpretation of this data we form a conclusion that our subconscious accepts as fact. The mind combines and structures these tidbits of facts to form a personal version of the real world informing what is real and what is not providing us with our personal map of reality. This map is our own unique version of accuracy and everything is measured against it and when something causes a disruption we are willing to reject as false anything that cannot be found in our belief system. The map may or may not be real, but we have made it so and when the map seems to unravel a bit as our views of God change we lose hope and direction because we keep focused solely on the map. When this happens, we feel our map is being destroyed but we are simply downloading a new version that has additional roads, towns, and places of interest that the previous version was lacking. So, updating our beliefs provide a better and more detailed map of what is real further pointing us to our origin in God.

As we define, defend, and depend on our map we tend to become restricted by its boundaries. Those limitations place real restrictions on the life experience and we must remember it is based on vantage point and line of sight. If I look at the earth in Google Maps, I see a distant orb on which I can see land and water but as I zoom in the structures become more enhanced by the amplified view and increasing amplification again and I begin to see actual roads and trees allowing me to lose my perception of the roundness and distance of the earth and focus on one street corner as intense detail comes into view. In the same way, the congestion of too many superfluous details in our belief system causes us to lose perspective and interpret wrongly as we attempt to focus on a single detail forgetting the journey.

The construction of a map of our beliefs is like a treasure hunt. We need certain beliefs to empower us and keep us on the hunt by keeping us intrigued, fascinated, and awed and at the same time we need to be wary of too many precise boundaries that destroy the sense of adventure and wonderment of God. Life is an ever-changing map and open to discovery allowing us to approach people and experiences as a child trusting God to unfold newness and intrigue. In looking at the earth from space there are no boundaries, no countries, no agendas, no rival governments only beauty and awe. If we can learn to live life beyond the map and see the world as one creation by a loving God realizing we get to participate not in an experiment but experience.

Non-duality is not a belief system but it is simply resting in the reality that you are His and always have been. It realizes that in every moment you are in His presence and He in yours and separation does not exist. A person who is at rest in God does not spend time searching for God but rests as a son on the Father's breast listening to the heartbeat and seeing what He sees and desires. All are one—not all is one.

The Illusive Identity of Death, The False Security of Immortality, & The Misapplied Hope of Resurrection

The major scrimmage of duality in Western religion is portrayed in the battle of good and evil and by default, life and death. Nowhere and in no greater depth does duality touch humanity than in death and evil. It is difficult to define death without first referring to what life means and vice-versa in the idea each reflects the other. Are death and life a dualistic concept? The concept of eternal life which is life in union with God while death is separation from Him and it is in this form the dualistic influence enters and takes root. It was Augustine who, in the fifth century, added the concepts of guilt and punishment into the creation narrative promoting the view our mortality is proof of our missing the mark. He also said it was only by the mercy of God who judges all mankind that one may hope to escape his anger. Augustine summarizes since Adam was created and chose to sin, he brings death to himself and contrarily if he had not sinned he would not have died. This agrees with Thomas Aquinas and John Calvin who also affirmed loss of life occurred at the fall of man through Adam which was due to judgment of God (Hick 1976, 207). This view carries the overall idea that our vulnerability to death is the result of human action and should never have come about but because of choices death is the effect and passes to all men. The alternative concept stems from the Eastern church which says man was not created in a perfect state from which he fell but was brought into being as an immature creature who began a long process of growth and development. In the progression of this view man did not fall from a better state to a lesser one into sin with death as punishment but rather man is still in the process of being created and forever learning through his experiences on a spiritual quest to enlightenment.

The Divergence of Greek & Hebrew Thought

The dualistic principle was the basis for the Greek view of man yet was a foreign concept to Hebrew thought which is founded in Hebraic holism. While dualism insists division increases clarity, it also implies a repair is necessary to fix an error or missed mark. In other words, it divides to point out the error and then requires a restoration to bring a union of the effected parts. The Greeks partitioned man into parts and gave each part a purpose and a final destination. In Hebraic understanding man was a single entity created by God. Holism insists the parts of any whole cannot be understood except in their relation to the whole. Its focus in humanity is the indivisible union of man and insists man cannot exist apart from his whole being. The Bible uses various titles to describe human nature for example; when Paul speaks of body, soul, and spirit he is not saying man is made up of three parts as distinct substances any more than when Jesus and Moses told us to love God with all our heart, soul, mind, and strength. These ideas do not serve to compartmentalize man but to unify him. These statements are simply demonstrating by repetitive language the Hebraic concept of non-delineation by emphasizing the functional unit which is man. The Greek concept of partitioning man into parts caused a loss of our created structure and value in the image of God; then, we use a similar concept to divide God which produced the trinity.

The dualistic principle presented man with his immortal soul as Greek thought made inroads emphasizing the soul's immortality and value by devaluing the body as something impure and an accident. As this ideology became anchored in theology, it seemed to negate the Hebraic concept of man's infinite worth and instead establishes a value on a possession called the soul. However, in the New Testament Paul seems to preserve the Hebrew form in most cases by using the word "soul" (Greek *psyche*) to mean life. The separate soul concept was foreign to Paul because to the Greeks man was an embodied soul or a soul placed in a body but in Hebrew thought he was an animated body or a body brought to life. There is a vast difference as Hebrew thought considered God to be a God of the living because death was viewed as an enemy opposing God. To live is to participate in relationship with the Creator while death causes separation and a breach in relationship perceived as disunity.

The Old Testament's declaration "in dying thou shalt die" found in Genesis 2:17 was understood to apply to life while the heart beats only. It meant man would live out life and in the end, would die and go to *Sheol* (grave). There was a conceptual idea of an afterlife expressed as hope in the resurrection "at the last day" because of the eschatological thought of the day. Jewish thought understood alienation due to sin in light of the completion of life on earth. The penalty for sin was death, plain and simple; no eternal punishment, no disembodiment, just loss. Death in the Judaic culture was considered a tragic loss even when it occurred early in life but was a natural process in the plan of the Creator. The process of mourning in Jewish faith was not an expression of loss and regret but in honor of the dead and to be a comfort for the living.

The next flow of understanding regarding death arose through the Platonic portal making the body the prison for the soul. The characteristic Greek concept of life after death is not necessarily a resurrected body but an immortal soul. Regarding the Greek concept of sin, Plato said it entered due to lack of harmony and was separation from purpose according to Aristotle; while the Hebraic concept of sin was rebellion of man against his creator. The soul, according to Plato, existed before the body and would continue to exist after the death of the body and he is the source of the metaphysical concept of remembering what we have forgotten in our earlier state. Where did the concept of immortal soul come from? It seems, according to historians, the Greek concept of an immortal soul originated from Egyptian mythology some 3200 years before Jesus' birth. The primary proponent in the Greek world of the immortal soul was Plato who was the student of Socrates (Law 2007, 32, 33, 245-249).

Interestingly, history assumes the idea of the soul living on after physical death would be acceptable reasoning, however, some Jewish scholars have a differing view. For example, The Jewish Encyclopedia states in an article on the immortality of the soul saying: "The belief that the soul continues its existence after the dissolution of the body is...nowhere expressly taught in Holy Scripture. The belief in the immortality of the soul came to the Jews from contact with Greek thought and chiefly through the philosophy of Plato its principle exponent, who was led to it through Orphic and Eleusinian mysteries in which Babylonian and Egyptian views were strangely blended (Kohler 2012)." It was also apparent the early church fathers such as Origen, Tertullian, and Augustine were familiar with Platonism. Augustine of Hippo, who was one of the greatest Christian thinkers taught the power of the human soul "fused the religion of the New Testament with the Platonic tradition of Greek philosophy (West, R. 2011, 418)." There were several accounts in history pointing to early Christianity quoting Greek mythology to support the immortal soul concept. Why? Is it because it's difficult to see in the New Testament without extra-biblical support? Traditional Western philosophy, which is sourced in the ancient Greeks, was based in Egyptian mythology and this background brought the immortal soul to Western religions.

The Illusive Identity of Death

Why does death seem distant, illusive, yet imprisons us in fear and dread? Leander Keck stated, "death is a problem today partly because the language we inherited to talk about it no longer says what we think about it; we use this language because it often has residual psychological power in times of crisis and grief (Keck 1969, 96)." Throughout history the perception of death changed in relation to the cultural view of God which itself was altered due to climatic events in that person's life. These occurrences were then documented and explained, again with one's cultural view in mind becoming "gospel" for those living after them flowing into a people's tradition and ritual forming a basic religious tenet.

Is death the end result of a life? Does it signal that the life lived accomplished all it was meant to? Or was something stolen? Did an enemy intervene and cut short God's plan? But if something was stolen from us then God was not a good protector, was He? As one considers these questions it all seems to hinge on what is one's definition of death. God told mankind that he was free to eat from any tree in the garden; but he must not eat from the Tree of Knowledge of Good and Evil, for when he does he will surely die. Genesis 2:16-17, which is the basis for one's formula of death and its meaning, does not say the body would die and the soul would live on. It was also not a curse but a description of what occurs if a choice was made. It is recounted by the satan in Genesis 3:4 when Eve was told she will not surely die but God knows that when you eat from it your eyes will be opened and you will be like God knowing good and evil. Did the adversary know more of God's intention than those made in His image and walked with Him in the cool of the day? Or, did mankind simply not understand the actual meaning of death? Did what the serpent said come to pass? Did the serpent attempt to deceive Eve by telling her that she would possess immortality and not be subject to death of the soul which seems to be the prevailing concept in Christian circles today? God does confirm the serpent's statement in Genesis 3:22 when He says the man has become like one of us, knowing good and evil. He goes on to say man is removed from the garden so he cannot partake of the Tree of Life for a period of time and live forever. Man did not have immortality or he would not have been removed from the metaphorical fruit that could give it to him.

Did God pronounce a curse being an appeal for evil, misfortune, and doom upon mankind sentencing him to death? Or was death a penalty being a punitive measure exacted by the one offended resulting in a judicial decision for breaking God's law? Was death solely the effect following a cause initiated by one man yet inherited by all men—a consequence being something produced by a cause being neither a curse nor penalty; but a self-inflicted response arising out of choices made.

The Many Faces of Death

The traditional religious view of death indicates it is the judgment of God exacted on sinful man. God then, condemned man eternally for an act which occurred in the span of a mortal heartbeat. The Bible is portrayed as saying this act put the entire creation in jeopardy, until both parties accept the blood of Jesus. The incident causing death set up man's redemption requiring a deliverer. Yet Paul insists death came by man and Genesis says God repented for creating him.

A Course in Miracles indicates, "Death is the central dream from which all illusions stem (Schucman 1992, 82)" posing the question does man live just to enter the process of death? Does the life of humanity travel to the final fate of cessation? If death is the final result of life then where is God? The decree of God passing to dust through fear, pain, and despair does not point to a good God. If death exists, is peace really possible? A Course in Miracles implies death is the symbol of God's judgment and death is real for mankind then life becomes illusive as this construct empowers death over life. Paul considers life to be the final victor and the defeat of death is accomplished, but death is still present and exerting dominance over mankind.

Death tends to be accepted in the Judeo-Christian worldview as God's judgment for an act within the heartbeat yet effecting eternity. Does the Bible imply the dead are alive in heaven or hell or does it attempt to make it clear the dead are not alive in any realm and there not being sensation or experience of life after the heartbeat? The bible speaks of the dead as destitute of knowledge and speech and as knowing nothing making it clear that death is clearly death and not life in some other form according to biblical understanding. Death is a return to a state prior to life and it is not a location (Knoch 2013). Vine says the Greek word *apollumi* does not insinuate extinction but of "ruin, loss, not of being but of wellbeing (Vine 1985, 164)."

Barth considers death itself not to be the judgment of God but is the sign or evidence God has rendered judgment (Pannenberg 2004, 138-139). It is the standard Christian worldview that death is said to be punishment for sin, then is it also reasonable to assume if death were part of the original plan then it would not be painful or fear-inducing? Therefore, death is not God's intent yet this cosmological stance places the entire race of mankind in search of deliverance from an act supposedly inflicted by God as it is said at death God "calls us home." Another interpretation of death is the view that is posited by Ted Peters, a Systematic Theology professor at Pacific Lutheran University who says death is "a gift of divine grace because it marks a point when consequences of sin come to an end (Peters 2000)." He also adds death is the work of God as He demonstrates mercy utilizing death as a gift of His Divine grace because it marks a point in time the effects of sin come to an end as there is no suffering in the grave. "Death is the door that slams shut on evil and suffering within creation (Peters 2000)." This interpretation removes the traditional view of death being an enemy and renders death good and almost a blessing as Peters refers to Revelation 14:13. So this concept brings about the question does God utilize death for His purpose?

Jurgen Moltmann emphasizes death is a completion of life in that living as if there is no death is to live an illusion. Moltmann attempts to make death less bitter and tamer by implying it is out of love we quietly surrender to death as if it is love which allows us to experience the "livingness of life and the deadliness of death (Moltmann 1995, 46)." He says that it is through this lens of love that we can understand the entire human experience where both life and death are a part of God's plan which he brings about in our lives. Is death an acceptable avenue of God's plan for man? It is the traditional concept of the resurrection that ensures death is not the end.

One of the challenges in defining death is distinguishing it from life. It sounds easy as death begins when life ends, however, defining that particular moment requires precise conceptual boundaries between life and death. This is somewhat problematic because the difficulty is exacerbated due to on-going debates attempting to define life. It is not as simple as saying death is the cessation of all biological functions which sustain an organism because consciousness can remain in the absence of a functioning heart or lungs and the reverse is also true in that the organs can remain functioning in the absence of consciousness. It becomes acutely apparent that death is more of a process rather than a single event.

Historically, death was defined as the cessation of the heartbeat and of breathing but the development of CPR and the increased knowledge of the circulatory and respiratory system has rendered that definition inadequate because breathing and heartbeat can sometimes be restarted. Life can be sustained without a functioning heart and lungs by a combination of support devices, organ transplants, and artificial pacemakers. If the lungs and heart are forced to keep operating by mechanical means in which food is digested and waste is excreted then are these the actions of a dead body? Or perhaps a more correct question would be, "Is there a person there anymore?" Can CPR exert control over the traditional religious understanding of the breath of life? Can the paddles bring a life back even after according to religious understanding God has "called the loved one home?"

The previous ideas center only on the organic aspect of life and death, but what about person-hood? When is the person no longer in the body? This idea brings into to play the electrical impulse of the brain as the indicator of consciousness. Not only must life be defined but the definition of a person must be connected to the concept of death. Deciding when a person is no longer alive also has significant consequences for now one must consider what a person is defined to be.

Is death an enemy or the gateway to heaven and the presence of God? Philippians 2:25-26 details Paul's account of Epaphroditus who was sick "unto death" and Paul says God had mercy on him and he was healed. Was God merciful or cruel by keeping him out of heaven? Why does man do all he can to live longer even if it is in pain? If death is a friend, then why is it not welcomed and longed for? Why do we mourn and not rejoice over the death of a loved one if death is the fast track to God's presence? Is it not because mankind inwardly knows death is not a friend to usher us into

God's presence but is an enemy? 1 Corinthians 15:26 says death is the last enemy to be destroyed. Oscar Cullmann poignantly says "death in itself is not beautiful" and whoever portrays death in a favorable light cannot portray a glorious resurrection (Cullmann 1956, 12).

Is the death of the body the extinction of the person? Or does one survive as a continuing consciousness? Does the individual enter again into a greater spiritual reality like a drop of water returning to the ocean? John Hick says death is a vast mystery and is evidenced because it is a central concern to all religions of the world. It is contained as the major topic of nearly all the great religious thinkers and philosophers for centuries and these ideas are contained in a vast array of books. And yet, death remains "impenetrably obscure (Hick 1976, 21)" as no man can testify to the trip that occurs after death by whatever mechanism it is defined.

New Testament View of Death

The New Testament does not appear to treat death as a major theme but instead discloses death in relation to other subjects and by not so much as what is said but more so what is not said (Keck 1969, 33). It is from these implied statements the ideology of death is derived from Scripture. For example, when Jesus said to the thief next to him "today you will be with me in paradise," religious tradition has extrapolated many doctrines from this simple phrase rather than seeing the major theme was forgiveness being a restored union in the mind of the transgressor not location of the body. Death and life are intrinsically linked to the Christ event in the New Testament that immortality becomes the central theme rather than resurrection hope.

To the early Christians, resurrection was not an isolated event but was only a portion of the presentation of the plan of God (Keck 1969, 44). It presented a moment in a sequence of eschatological events and with this central focus it explained why early Christianity was not confused by people being restored to life such as Lazarus or Jairus' daughter who died again versus the resurrection. In the eschatological viewpoint presented in Acts 3:20-21, which is likely the earliest account of the resurrection, the abode of death had been ruptured and with the early Christian understanding of death being an enemy then Jesus' resurrection was the conquering of a tyrant. If death is a defeated foe, then why do men still die? One possibility is our understanding of death stems from a misaligned view of God based on man's interpretation of God's actions in history. Furthermore, these interpretations come from writings that due to extraneous concepts prohibited a true unbiased portrait of the Logos of God.

It must be kept in mind the early New Testament writers were influenced by their geography, oral tradition, and mythical aspects of extra-biblical literature producing a diverse dualistic portrait of the Logos of God. The New Testament period flowed through the Hellenistic frame being dominated by Greek culture and folklore demonstrated by Paul quoting Epimenides the Cretan (600 BC) and Aratus (310 BC) in Acts chapters fourteen and seventeen. In my opinion, this is basic evidence that Greek concepts penetrated our developing tenets through the Hebrew mind and contributed to our understanding of death and life later forming orthodox New Testament doctrine. The oldest likely concept was the dead continued to exist in and around the graves and later it was conceived that the dead went to a place of subterranean origin known as the Greek *Hades* or the Hebraic *Sheol*. Under Orphic influence, the concept of reward and punishment was introduced adding the imprisoned soul in the body (Keck 1969, 52) and follow through to Socrates and Plato to whom the soul was an eternal alien being in a mortal body (Keck 1969, 53). Death, then in this vein of thought, was not an enemy but was a friend who released the soul from the body while the enemy was the cycle of life that imprisoned and destroyed the life of the soul.

Also during this period, Epicurus, a Greek philosopher who founded his influential school of Epicureanism in Athens in 306 CE, believed the world was a random combination of atoms and pleasure was the highest good added the soul was composed of atoms which disintegrated at death (Keck 1969, 54). The Stoics, who were part of a Greek school of philosophy founded by Zeno about 308 BC, believed God determined everything for the best and virtue was sufficient for happiness. Its later Roman form advocated the calm acceptance of all occurrences as the unavoidable result of divine will or of the natural order believing the soul was material like the body and returned to its original substance to be born again.

The Gnostics of the period acknowledged a divine spark in every man and his life's experiences were due to bondage of the eternal inside the mortal (Keck 1969, 58). While the Stoics regarded the orderly movement of the planets as evidence of cosmic law, Gnostic thought regarded the cosmic order not of providence but of fate in an inescapable tyranny of negative celestial energy governed by the planets (Keck 1969, 58). Both believed the death experience was a fulfilled purpose of someone or something with a higher purpose than themselves. It was this confusion over death as to whether it fulfilled a purpose (God eradicating sin by the flood) or was a reaction from a cause (Penalty for sin enforced by God) which birthed our New Testament's presentation of death through the mind of the early writers. Can death ever be purposeful in the Logos of God or is that a flawed perception?

Is death an interruption to life in opposition to God? Jean-Paul Sartre considered death deprived life of meaning. He posits that if the length of life were known then death would be endowed with meaning as death would complete life and give a mark of fulfillment in that life. Does history have meaning or provide the meaning? When considering death, does it close an individual's history or does it cause early termination of an unfulfilled life? Death, for Sartre, cuts arbitrarily and unpredictably across the line of life depriving that life of meaning removing fulfillment leaving an uncompleted history. Sartre concluded that death never gave life meaning but was that which removed all meaning and definition to life (Hick 1976, 101-103). Is death the consequence of an originally perfect creation? Is death a natural event in a physiological process or is death the true friend ending a hard life? With these questions about death the news of a potential resurrection as a correction of the death process was grasped in religion and become the answer for mankind in his search or hope for restitution.

Death seems to have evolved and shifted many times during history. It has changed from cessation of life through separation from God to an illusion of reality. These views provide a snapshot of death through a historical perspective and reveal a somewhat amalgamated concept proving the understanding of death is not a simple cut and dry construct. Does death offer the finality that we seem to give it? In considering the question, we must derive our responses from outside of preconceived notions and fears and our experiences. While this appears difficult, it seemingly causes a shift from the disdain and fear of death to the power of the Creator not only as deliverer out of death but also eradicator of death itself by providing a hope of death's destruction regardless of how it is defined be it cessation, separation, a return, or an illusion. Since death is so counterintuitive or not instinctively understood by humanity, then how is the soul seemingly the escape pod of man from death?

In attempting to understand the variances of Greek versus Hebrew concepts of death one may contrast the death of Jesus and Socrates. One of the aspects of death can be understood in the death of two individuals and their perceived aspect of their own death. How did these two men face death? The concept of the separate conscious soul can be seen in stark contrast in the death of Jesus versus the death of Socrates. Jesus died in the year 33 CE while Socrates died in 399 BCE, over 400 years apart each with surprising variances. Platonic thought considers the soul to be imprisoned in the body and goes on to say death is the great liberator. Plato shows Socrates' death, who, keep in mind, committed suicide, was in complete peace and composure demonstrating what Plato referred to as a "beautiful death." Socrates firmly believed that death was the redeemer of the soul and whoever fears death demonstrated a greater love for the physical world not realizing death was the soul's friend (Phaedo, 61c-69e). Jesus showed no camaraderie with death but an abhorrence to it. Why was that? If death brings him to his Father, then why would he disdain death and according to Mark 14:33 began to exhibit physical symptoms against it. Death for Jesus was not something divine but was something dreadful and painful and against life. He painted a picture demonstrating death to be abhorred and dreaded and not a friend to man.

Could there be a greater contrast in the views of death than those of Socrates and Jesus? Both had their disciples around them on the day of their death. While Socrates provided a very serene dissertation before his death; Jesus, on the other hand, was aware of what was before him displayed physical responses to his fear and dread of death and questioned his disciples about not being able to stay awake. According to the recordings of history, Socrates faced death calmly speaking on the immortality of the soul and Jesus was weeping and crying in physical distress. In the moments before their deaths, Socrates calmly drinks the hemlock but Jesus according to Mark cries "My God My God, why have you forsaken me?" One presumed death was welcomed while the other fought its onslaught. In consideration of this contrast does it not demonstrate two very different perspectives of death?

If we want to comprehend the faith in resurrection, then one must completely rebuild the historic understanding of death adopted through religion which seems to annul the power of resurrection in whatever form it occurs. For Jewish thinking, the death of the body was also destruction of created life as death was the destruction of a living being created by God. The purpose and scope of death will yield a varied viewpoint on resurrection and its meaning. If one's view of death is skewed, then that perception of the power of resurrection will also be misaligned.

So, one welcomes death as a liberation while the other sweats drops of blood (Luke 22:44). Socrates accepts and welcomes death as the liberator of the soul, while on the other hand, Jesus is aware of the finality of death and only the resurrection initiated by God can restore life. Yet the church teaches the soul is free and able to be present with God in heaven at death; not needing a resurrection.

False Security of Immortality

"You don't have a soul. You are a soul. You have a body."
????

The above was not quoted by C. S. Lewis as most suggest, but in a 1960 sci-fi novel entitled *A Canticle for Leibowitz* by Walter M. Miller, Jr. whose line states "You don't have a soul, Doctor. You are a soul. You have a body, temporarily." It has also been traced to an 1862 article in *The British Friend,* a Quaker publication in which the line is attributed to George MacDonald in which he states: "Never tell a child you have a soul. Teach him, you are a soul; you have a body." The C. S. Lewis Foundation indicates the quote is not in any of his published writings but there is indication Lewis was familiar with the writings of George MacDonald and it is perhaps a path that explains how the famous saying became attributed to him. ("C. S. Lewis Foundation" Facebook page. Accessed on August 10, 2014. https://www.facebook.com/cslewisfound/posts/1015152745350516 9. Posted March 20, 2013.)

Where did the idea of an immortal soul originate? According to the Jewish Encyclopedia it predates the founding of the major religions. It is noted in the 5th century BC writings of Herodotus, a Greek historian yet the ancient Egyptians were probably the first to teach the soul of man separates from the body due to its immortality at death. This concept was centuries before Judaism, Hinduism, Buddhism, Christianity, and Islam were formed. The Egyptians, in their belief in the dual nature of man, considered death to be a passage to a new state of life and the outcome of the exchange was dependent on the actions of the person before death. Their mythology considered the body to be evil and a prison for the soul. It was the Greeks (Pythagoras, Socrates, and Plato) who adopted the Egyptian belief of the dual nature and firmly planted the philosophy of the immortal soul in Hellenistic thought. The immortality of the soul was the initiator or founder of the doctrine of hell and immediate transfer to heaven upon death (Jewish Encyclopedia. "Immortality of the Soul").

Genesis 2:7 says, "And the Lord God formed man of the dust of the ground, and breathed into his nostrils the breath of life; and man became a living being." God did not insert an eternal soul into Adam instead Adam became a soul. What did God create from the ground? Adam was formed, sculpted, and dug out of the earth, and the union of God's part with the earth's part caused a sensational event for man was now animated, alive, and functioned as a soul. It is not something he possesses but something he is, an animated being, a being containing life and therefore living. The soul is the reaction of two parts being the human body and the breath of life. The entire aspect of man's formation and his creation was the original incarnation but seems to be minimized by the aspect of the fall. God entered creation long before the birth of Jesus or John chapter one.

What was given to mankind by God? Ecclesiastes 12:7 indicates that at death the body returns to the ground and the spirit or *ruach* returns to God who gave it. This verse is often used to interpret that the one who dies goes to heaven at death but that is not what is stated. It is interesting to note that nothing which was created or formed goes back to God. Remember, it was Adam's flesh that was created and a soul which he became after the union of earth and breath. When the breath returns to God the flesh dies, then the soul cannot exist as life (animation) has been removed. Job identifies the source of his life when he says he will not speak deceit if he is breathing and the breath of God is in his nostrils indicating his awareness that God sustains his life breath or his animation (Job 27:3-4). Paul says it in Greek fashion in Acts when he says we live and move and have our being in God (Acts 17:28); in other words, we are animated and continue to be because we are in Him. The *ruach* is the essence or life force of God and the Hebrew Bible emphasizes this spirit or breath of God is God Himself.

H. Wheeler Robinson, a British Old Testament scholar who wrote several works in the early 1900's, maintained there was little or no trace of body/soul dualism in the Old Testament. In Hebraic thought, there was no viable concept of the immortal soul as purported in the Greek frame of reference. There was no conception possible for the Hebrew mind of a disembodied human existence such as the soul passing into a heaven or hell upon death. According to Hebrew thought the soul was the whole person (Robinson, H. 1934, 11-26). In other words, neither soul nor body could exist apart. The soul is man thinking, willing, living, loving, and being. It is the life or the self of the person. The body is the same whole person seen from a prospective of form and substance, or said another way: "the body is the soul in its outward form (Gundry 1976, 119)."

Is immortality inherent or gifted from God? Romans 2:7 says those who will seek after glory, honor, and immortality will gain eternal life. If we have it now, then why are we to seek it? 1 Corinthians 15:53 says we are to put it on. The contrasts arise with the idea of an immortal soul with immortality resident in the soul or an act of God that provides immortality at a latter event. The latter concept places the full weight of life both mortal and immortal on God alone and not an endowment inherent in a component of man. Oscar Cullmann says: "Only he who apprehends with the first Christians the horror of death, who takes death seriously as death can comprehend the Easter exultation of the primitive Christian community and understand that the whole thinking of the New Testament is governed by belief in the Resurrection (Cullmann 1956, 11)." Immortality is a negative assertion regarding the promise of resurrection if the soul does not die then the resurrection is a moot point, an unnecessary aspect in the affairs of God and men. Alternately, the resurrection is a positive assertion if the whole man who has died is recalled to life by a new act of creation by God. It resets the apparent finality of the death process where life formed by God was destroyed and now restored by God again. Inherent immortality contrasts the view that man was created by God as a mortal creature who would perish if God did not hold the mortal man in existence during his heartbeat and then forever which may represent a fuller portrait of Creator/Progenitor.

Flow of Immortal Thought
Through the History of Religion

The doctrine of the resurrection was mainly developed in the apocalyptic writings of the Jewish nation between the Old Testament prophets and the historical life of Jesus. It was also during this time that the ideas of a resurrection formed the background for New Testament eschatology becoming the basis of doctrinal belief today. It seems in the Greek culture the idea of a blessed life came through the flow of the mystery religions. Edward Fudge notes the words "immortal" and "soul" are not paired in the Bible (Fudge 1982, 22). It is simply assumed the Bible teaches the immortality of every soul. Most current religions hold to this doctrine even though it is sourced in ancient mystery religions earlier than Judaism. The New Bible Dictionary emphasizes the non-biblical basis of the immortal soul concept and stresses its origination in the Greeks and further back, coming from Egyptian civilizations.

When and how did this concept of immortal soul enter Christianity? It did not seem to appear in the Old Testament as The International Standard Bible Encyclopedia says, "we are influenced always more or less by the Greek Platonic idea that the body dies yet the soul is immortal (ISBE 2014). While The Interpreter's Dictionary of the Bible states that the departure of the nephesh (soul) must be viewed as a figure of speech "for it does not continue to exist independent of the body." It goes on to say, "no Biblical text authorizes the statement that the soul is separated from the body at the moment of death (IDB 1952)." The Christian texts are at sharp contrast compared to traditional theology regarding the life of the soul.

Immortal Soul – Created or Pre-existent?

In considering the pre-existence of man and Jesus one must first be more articulate in terms. The Logos of God seems to pre-exist but man as a soul did not; yet the breath, the Ruach of God given to every man seems to return to God who is the source of Spirit. Aristotle considered matter and form existed together and man not only had a material body but also a soul in which the divine spark dwells. This divine spark in mankind is the elemental divine Logos which is the essence of God who is eternal and impersonal. The Stoics believed the Logos was a self-conscious world soul living within (Stanford Encyclopedia of Philosophy 2009). They considered the Logos to be God, the source of all life and wisdom, and as our human reasoning partakes of the Logos nature, humanity morphs into the "offspring of God" (Acts 17:18-29). Essentially, the Stoic philosophy said what God is for the world, the soul is for man meaning the human makeup is the universe on a smaller scale—a microcosm. As God is the world soul; He fills and penetrates the Cosmos. Similarly, the human soul pervades and breathes through the body informing and guiding it.

As one considers the Logos, it forces us to re-evaluate our concepts of the triune man. Does man contain a soul in his three-part makeup, or he is a soul? Eastern religion and Gnostic thought consider the soul to be an emanation portraying it as an extension of God flowing from God rather than a distinct creation and separate from God as Judaism and Christianity seems to indicate. Most Greek thinkers such as Philo and Origen considered the soul as sent from God and imprisoned in the body, awaiting freedom coming via death. Pre-existence is sourced more so from Plato than Jesus, Paul, or any other New Testament writer. In my opinion, the Bible does not teach a pre-existent soul but it does teach Spirit incarnated into flesh enlivening the body producing the soul. Creationism affirms the soul is created by God at the moment of conception and each soul is created *ex nihilo* for each person instantly and immediately. It maintains the soul is separate from the body and humans create the body while God creates the soul. It is in this vein of thought that the soul then becomes immortal when at death the body returns to the dust and the soul continues to another conscious state.

Is man a tripartite being? Can he function in any part separate from the others? God formed the flesh, infused life, and man became a living soul. The soul is not a part of man but is man. The soul ceases to exist if the heart stops beating, the flesh then decays and the spirit/breath returns to God. The soul is the result or reaction of the union of flesh and divine breath in that it is the resulting life force of divinity and humanity. Everything that exists does so because of a thought (cause) that initiated the effect — the physical demonstration of the thought. God imagined us (causes to be) and the living soul is the effect (evidence of being). The Body of Adam (mankind) was formed from the dust of the ground and fashioned into the physical form of God's intent then he infuses His life by His breath and man becomes a living soul; not a possessor of a soul. The Hebraic understanding considers man an animated body not an incarnated soul and this unit functions as a soul. The union of the clay and breath is a function of unity and value rather than parts that have various destinations at death.

My view of the soul it is not the part of man that goes to heaven at death but is the reaction of the body to the breath—the Ruach of God. The Soul is the experience of living/reacting to the Breath of God which is our animation whose purpose is to awaken man. I do not see the soul of man, the nephesh, as an entity or part of man but a reaction or evidence of animation of man by the breath of God. We have made the soul a concrete dimension with a beginning and end losing the truer abstract component of the life of God. Time sees the disintegration of the Breath of God but God never stops breathing. The Soul is evidence you are living. The nephesh is the proof of animation while the ruach is the animator.

The Hebraic ruach is equivalent to the Hellenistic divine spark and each seems to portray a different view of God's interaction with humanity. In one, God enters to enliven while in the other it's more ownership of humanity—God experiencing flesh. The soul is not an entity of man but is produced as an interaction between the flesh of dust and the Breath of God. The soul dies when the breath departs. Does God breathe into every man? Symbolically yes, and that is the implication of the Genesis account. Martin Buber said "Ruach Elohim, the breathing, blowing, surging phenomenon is neither natural (wind) nor spiritual (spirit) but both in one; it is the creative breathing that brings both nature and the spirit into one being (Myers 2013)." The Creation myth of Genesis is the understanding of God's union with His creation. Remember a myth is not a story of untruths but an account of the union of two worlds (spiritual and physical here) as understood by the storyteller. We tend to make a cut and dry translation of the Creation/Incarnation account to fit doctrine when it is multilayered, full of imagery, and embodied in the true meaning of myth.

Is the divine spark evidence of Incarnation? The belief that man has a divine spark implanted by the Creator is traceable to ancient mystical religions. The divine spark, implanted by the Creator, was the house of God in every human being. Although various religions have different names, Christianity posits the term incarnation and in this divine spark, in this incarnation, evidence of perceived separation between Creator and created is negated. The Bible is thought to support this concept in the idea of the breath of life. Does this mean that God gave man this life force or that this live force is inherently a part of him? Philo, a Hellenized Jewish philosopher, wrote in the beginning of the first century CE there was something divine in the human being. He considered the human mind incapable of knowing God if it were not for the implanting of divinity in humanity (Encyclopedia Judaica 2014). This concept seemed to initiate the doctrinal beginnings for Total Depravity for the Calvinists.

Did this divine spark pre-exist our birth? John 16:28 indicates Jesus came from the Father and came into physical existence and is to return to the Father. Christianity ascertains this means a pre-existence but it also supports the Hindu and Buddhist belief of reincarnation. They believe we progress through many lives on a path to total spiritual awakening at which point a return is no longer necessary. Another portion of Scripture used to point to Jesus' preexistence is John's Prologue which states the word was with God and was God and thus by implication includes our preexistence.

The Incarnation is the act of being made flesh, yes, but it is the Incarnation of the Logos, the intent of God's Mind that was implanted in humanity not Jesus. Becoming flesh is not only indwelling in blood and bone but to be fulfilled in expression. God witnessed his intent become flesh expressed in living color. He gave birth to his son. He "offspringed" himself in all creation. Because the account of the incarnation was applied historically to one man, it lost the beautiful and living account of the myth, the powerful Ruach of God indwelling and enlivening all men. The Incarnation was not a remedy for the perceived fall of Adam but the Incarnation was a plan of God alive in His thoughts from before the disruption of the world. This plan was not the soul of man engaged in Incarnation, Crucifixion, and Resurrection but man as a soul dancing in the movement of the Logos which includes Incarnation, Crucifixion, and Resurrection and other movements all involving humanity.

Pierre Teilhard de Chardin is credited with saying "We are not human beings having a spiritual experience. We are spiritual beings having a human experience (Jetmundsen 2005)" but this does not speak to my journey. It all rests in one's view of the soul. As I earlier stated, it is not a possession but an expression of being. I am not a spirit having a human experience. I am a soul experiencing something new—a new creation of spirit and flesh. The soul is an emanation of the union of spirit and flesh being an outflow of consciousness and its evidence. The soul is the animated living expression of this new creation.

The corporative unit of the breath, life, and the divine has been an ancient union and it was this concept that caused humanity to perceive the wind was a spirit linking it to the breath. The concept of the soul was nurtured in early Christian writings by Greek philosophy of the *pneuma* and the Essenian influences replaced the Hebraic concepts of the *nephesh* giving us the immortal soul trapped in Aristotelian matter later becoming orthodox doctrine.

The Power of the breath was enhanced through Pre-Socratic metaphysical concepts as it was both soul and intellect (*nous*) and if this breath departs then death ensues. Air was the predominate element and was the possessor of attributes such as intelligence having the capability to exert force, to direct, and incorporate reason and thought. In this Greek view, the air is breathed in and circulates through the blood and continuing in this view the human soul is air and therefore "a portion of God (Hillar 2012, 18)." When the Greek term pneuma was translated into Latin it was given the term *spiritus* thus linking breath with spirit. This union empowered the breath to be conscious and functioning as the vital source of animation.

The World Soul

The Greek metaphysical concept of the world soul was an intelligence that permeated the cosmos according to Plato. He believed it was the force that caused the motion of the celestial bodies and the source of intelligence given to the universe. It is this world soul and the emanation of souls that is the animating force in the cosmos and it is this same principle encouraging change, growth, and movement. He believed the human soul had a superior part or divine connection and it is through this inherent divine connection that humanity could understand the Divine Mind (Zeyl 2013). It was this Divine Mind who birthed the Logos which ordered the Cosmos. Plato considered motion a gift from the soul to the body and similarly the world soul was responsible for keeping the cosmos in motion; and too, acting as evidence or proof of life (Zeyl 2013). Philo of Alexandria believed man's ultimate goal is "in the knowledge of the true and living God (Hillar 2012)" and this allows the human soul to see the Divine Soul resulting in union with the divine. He accepts the concept of souls descending from God flowing through the celestial influence of the planets acquiring their astrological attributes on their migration to imprisonment in flesh where upon death the immortal soul is released from evil matter and the flesh to which it was bound and ascends returning home.

The Genesis account is characterized using Elohim in Genesis 1 as compared to Yahweh in Genesis 2. The Yahwist author expresses man as frail, mortal, and made from dust and then God breathes into his nostrils animating him. This conveys the Hebraic concept of the living person as an inseparable unity of body and mind made alive by God in contrast to the Greek idea of humans as embodied souls. This account demonstrates humanity requires more than physical life and makes God the means of existence of being. John Hands offers a great definition of consciousness in his book *Cosmosapiens: Human Evolution from the Origin of the Universe* in which he says, Consciousness is "the property of an organism by which it is conscious [fully aware] of its own consciousness [awareness], that is, not only does it know but also knows it knows" and humanity is the only species to have this reflective consciousness (Hands 2015, 430).

Hebrew Considerations of the Soul & Breath of Life

Creation is not an implantation of a pre-existent component into an animated soul but is the formation of a whole new being. A new creation could not have pre-existed but is a completely new being — the nephesh. The union of flesh and spirit has never occurred before and that is the formation of the soul created, structured, and ordered from dust and breath. Formation is the process and creation the product.

Man, in Hebraic thought is a unity—a soul made of many intricacies drawing life and activity from the breath and his being has no existence apart from his breath and his body. Our image and likeness of God is a cutting out or chiseling out as a pattern not indicating a division but similarity. Each human birth, according to the Hebrew mind, was a new miracle of creation as God was thought to influence conception of each child. So, as it says in Ecclesiastes 3, the body returns to dust and the divine energy, the breath, returns to God exactly reversing the creation process demonstrating the concept of God being active rather than passive in man's life.

Was the breath of life a magical substance or a gift sourced in the Giver? While man is alive the Bible says that in God's hand is "the soul of every living thing and the breath of all mankind" (Job 12:10). Literally? No, but in a metaphysical sense as the one who gave the breath to begin with as the absolute source of life. Yet, when man dies, the breath goes back to God who gave it. This is not saying God takes our breath from us but as the Giver of the breath it knows its origin, its source. Job 12 is not separating the soul and breath but is using a Hebraic rephrase saying the same thing but using different words portraying the intent in another way. Job 12:10 could be phrased "God holds lovingly in His hand the expression of life He created and is the source of all life being animated by His breath (Author's translation)."

Genesis 7:21-22 provides the effect of the flood by saying "And all flesh died that moved on the earth: birds and cattle and beasts and every creeping thing that creeps on the earth, and every man. All in whose nostrils was the breath of the spirit of life, all that was on the dry land, died" and in doing so provides a sweeping illustration of the influence of the breath of life signifying it is not only in man but in animal life too. Do the animals have an immortal soul according to tradition since it is the same breath as man was given? The only difference in the narrative is that God directly supplied the breath of life to man and it is not stated He did so to animal life also. Perhaps this is the benefit of being in His likeness and image.

What was God saying when he asked Adam who told him he was naked? There was a change of consciousness in man from the garden with God to the God who moved "out of the garden" convincing Adam God was now out there. This altered perception of God implying distance caused Adam to look outside of himself perceiving a disruption of relational harmony and in place of harmony, enmity signifying division, duality, and a more than one sprung up in the mind of man. Adam perceived he had been cast out of God's heart because of anger changing Adam's (mankind's) perception of creation to that of alienation and estrangement. These changes in Adam's consciousness, his false perception caused his death according to 1 Corinthians 15 which states death came by man—not God. I believe all the changes in Adam's consciousness were simply his perception and not grounded in reality and even though we carry those same perceptions they continue to have the same effect in us as in Adam, perhaps because we continue to see mankind in Adam rather than in Christ.

We are living souls composed of dirt energized by the breath of God. The physical and spiritual element were never meant to be separated or dualistic. God intended his creation to be in union with His intent and not a split image with divided components which seem to have varied destinations at death. The perception of the split seemed to have occurred when Adam realized a change in awareness and this, in my opinion, was the birth or manifestation of the ego. I do not think the ego was a gift from God but another byproduct or reactionary event due to circumstances. Perhaps it was a consequence of Adam's choice, nevertheless, it caused man to see himself outside of God. Animals are said to be souls and biologically their instincts are equal to our ego being formed at man's shift in reality. The mind is not the brain but a function of the brain and is activated by stimuli. The mind involves the spirit or ego and whichever one is empowered (carnal—Adam's mind or mind of the Christ) will dictate the outcome of our thoughts effecting our life.

Spirit versus Breath

The term spirit from the Old Testament is ruach and is translated breath or wind and not soul. Spirit in the New Testament is the Greek word pneuma also translated as breath or wind and not soul. The infusion of the breath of life into man formed from the dust resulted in an animated being. This breath of life (ruach or spirit) is the common possession of man and animals according to Genesis 7:14. In verse 22 of the same chapter it states, "all in whose nostrils was the spirit of life died" which confirms the statement in Ecclesiastes 3:19 which say that which befalls the sons of men befalls the beasts adding "as one dies, so dies the other." The verse also states that man has no preeminence over the animals in death by asserting both men and animals go to one place as all return to dust. Ecclesiastes 3:20 and 12:7 says the spirit—the ruach of man and animal alike also return to God who gave it. So where is the immortal part of man that does not die?

What is the spirit according to Hebraic thought? It is the vital force which animates living beings. It is the source of life yet not the life. It is the impulse which initiates thought, tells the body to breathe, and converts sensation to joy or pain. So, at death when the ruach is withdrawn the creature dies and this life sustaining impulse figuratively goes back to God who initiated life. While the New Testament seems to portray death as the surrender of the spirit it does not convey the notion that man rides on or in that breath back to God. So, the departure of the spirit cannot mean man himself departs fully conscious to another location and to read this into Scripture is mixing two worlds: that of Hebrew with Greek thought which assumed the soul survived the death of the body.

According to Jewish tradition, it is the breath of life which goes back to God at death. This concept stands in complete opposition to the unrighteous going to hell at death and the saved to heaven. The Bible does not declare the Breath of Life of the saints goes to heaven while the Breath of Life of the unrighteous goes to another location. So, what is one to do now with the Breath of Life at death? It is interesting to note when the term spirit is used it is never said to have life, personality, feeling, or wisdom. Why? Is it because the spirit is simply the breath of life, the animating force in man and animals?

Interestingly, The Shalom Center in Philadelphia conveys the pronunciation of the Hebrew tetragrammaton is not necessarily forbidden but in its speaking, reveals a hidden truth. As one tries to do so—pronouncing these four strange letters (linguists call them aspirate consonants) without the understood vowels of 'a' and 'e', one simply breathes. This emphasizes that the real name of God is simply beyond pronunciation unless you consider breathing pronunciation. The Jewish Siddur (prayer-book) says, "*Nishmat kol chai tivarech et SHIMCHA.*" ("The breathing of all life praises your Name.") For the Breathing of all life IS Your Name. The name of God then is the sound of our breathing and we speak His name every time we inhale (YH) and exhale (WH) (Phone conversation with Rabbi Arthur Waskow, The Shalom Center 6711 Lincoln Dr. Philadelphia, PA 19119. Theshalomcenter.org. August 2014). In a seemingly profound thought of God's logic, He causes His name not to be a Hebrew word, nor a word found in the Egyptian, Latin, Greek, Arabic, Sanskrit, or English languages. He did not place His name in any single language but in all of them but more accurately in a form that transcends language in that all you must do to call Him is just breathe (Waskow 2004). Mystically, the breath of God is more than air; it is also what animates man fulfilling reflective consciousness by enlivening the soul with the resulting action of the soul knowing it is enlivened.

In thinking about the forming of man from the dust, it was his body that was formed. There was a heart but it was not beating. The brain was there, but there was no mind yet as it was not thinking. There was blood but it was not providing gas exchange in the lungs—for there was not yet breath that initiated these operations. Then, God breathed and man became a living soul. His breath filled all parts of man with life and man now functionally alive became a living soul. The ruach or spirit is not man in the same fashion the body is not man but their union—their synergy is man. When God's Ruach incarnated humanity it caused animation—the heart began to beat, the brain woke up and respiration began. God's Ruach touched the physical brain enlivening it, forming the mind, imparting intellect and personality. That is what is meant when Paul said let the same mind that was in the Christ be in you. This account is also demonstrated in Luke the daughter of Jairus who sent for Jesus telling him that his daughter was "sick unto death." Because of the crowds, he did not make it to the house before the little girl died so Jairus sent messengers telling Jesus not to come because it was too late. Jesus still proceeds to the house and he puts out the professional mourners and raises the girl back to life.

According to Luke 8:52-55 it says, "her spirit came again" and her spirit or breath was called back into her by Jesus once again animating her body causing it to be alive by possessing life and not possessing a soul but by becoming a soul once again.

Is there a difference in the breath that was imparted to man versus that of animals? In Genesis 2:7 when God created Adam, was that which was breathed into him distinct from that of other breathing creatures? According to Hebrew history it was the *nishmat chayim* given to Adam which was not passed on to animal life. It is also important to note that according to some historians the ancient Hebrew language did not have a vocabulary for the mind, consciousness, or reason. In looking at the Genesis account of the flood it becomes apparent that creatures which did not receive the breath of life from God suffered also in the flood as their preservation was also effected by them entering the ark. So, what about Genesis 7:22 which says that death occurred to all creatures on dry land in whose nostrils were the breath of the spirit of life? Is this verse talking about animal life or just human life? Whether or not animals possess nishmat chayim leaves the possibility that animals and humans are innately different. In the universal application, the breath of life is the process of creation while the personal ruach, the forceful breath of God is the animator sustaining the soul.

As an illusion is an improper reflection of reality so death is an improper reflection of life. It is death which causes a loss of purpose in the resurrection being replaced by a false security caused by inherent immortality making the resurrection an unnecessary intrusion. Christian theology being greatly influenced by platonic Greek dualism impacted the concept of man as it is this dualistic concept that entered causing a division and the compartmentalization of man.

The Inner Man's Framework and Awakening

The framework of man is typified by the diaphragm in ancient physiology and Paul links the concept to the mind of man. In Romans 8:6 Paul used the Greek word *phronema* for the spirit of the mind which is named from the Greek after the muscle that separates the heart and lungs from the abdomen. The phronema, according to Greek understanding, was the seat of passion and fear. What is the outward symbol of passion and fear? The breath which is physically initiated by the diaphragm. What is the correlation then? It constitutes the process of thinking which is going beyond what we think to the way we think. For example, you do not have to mentally think to take a breath, and breathe again, and again; because breathing rests just below the threshold of consciousness. Therefore, the phronema is to our being as the framework to a house. The frame holds up the walls and openings giving shape and definition (Corley 2012). Our phronema or our spirit of the mind supports our thoughts, ideas, and feelings; and has an enormous impact on our worldview which is the way we think. Our spirit of the mind is the control room of our being.

The phronema of man connects with the Ruach/Logos not in physical breath but in conscious awareness. Does the Logos effect the phronema being the spirit of the mind or is the Logos affected by the phronema? Awakening is the cessation of separation and division yet differentiation is fully functional and appreciated. It is a way of perception free of duality especially between world and absolute. With this mindset phronema is only a state of uninterrupted creative potential yielding an awareness of the cosmos and consciousness. The soul is not a thing, it is however, consciousness—or the act of being conscious. Man became a living soul—he became conscious—he woke up.

Paul Ricoeur said it is the breath of God that was expired into the mouth and nose of man making the human a living nephesh (Gaiser 1999). Nephesh originally did not refer to a disembodied soul as it later came to mean due to its flow through Greek thought patterns of the word psyche. According to Hebraic thought, there is no nephesh that is not both body and spirit, or flesh and breath, as they are incapable of separation and being. The meaning became absorbed through the Hellenistic traditions as it became possible to kill the body and not the soul (Matthew 10:28). Translators continued through Paul to distinguish between flesh and spirit as the anthropological dualism of the body and soul overcame the original concept of singularity of the whole person.

What is the reactive influence of the soul in conjunction with consciousness? Reflective consciousness, being already defined by John Hands, is the result of a functioning central nervous system and is based on neurons, chemical reactions, hormones, and impulses; in short, biochemistry which is aligned with established physical laws and the awareness of this cohesive force influences the soul dynamic. When the cue ball is hit in a game of pool the motion of the balls is not under their individual direction nor the one shooting the game. The balls move because of an initiating force. Similarly, the operation of the brain is not the result of free will either meaning it is not the first cause in thought and action. Just as the balls on the pool table responded when they were struck so the neurons in the brain fire when they should due to an electrochemical response, being under the influence of external environmental stimuli. The processes of the mind are the end responses of biochemical stimulation which are the initiator of our choices. Then, our supposedly free will rests at the final cycle of sensory stimulation processed through a cause and effect principle and the choices we make are the result of very impersonal, mechanical, and biochemical forces. Our neurons respond not due to a free will impulse we initiate but rather to the rules of biophysics in corporation with laws beyond our control to manipulate.

Based on the above precepts the biochemical initiators can be traced and measured and as science has discovered, they are present before the person is aware of his thought in response to the stimulus. In other words, biochemical reactions and pathways are the initiator of choices and our feelings of having made that choice is an illusion which comes after the biochemical patterns that initiated them. Because of these discoveries, neurology has postulated the concept of philosophical free will cannot exist. The studies of Benjamin Libet, using the electroencephalogram incorporating brain activity, found compelling measurements between the moment the subject became conscious of an impending physical response versus the initiation of the physical response. His findings indicated the subjects actually made unconsciously the decision to act measurably earlier than when they became aware of it consciously. The conscious decision to act was not the instigator of the action but was the agent of a decision already formulated but not acted upon in time. These moments of insight were detectable through EEG up to eight seconds before the consciousness was aware of it. Conscious volition or will seems to sit on top of the process, not as an originator but effected by the biochemical pathway influencing our conscious response (Crabtree 1999).

The article goes on to suggest the human brain knows before the brain's owner does as Libet's conclusions also demonstrated that simple physical decisions such as the movement of a finger were made approximately "three-tenths of a second before the brain's owner is aware of them, and subsequent work has found that the roots of such decisions can be seen up to ten seconds before they become conscious. But this is the first occasion that such a long lead time has been shown for more complex thought processes (Crabtree 1999)." So much for the free will premise, right? Or does this simply explain the process of choice in contrast to free will? Free Will presupposes no external or internal stimulus while choice requires it and then exacts judgment.

The Misapplied Hope of Resurrection

When studying resurrection and death and considering early understandings of the topics one finds a battle in history between the mystical and literal. Did history shade the resurrection of Christ or misapply its intent? As the literal approach took hold, did man accept a distorted overview of death and the resurrection? It is history as opposed to religion that tends reveal a universal God over a God who favors a particular people.

Is history simply a recording of events or the story of a process? History is often perceived as having no ultimate meaning, no pattern or direction, and is essentially insignificant unless a point of absolute importance can be identified. Many religions name their pivotal point which invaded history and changed their story as Christianity did with the resurrection. According to theologians then, history was an endless cycle without real meaning until Christianity identified their pivotal point—being the intrusion of God in man, claiming this encounter for humanity—exclusive to Christianity.

We often remove the mystical and symbolical aspect of the story not realizing truth lies between the symbolic and the literal. When all facets including the literal, mystical, and symbolical are interlaced we have a richer and clearer tapestry of our heritage. It is trying to see the resurrection through this tainted piecemeal historical literal approach which causes a misapplied hope forcing one's trust in a fabricated history rather than the revealed Christ, Logos, Tao, Maat, and others who were and are present in all civilizations.

The diverse opinions that arise out of a resurrection study are steeped in tradition, culture, and concepts of a people's understanding of God or to be more accurate—a people's understanding of how they perceive God treated them. Just as there are layer upon layer of the ideologies of death, it is also the same for the resurrection. For example, is it a resurrection yielding a transformed body or resuscitation of the old one? Is it a physical event or spiritual? Or, is there no historical resurrection at all? One's base view of this topic seems to be anchored in one's concept of the value of man and included in this evaluation is the idea of redemption and its dependence on a resurrection. Cullmann says the early Christian concept of the resurrection was incompatible with the Greek concept of the immortal soul (Cullmann 1956, 6). Is death the last enemy as dictated in the New Testament or is death a friend that catapults man into God's presence? What was the original hope of resurrection? Resurrection was a calling back of the whole person a restoration, and not a calling back or promotion to endless life as Plato taught becoming a deathless state. Mark Eaton says: "We are so addicted to terminology. If we use the term 'Resurrection' people don't resist it. If we use the term 'quickened and raised,' there's no resistance. But if we use the word 'awakened' the walls go up (Mark Eaton, e-mail conversation with author, November 2014)."

The Midrash concept moves the resurrection of Jesus from a man of history to the ever-present mystical Christ. Even though history is recorded words describing events, the mystical concept posits words are never neutral nor the truth of the experience one is trying to relate. Said another way, words are not the truth itself but are placeholders of truth as man attempts to relay the experience he holds as truth. An example can be found in the prologue of John which states the word became flesh and literalistic methods dictate this was a single occurrence rather than the Logos being the intent of God and dwelling in all flesh not just the flesh of the man Jesus. Dermont A Lane said, "thus for the Jew the word/Logos was a form of God's presence active in history, whereas for the Greek, reason/Logos was the underlying reality which explained the structure of the universe we live in (Lane 1975, 96)." The mystical concept of the resurrection removes the focus on the historical aspect and places the focus on the effect of the resurrection making it a universal event for all men rather than a single historical event for one man.

Man can consider the origin of the universe, comprehend the mathematical concept of infinity, and desire immortality. We also can entertain the possibility of overcoming death and participate in life with an immortal God. Did God create the world as part of Himself or separate from Himself? Is He up in heaven looking down watching what transpires or is he involved in the affairs of man? Another point of contention, does the concept of a resurrection require a redemptive element? This concept is strengthened if one considers death a violation of God's rules, making death a curse thereby requiring a redemptive element to restore man to his original state. Or was death just a natural occurrence as assumed by the Greeks? Paul's idea of death was more encompassing as it was fourfold to him. Death is the consequence of sin, a means of atonement, an intrusion in the divine order, and a terror in the present age.

It seems we have lessened death's impact thereby negating the power of resurrection in whatever form it may take. In man's standard religious view of the soul which is going to God and living in heaven immediately after death makes the biblical concept of a resurrection unnecessary. Religion has removed the deadness of death with the idea of an immortal soul—a soul immune to death. If one is to restore the power of resurrection, then one must also restore the deadness and finality of death. While religion has softened death, Jesus demonstrated the powerful effect of death and its cessation of life, consciousness, and fellowship.

Is the resurrection simply a historical event on in the mystical aspect an ongoing event? In the definition of mysticism, which carried the mystery or secrecy of an order holds fuller etymological meaning being a deeper search for wisdom motivated by love. It causes us to rise above the religious rituals and rules and pursue God from a pure desire of love. Paul understood the awesome difference between being stuck in history versus living from the meaning of history. He did not see the resurrection as simply a past event but also as an ongoing mystical experience in the present moment. Resurrection is not a dead moment but exists as an eternal spring of life in every moment.

What does this mean to me? It is moving resurrection out of history where it was passive and only a memory and bringing it into my life and in my present moment activating the power of resurrection for me now—a dynamic reality.

I think we lost the power of Resurrection when we sit down to read about it in the Gospel accounts. We tend to see it as happening about 33 CE and we fail to see we were raised with Him, which, incidentally, is not revealed in thought until the Pauline writings in the Bible but did exist in older concepts. In seeing it as a historical event alone we lose what was also intended as a part of us and for us and for all mankind. Resurrection is not meant to stay in the historical past in the life of one man. It is not intended to simply fill the pages of a children's Bible to explain the Easter story. It is not purposed to be simply a belief.

We must remove the definite article "the" resurrection and allow its meaning to enter our lives continuously. Resurrection redefines humanity and we are invited to enter its mystery and experience the hope of all men and to connect in a mystical and spiritual way to our God motivated by love to know our Creator/Progenitor. Resurrection is not a past event but a person and not one person but a people—it is the definition of all mankind as man functionally becomes the realized intent of God.

Collapsing Duality

As dualism entered Jewish history through the Platonic portal in the form of soul-body dualism, it fostered the belief of the eternal soul. The soul became separate from the body and immortal. Fast forward to the "Early Church Fathers" we find Augustine who defined the soul as the ruler of the body, as independent from the body and outlives it.

Duality only exists in our perception due to sin consciousness until we see all mankind mirrored in the Christ—the full intent of God. We suddenly realize the God in our head, who we usually align with the doctrines we have decreed as truth, does not match the God in our heart which flows with intimate experience. We experience the God who loves, the God we come to know because of relationship. What do we do when the God we have fashioned in our head through the filter of our beliefs and doctrines is not the same as the God we feel, as the God we experience because of intimacy? It is at this point dualism has made a full disclosure. Dualistic concepts cause us to miss the beauty in the little things. We have forgotten that we can see God in the stars and the birth of our children. It has diminished our freedom to enjoy the arts and music in a religious attempt to be holy. It also causes us to see our different personalities as something to overcome rather than embrace.

Duality and Differentiation

Man created his own duality separating himself in his own mind from God and the Law was one of the many ways that man could point out this divergence for his own purpose mainly to resolve his guilt, shame, and lack of seeing his true image reflected face to face out of relationship. Until we realize we established the law to justify ourselves before God then we will continue to have difficulty in seeing God's continual interference to demonstrate His love restoring us to the true image of God being expressed as the Christ. Duality is not reality but the contrast or divergence it manifests can be perceived as one. Five days a week I enter the employee entrance where I work and on the wall in the hallway is a thermostat displaying the temperature. It is always set to 73 degrees. In July, when I enter the door the hallway is very cool and is a relief from the heat outside—but in January when it was 4 degrees, that same 73 degrees felt very warm and drove the cold away—yet it was the same 73 degrees but presented itself with a dual role—that of warmth in the winter and coolness in the summer. One temperature but different effects on the body. One temperature serving two functions; coolness and warmth, not opposites but differentiation the same entity but set to function differently.

Non-duality simply institutes equality which is uniformity in character, value, and ability; and homogeneity being the state of having identical functional value. To ascertain this concept, consider homogenized milk which causes the fat molecules to be

:ed in solution so no separation occurs. All components ɔn in harmony so no variance is evident. There are many universes, suns, stars—and all made from star dust producing differentiation not separation as portrayed in the New Testament as the many membered body of Christ. Oneness does not negate differentiation.

In cellular biology, differentiation speaks of a cell evolving into a more complex cell with organs and systems. In other words, the simple cell through certain processes (learning/maturing) can take on multiple functions but the DNA does not change therefore, no separation from its origin. The idea of separation may be the sole culprit of our concept of God. Differentiation is not duality because differentiation speaks to purpose and function while duality is a number, an opposite, and must be compared with another to be understood. The error is not duality's perception but that we consciously ascertain it to be reality. We make it reality and build our world and our responses to life around it and make judgments from this center totally constructing our worldview. Just because I am differentiated from God I can still have His stuff while I am learning to function as His offspring. I am from Him and of Him but not Him. This is not dualism but noting differentiation which manifests in maturity and specialization.

How is duality collapsed? What is the mark of non-duality? As duality is manifested from perception it must be negated from within—the same place the present moment is realized. Rest is the cessation of work, the absence of required motion whose purpose is to complete a task. It also has another meaning: that is to be supported or firmly based as in "the car rested firmly on the jack." Another is a legal understanding when rest means to voluntarily cease the presentation of evidence in a case to settle an issue to release the offender as in "the judge put to rest the dispute between the two parties." Rest is the aspect of fulfillment as no task is left unfinished.

When this moment is eternalized then time is no longer marked and duality will have collapsed. When law is perceived as the fracture of time then fulfillment is discerned correctly—nothing left to fulfill. History is thought of being static and dead based in translating facts while myth is dynamic and living and based on interpreting the union of God and man. When the moment is eternalized time will have lost its influence and duality is quietened. But when perfection comes we see without distortion, without illusion—we see face to face. We see reality. Dualism requires judgment while non-duality renders judgment meaningless.

Considering the previous chapter, the divergence of myth, history, law, and time is sourced in duality. Duality arose out of a perceived infraction and out of this fractured law man used myth telling the story of this fracture; yet the true is occulted in the myth as myth seeks to make atonement. Did myth propagate dualism or try and correct it; or even dismiss it? Myth gave man an out, a method to deal with his dualism issuing from a perceived breach. Man needed a remedy and he found it in myth, therefore, myth is the story of reparation. Myth is truth solely according to man's story which in most cases include dualism, a more than one. And that is just what Adam did, he asked for another, then he blamed her as his remedy for his perceived breach—his sin. Duality fully resides in the dichotomy of myth, history, law, and time.

-III-

THE DANCING MYTH ENTOMBED IN TIME

Retelling the Myth

The divergence of myth, history, law, and time rests on the fault of duality that has entombed the perichoretic myth, the story of us. This process has silenced the music but the orchestra continues making amazing harmonies yet we cannot hear them. Duality is time oriented and does not exist in the present moment.

Rollo R May, an American existential psychologist quoting Campbell said, "myths are archetypal patterns in human consciousness" and himself adds, "where there is consciousness there will be myth (May 1991, 37)." He goes on to add "in the moments when eternity breaks into time, there we will find myth (May 1991, 297)." Myth then, allows the first glimpse back into history and forward into the future as the story tellers interpret the past and foretell the future.

For example, as the creation myth is recounted, it is relived as creation takes place in every moment or an unending moment is realized in which evolution, incarnation, eschatology, and history are all one and the same moment even though time has determined how we define them. In the moment, time is not recorded and unable to enforce boundaries; therefore, no history or future as *chronos* yields to *kairos*. A kairos moment is presented as a gateway or portal to a monumental event, action, or decision point. A myth is not defined by whether it is or is not true but whether it functions to relay a story that serves to link or explain the interaction of two realms such as physical and spiritual or divinity and humanity; and in this manner, a myth is not bound by the laws of space and time but supersedes them.

Christianity, in its drive to literalize the life of Jesus, has removed the metaphorical meanings of those events which were designed to guide each of us on our journey. This process altered the envisioned operation of the Logos movements which were proposed as a guide for each of us on our journey. The restoration of the intended function of those movements would break the entrapment which caused us to perceive separation, division, and disharmony between God and man.

Mythology has been said to be the story of what is practiced in religion. The intent of myth seems to be an indicator that man is awake and conscious and because man is self-reflective he can relate his story through myth. While myth allows us to approach the mystery, it is also the means which allows us to explain the experience. Myth, as it explores the mysteries, offers explanation through human influences and perceptions. According to Joseph Campbell, mythology causes us to remember we are human acting as a mirror reflecting aspects of our being that we often try to forget (Neuendorf 2013). In other words, mythology causes one to reflect inwardly by exploring the innermost areas of time and space and viewing the consciousness. This concept echoes the thought of William Irwin Thompson who remarks "myth is the history of the soul (Neuendorf 2013)" as myth is the depiction of the drama similarly as music to a play, as history is nothing more than a mood setter for myth to unfold. Religion is the means of explaining how to adhere to a belief while myth is about why we perform the rituals. Myth will never seek to end the mystery nor explain it but it leaves the mystery open and alive seeking experience rather than explanation.

The Enigma of Time and its Redemption

"Time, is what keeps the light from reaching us.
There is no greater obstacle to God than time."
Meister Eckhart

This section will postulate time functions as a concealer, it is only real to the one who created it. Time's impact is completely transparent in the present moment. An enigma is a form or shadow which is imperfectly seen and indistinctly reflected but never in the sense of being non-existent positing time is muted in myth. 1 Corinthians 13:12 portrays a mirror of reality and it only reflects a dim or blurred image, keeping what is real as a distant riddle or enigma—something that cannot be brought into focus. When reality is made clear and brought into perfect focus we will see all reflections as face to face, in their true form as God sees them.

To redeem the time is to buy back what time holds ransom. Time holds ransom the present moment preventing it from being timeless and moving from an enigma to clearly seen. This verse indicates the present moment can be hidden because of distorted perception caused by the incongruity of myth, history, law, and time. When the moment is eternalized time will have lost its influence and duality is quietened. But when perfection comes we see without distortion, without illusion — we see face to face. We see reality. It is when this moment is clearly distinguished and time loses its function of concealing then realization becomes one in the One.

Meister Eckhart, a German Philosopher and Mystic from the early 14th century whom I quoted earlier implied time entombs the light thereby causing God problems. Time is not an obstacle to God but to man. Why does he say time hinders light? Light can only be seen if it's reflected. A mirror does not reflect an image in the dark. The mirror is still functional but a needed component, light is missing to fulfill its function. Why is time so powerful that it can cause a distortion of reality, of the light reaching us? Time is not an obstacle to God but to man.

Tic Toc

What really does the clock measure? Is it really measuring the passage of time? If the clock indicates it is 4:00 pm, what is it really telling us? In considering the concepts of time one must also entertain the process of history. If nothing memorable occurred then time goes into the past and forgotten; but on the other hand, if something did occur then time or the moment in time is memorialized and etched in our minds.

Try this exercise to illustrate the above statement. Search on the internet for the day President Kennedy was shot and you will find the date of November 22, 1963. Search for the date the space shuttle

Challenger exploded and you will be presented with the date of January 28, 1986. Next, search for the date Nero was born and it will report December 15, 0037. What about the year King Tutankhamen was born and it will tell you 1342 BC. But now, search for the day Jesus died and you will not be presented with a date but a myriad of reasons that day is not defined in history. Why is the date of his death not recorded?

Where were you on September 11, 2001 at 08:46 am? What about the day before at the same time? Recorded history is based on the perception of the narrator and masks truth usually to support a specific agenda, doctrine, or dogma. It is not that history has lied to us but we have given it power over us just like in the movie, "The Matrix" when Morpheus tells Neo: "You take the blue pill, the story ends. You wake up in your bed, believe whatever you want to believe. You take the red pill, you stay in wonderland, and I show you how deep the rabbit hole goes. Remember, all I'm offering is the truth. Nothing more (Wachowski 1999)."

How do we recall history? Do we not say, "remember the time when…" or we give a specific date and time when the specific event occurred? Did creation occur in time or did creation begin time? The universe is still expanding and limitless, why is that? Perhaps God is still creating and the act of creation was not a historical event in time but a continuous moment. Creation takes place every day because God's word proclaiming "Let there be…" has not returned to Him. God has not retracted His command to "Let there be…" and never will. Was time a creation of God who created all things or is time a derivative instigated by man to mark what he is trying to understand regarding the process of discovering his purpose? Time is a delimiter, serving as a boundary between the present moment and any other possibility we imagine for ourselves. For example, time sets love in the past or yet to come but when time is removed or more correctly muted; love is ever present and dynamic and will forever be. How do I know? Do you not still love someone who has died? Love is not limited by time or space.

What gives evidence that time passes? We perceive the passage of time because we monitor change. In this way, we count heartbeats per minute, the years from birth to death, and estimate the time from the Big Bang to now in millions of years or ages/eons. What am I saying? Time creates history. Plato says time is the moving image of eternity (Timaeus, 37c-e). Did you catch that? He said eternity is reality and time is only an image. Eternity is real and time is elusive. When one considers the religious concepts of time, it most often comes to us as subjective experiences such as intuition, revelation, and spiritual insight while in the scientific aspect it arrives in objective observation including quantitative measurement, mathematical and physical data, and through logical or rational thought.

Oscar Cullmann implies the New Testament word *aion* and the Old Testament word *olam* indicates a temporary duration (Cullmann 1962, 39). He goes on to say eternity is simply unending time and is unlimited in both the backward and forward direction (Cullmann 1962, 18, 48). He also speculates that time came into operation with the created mind (Cullmann 1962, 61-68), in other words, a derivative of man being a byproduct or consequence.

My earlier view considered time and eternity to be opposing ideas. I once thought time to be created by God therefore having a beginning and also will have an end. In time, there is change, but in eternity there is no change as all change and development must occur in time. Eternity, then, is without time as it is not composed of time nor is eternity time standing still. I viewed time as being governed by eternity and creatures governed by their Creator in time.

To re-assess the question; What is time? Is it just numbers on a clock? Time can be defined as a non-delineated flow of existence and events as our perception places them in past, present, and future categories being forms of time and as we number those events we use seconds, minutes, hours, days, months, and years which are parts of time. Lawrence W. Fagg in his preface writes: "In our quietest, most thoughtful moments, we can watch the second hand of a clock precisely tick off the seconds and at the same time, resting in the living present sense one moment gently and indistinguishably merge into the next. Time is an enigma. Trying to grasp and look at it is like trying to grasp water in one's hand (Fagg 1985, vii)."

Now other pressing questions arise which asks is time created by God or is it a derivative of man? Is the present moment encased in time? In looking at time versus the present moment we can first look at the concept of love. We attempt to lock love in the past or yet to come but when love is realized the past and future are merged and no boundary or delineation exists. What gives evidence that time passes? We perceive the passage of time because we note change. The delimiting influence of time issues a boundary that envelops the myth making it nothing more than a stagnant fairy tale of yesteryear. As the myth migrates through its time capsule it loses its mobility and life as it becomes a misaligned story of how man once perceived his God. This can be seen as Israel adapted the Canaanite festivals moving them from god worship to celebration of an event in which Jehovah intervened for the nation effectively locking that event in the nation's history. They were regarded as an event or "a time when God..." making the event a past occurrence only to be remembered and not re-lived as time denoted an event or a moment in time when God moved in favor or disfavor for or against Israel. This is pictured perfectly in Ecclesiastes 3 which observes:

> There is a time for everything, and a season for every activity under the heavens: a time to be born and a time to die, a time to plant and a time to uproot, a time to kill and a time to heal, a time to tear down and a time to build, a time to weep and a time to laugh, a time to mourn and a time to dance, a time to scatter stones and a time to gather them, a time to embrace and a time to refrain from embracing, a time to search and a time to give up, a time to keep and a time to throw away, a time to tear and a time to mend, a time to be silent and a time to speak, a time to love and a time to hate, a time for war and a time for peace.

In the early Greek period of the New Testament this was carried forward as events such as the Transfiguration and the Resurrection were placed in time and locked in the history of the church losing life and purpose placing them in one man in history rather than all men.

Time in its metaphysical aspects is not regarded as hours, minutes, and seconds on the face of a clock but is in a metaphorical sense a bondage to reality. The Metaphysical Bible Dictionary says time signifies the measure of events and degrees of unfoldment (Fillmore 2014, 679). The only power that time possesses is that which man gives it and as he comes into the understanding of the Absolute he will then be free from all bondage of time and will then be able to declare time shall be no more and deny it entrance to his mind, body, or affairs (Fillmore 2014, 679). Fillmore provides a powerful declaration for humanity as he states: "I am not in bondage to any false idea of time. I, with God, inhabit eternity, and the divine order of God's universe is manifest in my mind and in all my affairs (Fillmore 2014, 680)."

Time can be compared to a limited consciousness of the past, present, and future which is the effect of the ability to memorize as we place events in relation to each other. Memory is information compared in time, encoded by the mind and filtered through perception residing in consciousness. As a human being, we generally exist in three states of consciousness. First, we are awake in which the senses are active retrieving and transmitting stimuli from the environment and time is actively measured. Second, dream sleep in which outside stimuli are absent but the imagination is active and time is skewed. Last, deep sleep which is a sound sleep where the senses are inactive, where nothing is felt nor time is perceived. The present when based in time is not permanent and is only experienced in the wakened state. In the dream state, however, we create our own world from impressions or experiences derived from the subconscious mind. During the dream state, we note that often large expanses of time have past the mind all in just a few minutes of actual dream sleep. The dream sleep time is not permanent as it fades upon wakening. In deep sleep, we are not conscious of any stimulation from our senses nor are we conscious of time. In this sense, we exist but in a state of unreality. Consciousness is the source or more precisely the cognitive factor by which we track the passing of time. It is important that in the present moment we must distinguish between perceiving the present versus perceiving something as present in the moment. The true present moment is experiential demonstrating peace and relational harmony versus a perceived intrusion of incongruity such as fear or dread.

As I have previously stated, time is the great delimiter enveloping myth causing it to stagnate becoming a fairy tale. As myth maneuvers through history locked in time, it loses mobility and life becomes a misaligned story out of sync with reality. The delimiter concept that we see in time is illustrated in language and math and will assist us in applying it to the myth entombed in time. In explaining this concept and by looking at language a delimiter is a sequence of one or more characters used to specify the boundary between separate and independent regions in plain text or other data streams. An example of a delimiter is the comma character which acts as a field delimiter in a sequence of comma-separated values controlling the flow of the sentence. In considering mathematics, a slightly different concept arises. In equations, a parenthesis or bracket acts as a delimiter in an algebraic equation as a guide as to which function is performed as a unit or set. In math, it may be visualized with the following equation: "$(3+2)*3=X$" compared with "$3+2*3=X$" in which "X" is two different computations as Algebra follows the abbreviation of "PEMDAS" expressed as "Please Excuse My Dear Aunt Sally" which mathematically stands for "Parenthesis, Exponents, Multiplication, Division, Addition, and Subtraction" providing the order of mathematical operations in an equation. In both language and mathematics, a boundary is dictated offering an accurate description of time as it sets a boundary and then dictates the order of operation (perception).

Historical Time, the Timelessness of Myth, & Time's Redemption

In Greek terminology, a concept of time is expressed by the word kairos meaning a decisive moment marking a sense of fate or a crisis point—a point of decision or action which incites judgment and because of this concept time carried a weighty aspect of judgment. I was asked if mercy was an eternal attribute of God (Mark Eaton in e-mail to author, July 2015)? My response was as judgment existed only in time, therefore, so must mercy. His mercies are new every morning said the psalmist in time. Mercy is only demanded when something is not equal, therefore, only needed in duality. God's defining attribute is love and love does not include mercy as love removes duality thereby eradicating mercy. We only needed mercy because we do not understand love.

A kairos moment being the present moment or now is presented as a gateway, a boundary for which a radically new state exists to a monumental event; it is the day of action. Then, does history simply consist of chronos periods of time rolling on without purpose and direction? The Greek concept was a wheel of time without beginning and man was trapped in this eternal circular course in which history repeats itself.

It is because of this concept the Greek philosophers studied history to learn the future. They looked at reoccurrences to see and understand their current stage of life and to plan the future. Are the chronos periods then old and stagnant and the kairos point new and fresh? Was the Crucifixion a turn of events by angry Roman soldiers in alliance with the Jewish rulers or was it God decreed? If God decreed the Crucifixion and directed this historical event; did he too direct the Holocaust and other atrocities in human history? Ones view of the flow of history will indicate one's concept of God's sovereignty.

As stated earlier in Greek thought, time is not conceived as a progressing line with beginning and end but rather a circle and man is enslaved to this path of re-occurrence. Therefore, the philosophical thinking of the Greeks is so focused on the problems of history and time.

Time suggests a temporal presence while eternity is an abiding presence not necessarily unending but exceptional quality. Eternity is unmeasurable, not outside of time but without and regardless of time. In other words, when seizing the full scope of the moment, the intensity of the moment causes the innate necessity to mark time redundant. The traditional concept of eternity versus time is that both coexist. Time has both beginning and ending but eternity has neither. Time seems to pass through its forms (past, present, and future) while eternity is ever-present.

Aristotle says time is only measured in the mind and everything that happens leaves an impression and that impression remains after the event has ceased to be as a mental image. He says it is this impression that is measured since it is still present and not the thing itself (Aristotle's Physics (Book IV, part 10-13)). Therefore, time is the measured distance between events or impressions of the mind. Cullmann implies that for Christianity, these events are Crucifixion and Easter as the two main events in the past, a now moment entombed in past time (Cullmann 1962, 81-93).

Christianity has set the resurrection as a point in history frozen in time removing it from mythical flow causing it to be a stagnant event rather than a quality enriched eternalized moment. It has become the motionless resurrection of one man over a dynamic resurrection for all mankind.

To redeem the time is to buy back what time holds ransom. Time holds ransom the present moment preventing it from being experienced in timelessness. 1st Corinthians indicates the present moment is out of focus because law and time hinders perception distorting the clear/true view making the present moment ineffective. It is when this moment is clearly distinguished and time ceases its purpose then all becomes one in the One.

Is the Bible more a mythical book rather than a literal book? If it is mythical does that make its contents false? Absolutely not, but it intensifies the desire of man to unite with his beginnings in God however God maybe described. The creation myths of Genesis one and two express the belief that all things depend for there being on the creative acts of God. That belief can be expressed in doctrine even though the concept of creation was not intended to be doctrinal. The doctrine extracted from myth is very rigid while myth maintains fluidity. A myth is the interpretation of an event and not the linear facts of the event.

A powerful aspect of myth is its ability to exist over many ages and throughout many cultures. Even though the story may not be the same, the truth remains rich and vibrant making it seemingly timeless. Timelessness of myth means it is not encapsulated in the past, present, or future but remains outside of time's forms. For example, what makes the Incarnation a myth? An account of the divine incarnating into humanity is not solely historical truth as an event which happened in the past to one man; but its mythical aspect is seen in its continual function in the tradition and culture of all humanity. While Christianity sees the Crucifixion as the tragic death of Jesus, the Son of God; in its mythical aspect, it is the interaction of God in humanity. As the Bible is opened as a mythical book of man's journey rather than a literal view of man's history depths begin to unfold detailing a richer story of God's visitation and if allowed to be our own, morphs into our personal journey of discovery and mystery.

History is a chronology of significant events as determined by the storyteller. Is history always true or is it influenced by the recorder's culture, beliefs, and perception of the events? History is based on perception being input via the senses translated and interpreted by the narrator. Religion manipulates history being recorded time intended as a spiritual path for learning our origin and replaced it with a rigid structure of do's and don'ts and called it God's Law. When distance from the Creator is perceived man established laws to return him to his origin. The Hebrews proclaimed God revealed Himself to them throughout history not as ideas and concepts but as movement and action. They saw Him as He created. His being was not learned through laws and propositions but in action and in His interaction with His creation. History to them was a movement toward a goal and that goal was set and achieved by God with His promise of blessing as He supervises and intervenes as necessary.

In the Hebraic mind, the words effected or caused to be while in the Greek concept the words describe the state of being. An example is demonstrated the attribute of love. Hebrew concepts express "the God who loves me" while the Greeks conceive "God is love." Neither is wrong but each portrays a differentiated concept of God's love. One makes it personal and the other is more generalized and distant. One makes it truth experienced and the other is stating a fact known. In Hebrew thought, it is God who causes me to experience love. For the Greek, it is God who initiates love. Inevitably both are true.

Does divine intervention change the outcomes of human history? If God intervenes, it becomes God's show and not man's. It is no longer the history of man but God's story as He dictates outcomes. Or, does God set the stage, providing a kairos moment and then allows man to act and react thereby creating his own history? A kairos moment is a point in time that is presented for a monumental event, it is a fixed day, or in modern jargon, it is "D Day," the day of purpose and action. In Divine Presence, time stands still and we experience the moment eternalized—the kairos point—the Now of unbelievable quality over quantity. In this way, the divine intrusion into creation sees quality time rather than a sequence of events over a period of time. It sees a divine visitation and the creation myth is man's story of the encounter.

The Power of the Breath:
The Interaction of Divinity Placed in Time

The *Sefer Yetzirah*, paints an amazing picture of the Creator carving out a place forming and creating an empty space to implant the intent held in his mind. The process of creation was the vocalization of the image formed in his mind becoming materialized initiated by the Ruach of God (Kaplan 1997, 13-14). A glass blower will apply pressure to the formable glass producing not multiple images but a single image to which he gives form and function. In the Hebrew mind, creation was not a creation of many but an event of union speaking not to number or quantity but to function and quality. God announces the intent held in His mind and this force or pressure expressed by His breath activates the physical plane causing His intent to breach multiple dimensions.

What is the product of the breath, the intention of God called? The Christ or the Logos is what is formed and carved by the Ruach universally for mankind but religion has limited the Logos to that of one man, Jesus. Origen said, "As our body while consisting of many members is yet held together by one soul, so the universe is to be thought of as an immense living being, which held together by One Soul—the power and the Logos of God (Freke 2000, 84)." The words of God were formed as He breathed. He breathed to express his mind and forced the image to be formed as does the glass blower. The Christ is the expression of the word spoken so long ago that has not returned void. As the Christ is in all of us being universal, this is the divine nature that we share. It is from this perspective that the Son of God is not simply a historical figure who lived in time, but an eternal philosophical principle, the breath who infuses us with our identity. As Origen also declared: "The Father did not beget the Son, but is ever begetting him (Freke 2000, 84)."

The perception of the Hebrew man is not like the Greek man. The Hebrew man is a union of spirit and body and related to the two worlds. He is flesh animated by God's breath, the Hebraic ruach, who is then declared to be a living soul, the nephesh. Man does not have a life but he is life. To the Greek mind, man is a soul imprisoned in flesh who embarked on a circle of continuous learning. The Soul is divine and must be released from physical existence to make its eternal home in the realm of reality once again. The Greek concept is God can only be known by the flight of the soul in ascendance to the spiritual realm, while the Hebrew view says a personal God gave of himself by invading history to meet man in forming a historical personal experience exemplified in redemption.

What is the soul? The soul is not the part of man that goes to heaven at death but the reaction of the body to the breath—the Ruach of God. The soul is the experience of living/reacting to the breath of God which sustains our animation. I do not see the soul, the nephesh, as an entity or part of man but a reaction or evidence of the animation of man by the breath of God. The soul then, is the evidence of life! Nephesh is the proof of animation while the ruach is the animator. Death is simply the inability of the body to no longer respond, house, or react to the breath of God.

The incarnational infusing of breath was applied historically to one man named Jesus thereby creating a literal historical record causing a loss of the beautiful and living account of the myth, the powerful ruach of God indwelling all men. Why the mythical incarnation? It acknowledges the viable Perennial Philosophy which carries the kairos moment for all cultures, the timeless and universal experience of God interacting with humanity in a personal and direct way as told from the viewpoint of many civilizations with their own unique perspective of the event. In interpretation of the myth, there is no right or wrong; but is a living account of the divine visitation in humanity. The myth does not account for how it happened but why it happened—as the truths expressed in ancient times are the same intent as they are in any present moment. The *Philosophia Perennis* points to a higher reality and principle pulling all men to their origin in God regardless of how He is described. Even though the interpretation of the truth may vary, it still points to the power and beauty of the One in which no duality dwells.

God is, mirrored in the Logos of the Greeks, the Ma'at of the Egyptians, and any of the other expressions of the principle order of the cosmos upholding and directing through appropriate acts the world and especially mankind to a goal. Also, God as the Absolute, is disclosing himself to us and to the world through a system of symbols. God's essence being the effects of his word and action, is experienced while in the second instance, the being or intent of God is perceived. The first is a portrait of linear history and the second is mythical enlivening the mystery. During history and time, one can see evidence and perceive occurrences of divine intrusion displaying will and divine meaning. Seeing God in the divine will expressing His actions and perceiving God in symbols presents a differentiated image and in both cases God is active in self-disclosure. The Western mind tends to see God in a linear process and seeks to find solutions for perceived inconsistencies while the Hebraic mind is filled with wonder and seeks to enter the mystery of God rather than trying to explain it.

As man attempts to understand his role in the cosmic structure, he seizes that moment and encases it causing him to experience the mystery of divine intrusion. When he bypasses the mystery of myth, and to control the experience, he establishes rules and laws to govern this process of experience ritualizing it in time. Ancient man who listened to the declaration of the heavens felt the need to be governed by mimicking and adding to what he heard the stars say and turned it into law, religion, and doctrine. As the voice of the heavens, which was the basis of the early myths, became faint being mixed with doctrine, man established law attributing it to God as its Giver to enforce obedience. As the stars told of the Christ, the mythic anointing of union, man began to tell of his humanity conceiving separation enlarging himself in his own mind. Man, to copy the voice of the stars placed himself in the Zodiac striving to see his individual future overriding the declaration of the astronomical heavens which uttered/declared without words the Divine union of man and Creator—the journey of all mankind. This concept, for me, arises because I see the Zodiac, Astronomy, and Ancient religions as a picture of God showing Himself to man and they represent the interpretation of the show being man's journey. It ensures that God has been in intimate contact with his creation and will continue to be. Now, is there a hidden secret in these things? Perhaps, and, I really hope so.

The Institution of Law Implies Separation

"The law attempts to make us keep score in a game God isn't playing."
(Don Keathley's Facebook page, accessed March 2015,
https://www.facebook.com/don.keathley)

Duality is the divergence of point "A" and point "B." Time, then, is the evidence or the measurement that duality and contrast exist being the distance of point "A" from point "B". The ratio aspect of Logos is not how divergent the two points might be but is a relationship of differentiation; or more precisely, expressing how one is contained within the other. Judgment is time relational as it gives us how much, how wide is the variance, and by how far did we miss the mark. But in Oneness there is no duality, no judgment, and therefore no time. One is relationally contained within the other. In the fullest aspect of being one, duality and time lose their expression.

First and foremost, man judges while God decrees. God proclaims man's reality correcting perceived judgments as man outlines how he failed according to a misapplied law. Righteous judgment echoes the decrees of God rather than the judgment of man. Man's judgments, reflecting duality, harm and punish as the incongruent images are empowered. The decrees of God enforce the correct image of God's intent while judgment which issues from duality instills separation through laws that can never offer restoration.

The kairos moment attempts to remove the locks which time has placed on the Incarnation, Crucifixion, and Resurrection from their historical cages, releasing them to their true place of timelessness thereby enlivening and empowering them out of history to mystery. As past and future integrate to now, the divine intrusion becomes union. Said another way, myths were put in place in humanity's path not to provide a historical record but to provide an interpretation of what transpired as man comes to understand his journey.

Each time a myth is retold the truth of the event is relived and again effects the hearer. For example, as the creation myth is recounted, it is relived as creation takes place in every moment or an unending moment is realized in which evolution, Incarnation, Eschatology, and history are all one and the same moment even though time has determined how we define them.

For a law to be enforced a judgment must be rendered or at the least implied. In John 7:24 Jesus says do not judge according to appearance but judge righteous judgment. The judgment by appearance is a judgment based on a law after a determination of failure. It requires a comparison with a rule to determine if the rule was broken. Jesus was doing away with this type of judgment by removing all condemnation to project a correct image. Again, man judges while God decrees. God issues a proclamation of man's reality correcting judgment as they saw or perceived themselves to be due to a misapplied law.

Righteous judgment does not harm or punish like the law. One enforces the misapplied perceived image and the other restores the correct one. Righteous judgment being decrees, removes duality because it erases the depiction of the incorrect image restoring man's perception to that of the image of God; an act accomplished in the mind of God, indwelling and active in the awakened man.

Is the law a creation or derivative of man to remedy his own perceived failings or did God give us the law to prove we needed salvation? If we determine the law was our own fabrication, then we must wonder what else was self-created because of our wrong construct of God.

Religion implies God judged creation followed by punishment when no judgment was actually decreed as consequence is often confused with punishment. A judgment is pronounced by one in authority and in the issue of punishment the offender pays the offended for the offense (retribution). Judgment produces anger and resentment and does not restore the offender but simply trains him not to make the mistake again for fear of a harsher punishment.

A consequence is a true cause and effect event and is brought about by choice of the individual. A consequence is received not because of judgment by a failed standard but because of an action of one man. While judgment with its associated punishment produces fear, a consequence produces a true learned response.

God did not pronounce judgment on mankind but simply told them of a consequence—neither good, nor evil—that would occur as particular choices were made. In other words, judgment is enforced by the one who rules over you because they were offended by your actions and thus a punishment follows. A consequence on the other hand is encountered because of one's own actions and in time understanding and awareness is produced. In one you pay and in the other you learn.

Duality & Differentiation

Non-duality simply institutes equality which is uniformity in character, value, and ability; and homogeneity being the state of having identical functional value. There are many universes, suns, stars—and all made from star dust producing differentiation not separation as portrayed in the New Testament as the many membered body of Christ. Oneness does not negate differentiation. Mark Eaton said, "Oneness is not achieved; it is discovered and discerned (Eaton, Mark, e-mail message to author, July 12, 2015)." as oneness is a present moment condition. In cellular biology, differentiation speaks of a cell evolving into a more complex cell. In other words, the simple cell through certain processes (learning/maturing) can take on multiple functions but the DNA does not change, therefore, no separation from its origin. The idea of separation may be the sole culprit of our concept of God. Differentiation is not duality as duality is number. It is an opposite and must be compared with another to be understood; while differentiation speaks of quality and function, and an ever-increasing capacity to evolve. It is becoming more and more awake, aware, and alive. This shift resulting in increased awareness does two things. First, it reveals intense detail and then sets another course based in this new information.

The error is not being consciously aware of duality but that it is consciously ascertained to be reality. We establish it as real and build our world and our responses to life around it and make judgments from this center. Just because I am differentiated from God I can still have His substance while I am learning to function as His offspring. I am from Him and of Him but not Him. This is not dualism but noting differentiation which manifests in maturity. Man created his own duality separating himself from God and the law was one of many ways man diversified himself from his Creator. Man used law to point out divergence for his own purpose mainly to resolve his guilt, shame, and lack of seeing his true image reflected in the Christ of the ages. Until we realize we established the law to justify ourselves before God then we will continue to have difficulty in seeing God's continual interference to demonstrate His love restoring our mind's perception to the image of His intent. Duality is not reality but the contrast or divergence it manifests can be perceived as one.

Cosmology and Law

"We have been taught to believe in 'the Laws of God' and the 'Laws of Nature' when actually there are no such things, save those man makes."
(Graham 1975, 19)

Manmade laws, including the Mosaic Law, defines or more accurately sets limits and boundaries; while Cosmic Law describes observed behaviors and actions. It does not govern but declares what is. Laws of man, again, including the Law of Moses, instills division while God's decrees instill union and singularity. How are the cosmic laws noted in ancient cultures without scientific theories and descriptions? In my opinion, one amazing example is seen in Psalm 19.

It has been assumed two thoughts were expressed in this Psalm, one being the Glory of God and the other Law of the Lord? We tend to read it as two witnesses telling their own story rather than one testifying to the same truth. The effect of most religions is to force separation by instituting a comparison (a duality) rather than an expression of union. The Glory of God and the Law of the Lord are one and saying the same truth.

The Law, as we have understood it, seemed to demonstrate the need for remediation but the Law of God shows no remediation is needed. The Law of God in its original purpose emphasized no division and no separation. Instead of trying to read the Psalm as a lecture on the heavens consider the unique perspective of David, not a chapter to form doctrine but one who looked up and saw the stars one night and he simply expressed his heart and it is in this same way we should let the Psalm unfold.

The sun's Creator is directing the sun and establishing his realm--and his realm is total and completely all that is in the heavens/firmament. Verse 6 is not saying the sun orbits the earth, but he is saying as there can be no fixed position or no point of zero motion in the universe due to its constant motion the arbitrary fixed point is the current location of the observer as all measurements of surveyors, navigators, and astronomers the zero point is the earth's surface at the observer's location. Lloyd M. Graham said, "The

Creative Principle does not make time and space and put worlds into them; it makes worlds and time and space result from them (Graham 1975, 20)."

This psalm is an allegory of the Christ and its effects on the entirety of creation. As the sun is the life giver of all that is created so too is the Christ, the Son of God. This is not a historical Jesus but the Sophia/Logos, the Tao, the Great Spirit of the Native Americans, and the sustainer of all that man sees.

Psalms 19 is not about two separate viewpoints but two witnesses; the heavens representing dimensional space, and law representing dimensional time telling one story — our history. This psalm according to Hebraic language is about reading it and seeing the whole function as each part conjoins and interpenetrates revealing a mythical truth. What is that truth? A mysterious God who is self-revealing to his creation. Their simultaneous declaration is not how mankind has erred but is the declaration confirming the image of God in man. It is this divine seed that makes the heart shine and the eyes see clearly, without duality.

Judgment only exists in time and time being a derivative of man produces judgment. There is a record or more correctly a kairos moment that exists without time constraints and is a living moment without end bound to the Logos, the Intent of God in every man. This record is a decree not a judgment and is a testament to the divine intent experienced in the Incarnation, Crucifixion, and the Resurrection. It is alluded to in the verse that talks about the Lamb slain from the before the disruption of the world. It is also seen when Paul says the Christ was dead, buried, and resurrected; and we were in that experience too — all outside of time or more correctly regardless of time and more importantly due to the kairos or critical point, their purpose cannot be diminished or negated.

This kairos moment is not a moment in history but is mythical being dynamic and living. Could it be a divine intrusion (Symons 2014, 131) to coin a term I first heard from friend and author Barbara Symons. The Divine invests into humanity and it is in these moments humanity is briefly overwhelmed and the vivifying power waits on man to catch up and breathe. In other words, the mysteries of the Incarnation, Crucifixion, and Resurrection are not the historical single event in one man but in its mythical aspect are charged with layers of freeing truth for all men. Just as the Incarnation was set in time the same happened with the Crucifixion. The Crucifixion is the dying of illusion that implants separation and division. The cry is from man as he perceives loneliness. The Resurrection is the full awareness of union—no separation, no loneliness. The true death of death. Time implies distance and makes God "up there" but the myth of the incarnation is forever in you ending time and restoring the eternal moment. Said another way, as myths were put in place in humanity's history they were not meant to provide a historical record but meant to provide an interpretation of what past in time in man's perception—man trying to make sense of the interaction of divinity and humanity. History, then, is the linear story while myth is the personal experience enhancing the magnificent divine intrusion.

As previously stated, R. J. Stewart confirms: "The declaration or recounting of a myth is, at its deepest and most powerful level, a reverberation of the event which it describes. Thus, myths are not allegories but resonances or reflections of actualities, of occurrences or manifestations at the heart of being (Stewart 1999, 6)." In this way, creation takes place in every moment begating an unending moment in which evolution, incarnation, eschatology, and history are all one and the same moment—but time has determined how we define/limit them. In the moment, there is no time; no limits, therefore, no history or future. The myth is not about one man but mankind as chronos yields to kairos.

Are the stars still speaking? What did the author of Psalm 19 intend to convey? Paul Hawken brought a quote of Emerson's to the current time period by asking the graduates at the University of Portland "What would we do if the stars only came out once every thousand years? No one would sleep that night of course as the world would become religious overnight. We would be ecstatic, delirious, and made rapturous by the glory of God. Instead, the stars come out every night and we watch television (Hawken 2009)."

Retelling the Myth: Via Perennial Philosophy

The historical Incarnation is viewed as an act of God becoming flesh in one man. This en-fleshment was not only indwelling in blood and bone but to be fulfilled in expression. God witnessed his intent become flesh—expressed in living color. He gave birth to his son; He "offspringed" himself in all creation. Because the account of the Incarnation was applied historically to one man; it lost the beautiful and living account of myth, the powerful Ruach of God indwelling and enlivening visible creation. What is the value of seeing the Incarnation mythically? It acknowledges the "Perennial Philosophy" which carries the kairos moment—the Now for all cultures, the timeless and universal experience of God interacting with humanity in a personal and direct way as told from the viewpoint of many civilizations with their own unique perspective of the event. In interpreting myth, there is no right or wrong; but it is a living account of the tapestry of divinity indwelling humanity. The *Philosophia Perennis* points to a higher reality and principle pulling all men to their origin in God regardless of how He is described pointing to universality of God not multiple gods. Some cultures in personifying His attributes having en-fleshed them gave that culture a polytheistic concept; yet it was a single god whose attributes were enshrined and enlivened as entities.

The term Philosophia Perennis (throughout all Philosophy) is a term indicating wisdom is timeless and present in all civilizations. This wisdom or philosophy is timeless because the layers of truth it expresses was the same in ancient periods as it is in any present moment, and will, for the most part, be unchanged in any future time. The Perennial Philosophy is not "a" philosophy or one single concept but is the common foundation from which proceeds whatever is truly valid in all philosophies. It does not seek doctrinal status but it seeks to uncover and to articulate eternal and universal truth found in all cultures and philosophies as each strives to see God as they understand Him. No people or culture can claim ownership but humanity throughout history has detected this unchanging light and strives to describe this light in human language in their time and then apply myth to aid in understanding their purpose. The central idea of the Perennial Philosophy is Divine Truth being one in purpose, timeless in duration, and universal in scope. As this ideology reverberates throughout all times and places in human history, it is manifested in different civilizations so "that the different religions are but different languages expressing that one truth (World Wisdom 2015)."

Perennial Philosophy views all religion and its traditions as sharing a common single thread as a universal truth upon which is the foundation of all religions. This thread of truth has been recovered in each epoch of time by various saints, sages, prophets, and philosophers. Even though religious ideas are diverse yet in all of them is a stream of life which in full mythical form demonstrates an essence in all human life seeking re-union of spirit returning to

God who gave it in all humanity for all ages. Interestingly, this concept is voiced by Origen, who said: "the very thing that is now called the Christian religion was not wanting among the ancients from the beginning of the human race, until Christ came in the flesh, after which the true religion, which had already existed, began to be called 'Christian' (Watts 1968, 136)." Early church philosophers saw Jesus as the embodiment of wisdom as well as the incarnation or en-fleshment of the Logos; but what is the Logos? It was in this manner Christ became a far reaching mystical reality as the transcendent God created all things by self-expression as He becomes defined in the flesh and this creativity of God is resident within every man and all creation and man develops means to explain it utilizing myth.

Generally, the Perennial Philosophy assumes a loss occurred which Christianity calls original sin and is a consistent element in most if not all religions. It is the goal throughout time to return to balance made difficult by the Absolute God who is infinite not being bound by time and humanity who must exist and succumb to measurable time. Thus, Perennial Philosophy considers time an illusion pictured as a series of cycles in which man attempts to reunite with his Creator attempting to correct a perceived breach. Man seeks to escape imperfection by attempting to enter the atmosphere of God either in a dream, as a reflection, or escaping time and entering ultimate reality. This movement is often hindered by the effects of time which chains humanity to the finite. We find ourselves restricted by finite boundaries in which we are limited by a closed set of abilities and possibilities with our responses entombed by time.

It is generally assumed religion and myth are antithetical. Religion is belief concerning the sacred and the application of moral code, rituals, and values to support a set of beliefs while myth is a traditional story of historical events that serves to reveal a world view of a certain culture or people usually explaining a natural or supernatural phenomenon. John A. T. Robinson acknowledges Christianity would be better served detaching myth from the doctrine of God (Robinson 1963, 12, 32-35, 123) but that is based on the generally held view of myth as a fable, a story of untruths. Mircea Eliade, a professor of religious history, said myth was an integral part of religion as it offered a living element. The mythical aspect has served the Christian doctrine by stating myth was "an essential foundation of religion and that eliminating myth would eliminate a piece of the human psyche (Wikipedia 2015)." Eliade wrote about the sky god while Christianity was working out the death of god theology. Joseph Campbell comments: "People could not fully understand their purpose without mythology to aid them (Wikipedia 2015)."

People become offensive if elements of faith are labeled as mythical meaning outside the natural flow of historical events because of the current meaning. J. R. R. Tolkien combines his faith and myth when he marries mythology to the echo of divine truth saying myth is a sub-creation to God's creation. C S Lewis labels the Christ story as myth—as he understands that myth express truth on multiple levels. He says the Christ story is God's myth while all other myths are manmade. On the evening of September 19, 1931; C.S. Lewis was having a discussion with his close friend J.R.R. Tolkien in which Lewis said he could not understand how the meaning of Christ's life, death, and resurrection could affect him some 1900 years later. Tolkien replied that the gospel works in the same way as a myth. Lewis had no problem understanding the movement of myths and legends and he adds the gospels "are lies breathed through silver." Tolkien replies they are not completely lies but one must realize myth has elements of truth within the distortions and unworthy outer husk they often wear. Tolkien said, "Myths are echoes or memories of the truth that God had originally made known to Adam and Eve, the ancestors of the whole human race (CSLewis.com 2009)."

What is myth? A story of nothing but un-truths? Or an attempt at man trying to explain a concept which he has no explanation for? Modern day terminology says it is nothing more than the imagination of a storyteller and bears no truthful concepts. Was Tolkien right? Are myths simply echoes or memories of a masked reality that man cannot fully remember?

The Power of Myth – Time's Illusion

Is time an illusion? The contemporary concept of time is time does not exist; it is an unreality. Time is an illusion of the mind created by one's own cultural and biological evolution. In this sense, time is not independent but is a measurement of our mind interpreting the perceptions of the body as aspects of change in reality. One must first define illusion from its etymological roots. It seems illusion never meant unreal nor non-existent but wrongly perceived or interpreted by the senses. It means something that tricks the eye, but which eye? It is simply an erroneous perception of reality and not negation of reality. The Sanskrit term is even more revealing in its original intent. The Sanskrit word *maya* literally means magic and in this older language reveals an extraordinary display of power and wisdom. The spiritual concept is "that which exists but is constantly changing and thus is spiritually unreal" and it is the power or principle that "conceals the true character of a spiritual reality (Wikipedia 2015)."

Illusion is a mask and time functions in this aspect also. What is time hiding? The present moment is manifested when there is no time or time loses control by uncovering what is true, what is real. Does time cease in the present moment? Not really. But it ceases concealing, or loses its governing power allowing the view of reality, the place or locale where God is.

Eckhart Tolle says: "Through the present moment, you have access to the power of life itself, that which has traditionally been called God. As soon as you turn away from it, God ceases to be a reality in your life, and all you are left with is the mental concept of God, which some people believe in and others deny. Even belief in God is only a poor substitute for the living reality of God manifesting every moment of your life (Tolle 2005, 267)." God is not seen in the past or future. When God answered Moses in Exodus regarding His name, He said I AM that I AM—no past or future tense. The literal translation is "I shall be that I shall be." Rotherham's translation of Exodus 3:14 says, "I will become whatsoever I please (Rotherham 1994)." Who is in the present moment? Is it a lonely place? God solely resides in the present moment but as all are in God then that is the place teaming with life. The present moment is not plurality in the sense of everybody has a specific moment but is more unity in that all are present in the One—who is the power of the moment.

The present moment? It is undefined time rather than no time. Time is an illusion, but not in the sense of unreality but in the sense of a mask, for it hides or defaces reality. Is it an enemy? Again, an enemy must be defined. An enemy is an active opponent in the sense it prohibits a beneficial relationship. Time acts as a barrier to recognition of the present moment because the moment is only experienced when there is no time—or time is not manifested. What is the past and future? Are they not mental concepts as the past is the thinking or more correctly the remembering, a reconstruction of memories while the future is the projection of possibilities? This ideology seems to demonstrate that time is none other than a concept which marks events or marks change.

It seems time has distorted reality having caused us to realign our focus on temporal rather than timelessness. We claim no separation but divide and mark our lives by time. Once time takes its predominate role then we form love, hate, and other concepts around it. We strive to determine the beginning and end of spiritual events (Incarnation, Crucifixion, and Resurrection) and place them on a time line and in doing so, we lose their Present Moment mythical significance and they lose the ability to influence outside of time and history. For example, we see the Crucifixion as a historic occurrence and in doing so, we lose the powerful force of the ongoing crucifixion of duality in us. As with the Incarnation, we focus on the incarnation of one man in time and lose the fuller significance of the incarnation in every man allowing the Divine Seed (Logos) to produce fruit.

Religion determined God judged man based on laws He established and anytime judgment is instituted then division is the result. We claim no separation yet we seek to determine if the law has been fulfilled. If a law is in need of being fulfilled then a law itself being present indicates a miss; therefore, a separation existed and remediation needed as punishment must follow to appease the offended. Judgment is only warranted if an infraction occurred. If the Lamb was slain before the disruption of the world, then in effect no judgment can exist now, yet, that does not indicate consequences are not real. Judgment only exists in time and since the perceived infraction of the lamb slain occurred outside of time then no penalty can exist in time. If there is no infraction, then there is no judgment. Time is a soulical measurement appealing to temporal life. How was the lamb slain before the disruption of the world? By the power of myth.

A primary focus in ancient myths was the topic of creation. In Christianity, it is how we got here but the mythical account does not tell how but explores why. The Trees of Genesis are prime examples as Christianity seeks to know who planted them while the mythical concept deals with why they were planted and how they explain us. The Tree of Knowledge presents time as linear and its attributes exist only in time. A few of those being light and dark, good and evil, judgement and punishment: all exemplifying duality. Because we have eaten of (sourced ourselves in) the Tree of Knowledge of Good and Evil we then encounter what issues from it. Interestingly, Matthew 7:18 says a good tree cannot bring forth good and evil fruit—yet here is one that does and supposedly planted by God. The Tree of Life is timeless—Now. It stands in perfection, in singularity/union and presents its emanations surrounding it as that of an atom with its electrons surrounding the nucleus. Its emanations are light, life, and love and there are no opposites. Here is the action of the trees in the myth. A myth is not a static story but a dynamic recounting of an interaction between the spirit and the physical with a purpose of dismissing separation and demonstrating non-duality.

What emanates from the Tree of Knowledge? An emanation is an abstract but perceptible thing that issues or originates from a source and its synonyms are products, results, and consequences. Judgment is an emanation of law which is an emanation of time therefore making time the grand illusion. The decrees of God correct the illusion sourced in time as good and evil are also emanations or consequences of time which spring out of the Tree of Knowledge of Good and Evil.

Are evil and judgment illusions? Recalling illusion does not mean unreal or non-existent but wrongly perceived or interpreted by the senses; it is an improper reflection of reality and not negation of reality in that it hides or masks the truth of a spiritual reality. I think evil is a derivative of judgment solely existing in time, therefore, an illusion being something perceived wrongly indicates evil is not an illusion but an emanation or consequence of time from the Tree of Knowledge of Good and Evil. Time created good and evil producing judgment. Time is the illusion and good and evil are time's emanations or offspring.

Change is the mark that time passes as change highlights or makes contrast visible. The root of judgment is contrast and contrast reflects judgment which is resident in time. Our traditional view of sovereignty said God does not change and thus sprang our traditional view of eternity—that which is unchangeable. Bringing God into time birthed law and judgment as man perceived separation and a need to be reinstated into God's graces. Judgment lives in chronos because man misunderstood the declaration of the heavens. The chronological heavens are declaring the kairos moment—the now moment of a timeless God.

Good and evil cannot exist in the kairos moment as they are not reality but created perceptions of time yet they bring influence in the physical realm. We must learn to manifest what resides in the kairos nullifying the chronos.

As the precepts of the Lord clear up the eyes it also states in Matthew 6:22 in explaining the removal of dualism portrayed as seeing double; the eye that sees singleness or oneness causes the whole body—the whole state of existence to be full of light. The "law of the heavens" in Job 38 is not rules like the speed limit sign on the highway but are statements such as the law of gravity. They detail a truth about us and are not "do's and don'ts" that are man-made to satisfy a mentality based on judgment.

Faith is said to believe in God but the heavens are not telling us to have faith, they are telling us about the faithfulness of God towards us. Faith in the Greek mind is a mental concept and is more a mental maneuver being a persuasion of the mind to believe. This is not so to the Hebrew mind as faith is a verb not a noun as in the Greek concept. The Hebrew concept is to follow God and this demonstrates a reciprocation of faithfulness between God and man. The Hebraic concept is a glowing fire in the heart and this fire causes movement energizing to action. The Greek mind teaches us how to have faith while the Hebraic mind responds when faith is energized. In the Greek explanation, faith is the cause of movement while in the Hebrew mind faith is the effect of movement.

Time implies distance and makes God "up there" but the myth of the incarnation makes it forever in humanity ending time restoring the eternal present moment. The historical record of mankind is open to human influence, interpretation, and evolvement. God purposefully flows all historical outcomes into His plan and even with man's interruptions in the historical record, He had the extraordinary resolve to bring all interactions to his purpose revealing the myth—it is written in the stars.

Why did religion seem to divorce cosmology? The priestly account of Genesis describes a basic cosmology that has stood for thousands of years. Graham says it is because the Western mind cannot grasp abstract thought in that he is unable to ascertain metaphysical and cosmological concepts which caused him to "put the stamp of his own ego on everything including the Creator (Graham 1975, 2)" and we then create God in our own image. Graham adds that due to changes in cyclic law, knowledge was lost as "priests took the place of initiates and religion of metaphysics (Graham 1975, 2-3)."

Conclusion

Belief is a static concept and attempts to lock an idea within boundaries but truth is flowing and able to expand and breathe. This book is not about what I believe because I have realized I don't want to be locked down in belief. Richard Rohr was asked by Oprah "What do you believe in?" He answered "nothing (Barancik 2015)." Belief is like a stagnant pond while truth is a spring of life and is flowing, dynamic, and full of energy.

Is Jesus the Christ and the Logos? Is Jesus the Christ and not the Logos? Is Jesus not the Christ but the Logos? Is Jesus neither the Christ nor the Logos? The Logos was never meant to be a human Messiah who became God but is the materialized intent of God. The Logos can contain a Messiah but in my opinion the Logos contains the entire universe and is en-fleshed in all creation being the ultimate Incarnation of God.

The Logos is not a concept which first appeared in John 1:1 but it is resident throughout all civilizations. Christianity claims Jesus as God according to John's Prologue and thus, religion stalls the myth; stopping it in one man when John recognized the principle enlivening all. It was the Torah which, according to Jewish mysticism, preexisted the throne of God. It was the Aramaic Memra who created, saved, and Ma'at (truth) of the Egyptians who stood for justice, balance, and maintained the rational order of the cosmos. One cannot stop looking at John 1:1 for the origin and great mythos of God and man. It was this divine order and operation of the cosmos that was recognized and honored from ages past but it was Christianity who sees the God-man as one man and then claimed exclusivity.

In Christian terminology, who initiated this rational order? According to Hebraic thought it was the Ruach, the breathing creating impulse of God which expressed, produced, and materialized the Son, Logos, Torah, Memra, and Ma'at. The Ruach of God caused the Cosmic Whole of God to be seen, to become visible, but this expression of intent became deity through religion. The Ruach of God is the Effector of the Logos and is still effecting because God has not stopped breathing. It is not a breath but breathing. It is not the single breath breathed in Adam—but the continuous Ruach of a Living God.

The movements of this rational order regardless of the name each civilization called it demonstrates the continuous interaction of light, life, and love with creation. Although the stories and characterization of the Cosmic Structure may vary, the principle has remained intact through unknown years. The movements of the myth reveal truths of love and relationship and when held in history locks the story in the past leaving the truer promises distant to all mankind. The myth never ages and never loses its power as Light, Life, and Love—or God continue to touch humanity.

Does God really breathe? Did He really use His hands to create Adam? Did the Red Sea really split and the ground was dry? Does it really matter as the myth tells of a connection between God and man through the story teller's perception? Truths are present and are seen in the mystery of awe, God came down and interacted with His creation and man gets to tell the story.

The Hebraic concept of wisdom is an equal reflection of the Greek Logos. As the Hebrews personified wisdom, so the early church did to Logos. Philo said both were the "*eikon*" or image of God representing a light print, a reflection of the original. A trait of an image is its dependence remains to the original in that a mirror image disappears when the original steps away from the mirror. If God steps away from the mirror or He no longer intends then there is no logic (no principle, reason, or power) holding the universe together. You are a state of being because God who is Light, Life, and Love holds you in his mind. He is constantly thinking of you as you are the human intrusion into divinity.

Duality was the root cause for the incongruity of myth, history, law, and time. The perceived separation of humanity from divinity caused man to lose reality creating his own and in it man fell, God's rules were broken, and restoration will occur in the eschatological future. In man's fractured view of reality, he lost the divine intrusion of God and the relational awareness of divinity, the powerful Logos within. In this perception, man perceived he had a soul rather than is one, a new creation of divine living in flesh animating the human. This intrusion was what was hidden in the myth, as man attempted to explain what he intuitively knew was truth but relied on perception to convey the story. As man enlivened the perceived separation divergence ensued and union was lost in time.

Did myth propagate duality or try to correct it? Myth gave man an out, a method to come to grips with duality caused by a perceived breach to pay a debt that was never declared. Man needed a remedy to pacify his fears and bridge the distance which was propagated in myth; but, and a massive "but" here, he knew there was more, the spark of union was never extinguished. So, myth became man's story and according to the storyteller included dualism, a more than one, a separation he felt existed but could not explain. And that is what Adam did in the Genesis account, he asked for another; he blamed her as remedy for the perceived miss, the sin. Myth provided man with atonement, a means of maintaining the connection with divinity but with a price.

What is the myth that is entombed by time? The powerful myth of the creative force; Logos to the Greeks, Ruach to the Hebrew, Memra to the Aramaic, and traced to every civilization before was rendered powerless by being placed in a time line. The powerful myth of the intrusion of divinity was paralyzed by being placed in history and feared in religion. As the myth told of the incarnation of humanity by divinity, religion said it was the incarnation of god in one man. Max Planck speaks to this dilemma when he says "Science cannot solve the ultimate mystery of nature. And that is because, in the last analysis, we ourselves are part of the mystery that we are trying to solve (Planck 1932, 217)."

-IV-

THE MYTHIC COSMOS &
THE COSMOLOGICAL ELEMENT

The mythic cosmos implies the cosmos and the cosmic principle arose out of myth as creation myths told of beginnings in light of the storyteller and their perception of a world they could not fully understand. Psalms 19 is one such encounter that has been used to decry the union of what man sees being the glory of God with that of the stars, the heavenly declaration of man's story. The declaring heavens in Psalm 19:1 and the decrees of God in Psalm 19:7 are telling us not of a failed creation but a functional whole which totally expresses the Glory of God in and through the beauty of the works of His hands which is the manifestation of the intent of His heart. This psalm was not intended to be a scientific lecture of the heavens or to detail the cosmic laws of God but they, in their mythic form, portray the unique perspective of the author who is thought to be David, who, while looking up at the stars one night realized the mark of the Creator fully within his sight and awing his senses.

In reading this psalm, and as our Western mind tends to do; it pulls it apart in attempting to dissect the declaring heavens and the decrees of God rather than seeing the single message they proclaim. The Hebrew language is about reading it and seeing the functional concept as each part conjoins, reveals, and enfolds as they dance together in mythical truth. Are the stars still speaking? What did the author of Psalm 19 intend to convey? David realized his heart and his head agreed, no division between the mythological cosmos or the cosmic laws of God as both press the senses and logic of man. What he saw, what he felt, and what he heard in his heart were in unison, all were one.

Cosmic Light

In looking at Genesis chapter one we notice that God spoke in Genesis 1:3 creating light.

> [3] And God said, "Let there be light," and there was light. [4] God saw that the light was good, and he separated the light from the darkness. [5] God called the light "day," and the darkness he called "night." And there was evening, and there was morning— the first day (Gen 1:3-5 NIV).

But verse 14 of the same chapter God again speaks saying:

> …let there be lights in the vault of the sky to separate the day from the night, and let them serve as signs to mark sacred times [fixed times], and days and years, [15] and let them be lights in the vault of the sky to give light on the earth." And it was so. [16] God made two great lights—the greater light to

> govern the day and the lesser light to govern the night. He also made the stars. [17] God set them in the vault of the sky to give light on the earth, [18] to govern the day and the night, and to separate light from darkness. And God saw that it was good. [19] And there was evening, and there was morning— the fourth day (Gen 1:14-19 NIV).

The Hebrew concept is to always focus on function. Light came into being before the sun, moon, and stars were called into existence according to the Genesis account as taken chronologically. In the creation account on day one, light was called forth and separated from darkness which was not created but was already there. On day two the atmosphere was established and functioning. On day three dry land was formed as water was contained and vegetation was established. On day four the sun, moon, and stars were formed and called to function. On day five sea life and birds were created. On day six land animals and then man was formed from the earth. What was the light created on the first day—three days before the sun was set to function?

God, according to the Genesis account, called light from darkness, life from death, and function out of non-function (dysfunction). Days were established before the sun was in place to mark them. A day is defined by the earth's axial rotation to the sun and a year is determined as the earth orbits the sun. Genesis 1:14 says the lights were for signs—plural. A sign carries a message or reveals information acting as a bridge or an interpreter. How do the luminaries give information? Psalm 147:4 and Isaiah 40:26 indicates that God named the stars; and if literal, the stars only come out as God calls their name. Poetically, they are signs interpreting the character of God. In Hebrew thought when something is named it is done for identification by exhibiting the character in the name. When God determined the number of the stars and called their name He was indicating a complete number to fulfill a purpose. Incidentally, when determining their number and name He also placed them in their functional locations telling our story according to Hebraic thought.

God, through the book of Job, references astrological elements in Job 38:31-33 which asks:

> Can you bind the cluster of the Pleiades, Or loose the belt of Orion? Can you bring out Mazzaroth in its season? Or can you guide the Great Bear with its cubs? Do you know the ordinances of the heavens? Can you set their dominion over the earth?

The author of Job implies that God is in full control of the constellations of the Mazzaroth and there are laws that govern the heavens and exert influence over the earth. The Mazzaroth in Job 38:32 is referencing the Zodiac which in current dictionaries is defined as circle of animals but the primitive root through Hebrew to Sanskrit is *sod* and means the way or path. This circuit in the sky is the pathway of the sun through the heavens as seen from a fixed point of view on the earth.

Another mysterious and mythical concept regarding aspects of creation is that inanimate objects also have a message to the living. The declaring heavens in Psalm 19, the rocks crying out in Luke 19, the mountains and hills shouting in Isaiah 55, and the hand clapping trees also in Isaiah 55 are not proclaiming acknowledgment of a defeated creation but that creation is intimate with its creator. The signs carry a message revealing information of the union of creation. Are these talking objects to be taken literally or retained as a mystery? A mystery is not unknowable or impossible to understand and explain but a mystery arouses wonder and inquisitiveness bypassing the literal interpretation for the mythical one. It is not secretive in the sense of hiding from us but concealed for us and as the wonder and amazement is heightened then explanation comes and secrets are revealed for the sole purpose of enhancing relationship across multiple dimensions.

The ecclesiastical mysteries which include Incarnation, Crucifixion, and Resurrection are also cosmological depending on whether they are taken literally or mythically. The declaration of the heaven and earth regarding the Incarnation, Crucifixion, and Resurrection have the end mythical result of a shining heart and the decrees of God produce clearness to the eyes. The declarations and decrees are not proclaiming a fallen humanity and are not screaming what happened on a historical cross to one man but are proclaiming the results on a mythical cross to all mankind.

Fillmore provides the esoteric concept of crucifixion by saying the crucifixion is "the crossing out in consciousness of errors that have become fixed states of mind [and it is] the surrender or death of the whole personality in order that the Christ Mind may be expressed in all its fullness (Fillmore 2014, 151)." The crucifixion of Jesus represents the removal of self from consciousness by denying the ego or subduing it while humanity unites to the selfless. It also causes a refocus of man from that of flesh to spirit. The process of Crucifixion rather than the historical one-time event enforces the superiority of the Christ Mind as the ego loses its place.

The Crucifixion, according to the Manichaean view, depicts the Christ being God-actual proceeded from God-potential and descends into matter as the Divine sacrifice and has contained in himself the ideas and forms of all things that must be impressed into matter (Gaskell 1981, 190). In his involution or the act of enfolding, entangling, and interpenetrating of the Christ, he then becomes the evolution or unfolding of the archetypal man for all life. The Crucifixion portrayed the divine invading humanity as the Logos interpenetrated creation again, enfolding and effecting physical matter. This highly dual view typifies the Divine enfolding Himself in physical form and unfolding as a functional whole of a new creation. The unfolding of the Intent of God (the Logos) gives way to light as chaos births order.

As I have said previously, the heavens are not declaring what happened on a historical cross but are declaring what is happening in you symbolized by the cross. Nor are they saying God came into one man in history but incarnated or en-fleshed all humanity, birthing a new creation, a union of divinity and humanity of spirit and flesh. Also, they are not proclaiming a coming to life of a man from a tomb in Jerusalem only but a resurrection of a completely new type of life going beyond the heartbeat. The depiction of full life in the gift of immortality to the mind, body, and spirit being the whole soul devoid of duality and never divided or separated again. Time implies distance and places God up there but the power of myth tells you it is effecting you now and moves a moment in history to an ongoing present moment reality. While Christianity sees the Crucifixion as the tragic death of Jesus, the son of God; in its mythical aspect, it is the interaction of God in humanity. Just as the Incarnation was entombed in time the same happened with the Crucifixion losing its light becoming powerless in the lens of humanity. The light of the Crucifixion was masked, covered by the darkness yielding to the perceived power of death, sin, and evil.

The Perennial Philosophy Cosmology Connection

The Perennial Philosophy is a philosophical perspective of religion which posits all the world's religious traditions contain a single universal truth threaded throughout all cultures and it is this thread which enlivens the heart of divinity and humanity. Each religion however, has, through psychological, intellectual, and social needs, taken this thread and woven a veil that has effectively disguised it from the heart. This nugget of enduring truth is continuously recovered by humanity as it strives to point man to his origins. It is reinvigorated by the world's sages, mystics, theologians, priests, imams, rabbis, and preachers as they attempt to separate the ritual from the mystical seeing the ageless but masked light. Joseph Campbell says this beautifully when he observes "when one is ready to see the eternal flashing, as it were, through the lattice work of time, one can experience mystery (Campbell 2001, 15)."

How would one recognize the Perennial Philosophy? It is a concept extolling the *summum bonum* or the greater good of humanity, as it points to a vibrant union of divinity and humanity void of duality and division. The world's religions are clearly diverse as seen by their theologies on a superficial level. The Hindu faith is polytheistic, Judaism is monotheistic, while Christianity is considered monotheistic but only after manipulation of the trinitarian concept, Buddhism is non-theistic, while Islam rejects God having a son. The Perennial Philosophy mindset whose seemingly divergent views when laid against the spiritual, psychological, and cultural needs of civilizations in history can be easily reconciled through their metaphysical and symbolic meanings removing the dogmatic or doctrinal box in which religion has encased them allowing one to see the golden thread as each phase of civilization centers to touch their origin.

The meaning of Perennial Philosophy in simple terms is an undying drive or persistence to live with the divine and like a perennial plant is renewed to life season after season. It is a concept that cycles throughout humanity and this is best seen in the cosmological cycles of our existence pointing out our story. Cosmology is the study of the origin and development of the universe and simultaneously coming to understand humanity's role in it and this is accomplished by the mythos which develops from civilization to civilization and builds on each culture enhancing the mythic journey of humanity—the story of us. The *Philosophia Perennis* declares the wisdom of the ages is timeless and present in all civilizations and each layer of truth expresses what was true in ancient periods tempered with culture and tradition is also true in any present moment. It is not a single true concept but rather is a common thread of truth present in all philosophies as man connects to origin. As the Perennial Philosophy reverberates throughout humanity and is manifested in different cultures and religions it allows the varied language of religion to speak truth.

The cosmological principle is seen in the stars and their declaration over judgment. Psalm 19 says they declare the glory of God and they do so without error night after night, year after year, century after century and their words have abounded to all ages and will continue to do so as they do not declare humanity's demise but man's mysterious and glorious purpose bound in the Logos of God being God's intent and it is this intent that directs and gives form to the cosmos. It is not a completed or finished process in time but a continuous living process outside and above time. Even though Logos is a Greek term in our Bibles, its principles are also found in Indian, Egyptian, and Persian philosophical systems pointing to a rational living Perennial Philosophy as an unending ever-present reality for man to see God with each culture having various names for this principle. John Sanford describes the creative force of the Logos principle when he says, "the world-creating Logos could be seen in the movements of the heavenly bodies, in the majesty of the skies, in the great ocean with its abundance of life… but also could be seen in the tiniest unit of life but the most important place where the Word of God was to be found for the early Christian was within the soul herself, where it lived as an 'imago dei' like a spring of water from which flowed the knowledge of God (Sanford 1994, 23)." The Greek Logos reflected the age old Perennial Philosophy caught in time in the Greek mind serving to move humanity on their amazing journey of discovery.

The Cosmological & Cosmogonical Blueprint

As I stated earlier, cosmology is the study of the origin and development of the universe while also coming to understand humanity's role in the cosmogonical cycle as man becomes fully functional representing the tangible expression of God. How is this accomplished? By allowing the development of myth, the why of our journey throughout all cultures and at the same time realizing it has always and continues to develop. As we allow this process to engage us, we are admitted to a cosmogonical display of all ages as we gaze upon the magnificent tapestry that is the journey of man. The purpose of myth is not to explain the journey but simply make you aware there is one.

Cosmologies are either formed from chaos, emanating in unplanned evolutionary steps from an original formless state that is simultaneously nothing yet contains everything; or cosmic implying creation is a deliberate act by a logical creator. Chaotic cosmologies are found in the ancient cultures of China and Egypt while cosmic cosmologies are seen in Judaism, Christianity, and Islam. The differences are seemingly depicted by secular versus religious precepts but more accurately how each views time whether cyclical or linear. The Cosmological Principle posits the universe is homogeneous and isotropic and is dependent on the position of the observer. Homogeneity stresses the universe has the same properties at every point and it is uniform without irregularities or abnormalities. Isotropic concepts imply it is uniform in all orientations as isotropic means equal way or direction. The Cosmological Principle conveys there are no special places and no special directions and no matter where you look from an observer perspective you see the same distribution of objects which theoretically implies the universe cannot have a center or place of origin; therefore, no place for the Big Bang to have initiated. Is there an edge to the Universe? The idea of an edge suggests that everything in the universe is not contained in the universe invoking the concept of an outside property, a portion that is not resident in the whole. Empedocles, a Pre-Socratic philosopher, said "God is an infinite sphere whose center is everywhere and circumference is nowhere (*Liber XXIV philosophorum*)."

There is a difference in cosmology and cosmogony as one is the fountain head from which others spring forth. Cosmology is the study of the cosmos from its origins through how it was formed. Cosmogony is the study of the cosmos without regard to its mechanical process instead focusing on its metaphysical and philosophical approaches. It explores the functionality of the cosmos over its mechanisms from which it was fashioned. Cosmology is principled in time while cosmogony is timeless. Is the account in Genesis a cosmology or a cosmogony? Cosmogony is not solely the story of creation. It is not concerned with how creation occurred but why it occurred. Is the book of Genesis the only account of creation? Of course not. Each culture has their own account of the process but why did creation unfold in the manner it did? Was it by chance or by evolution? Or was there an Orchestra Leader, a director of the music which choreographed the dance offering a perichoretic interpretation of the interaction of divinity and humanity? What is the purpose of cosmos? It is so divinity and humanity can dance!

Consider the word endings of cosmology and cosmogony. Cosmology or the *cosmo-logos* is the origins, theories, and dynamics of evolution as they unfold and reveal the universe as perceived from an observer; the eye of the beholder. It is a study concerned with structural order and logic. Cosmogony or the *cosmo-gonia* is concerned with the idea of coming into being and is an endeavor to understand the purpose of becoming or coming into being which features function, role, or duty but more so focuses on the privilege of completing the task. Cosmogony reaches beyond the perceived form without religious, traditional, and other filters deriving truth accomplished through philosophy. Also, a cosmology is a narrative written to a specific people in a specific time inclusive of cultural traditions, while a cosmogony is generally poetic alluding to creation's purpose as an inclusive and flourishing environment. Cosmology seeks to convey the dynamic movement and articulation describing the motion of the universe as a quantity. Cosmogony, having the same root as Genesis, conveys the purpose of beginnings and deals with the purpose of origin and becoming of the cosmos as quality. Another point to consider is cosmology has Greek expressions while cosmogony contains Hebrew assertions as one builds the house and the other creates a home.

The Cosmic principle sees or implies there is someone bigger than you or I. Someone outside our ability to dictate or control yet not outside our ability to comprehend and experience and this principle is inclusive of all and in all dimensions. Lee Smolin said, "whether the talk is of God or of an eternal and universal Law of Nature, the idea that dominates is that the rationality responsible for the coherence we see around us is not in the world, but behind it (Smolin 1997, 194)." What is behind the failure to see a universal inclusive principle in the cosmos effecting humanity? There seems to be two schools of thought. One lacking interest of distant galaxies and having a singular focus for that which brings comfort and hope now with no concern for cosmic ideologies. The other emphasizes cosmology which effects the entire physical realm of our existence. The cosmos is trying to tell us something; about ourselves and about our Creator. "See that distant star? It is part of us and we are part of it!"

It was the Greek mind which afforded us with the idea of the cosmos being a portrait of beautiful and divine order. Brian Cox, a British particle physicist at the University of Manchester United Kingdom said, "we are the cosmos made conscious and life is how the universe understands itself (Cox 2015)." Plato said the cosmos emanated from a single creator, a supreme conscious mind rather than a personal god (Campion 2012, 152). To the Greek mind the entire cosmos was intelligent, divine, and conscious. From this consciousness or soul, the world soul birthed all other forms life. The World Soul was the organizing principle and life source for all souls flowing from the ancient philosophy of *tat tvam asi* (thou art that) as all cosmic particles originate in the one.

The cosmic principle is also beautifully expressed in the metaphysical concept of being and becoming which exemplifies two modes of philosophical existence. Being is structured and infused with life's experiences as continuously dwelling in the present moment. Becoming is experienced in the physical realm and is characterized by changes in time yet not locked in time. It is marked by openness, limitlessness, receptive to learning, and exploring the unknown. If a thing is perceptible such as visible and tangible, then it has become.

This cosmic concept of being and becoming presents an existence that is dynamic, full of movement, living, and responsive to all life and not a cosmos that is wondering, floundering without purpose and intent. Cosmically, being represents a cosmos of structure and self-reliance seen in the cosmic constants such as the speed of light and the force of gravity. It is perfectly ordered and functionally open. Being and becoming take root in the perichoretic dance of perception and experience. The loss of the dance occurs when we forego experience and look at perception alone and proclaim, "I believe." At this moment, all else must be excluded as you detach yourself from the journey losing awareness and wonder. They are both cyclic processes in the cosmic structure and can only be described in the language of myth. Based on these concepts, is God being or becoming? He is both as the initiator of the processes! In Being he is dwelling and instigating the present moment, he is structured, logical, complete, and self-sufficient. In Becoming he can be touched by time but not limited by it. He is open, unlimited and adaptable to change. But most importantly, he is relational and responsive to and by his creation as His attributes effect the cosmos universally.

The Cosmological Divorce

The cosmos is actively screaming "I am one with the Creator" as the rocks, hills, and trees raise their anthropomorphic elements while Paul in Romans eight declares the creation exhibits gut wrenching pains. Are these expressions by nature literal or are they mythically explaining the union of two worlds? The question is not how can they make these vocal declarations but why do they? It is solely because they are linked to the Creator. The cosmos is connected to deity. This union is also evidenced in sacred geometry seen in the golden ratio and the cosmic constants.

Why does religion seem to divorce itself from cosmology? Early Christianity depicts the embeddedness of cosmology in its beginnings especially in the Greek and Eastern arenas. Its primary rise is through the theological interpretation between Creator and creation as creation is stripped of its mythical value because religion stressed the mechanical creation story over the mythical which responds to the why of creation. Creation became physical and complete rather than metaphysical and ongoing losing the breath of the divine as the "Divine Magic" was lost and replaced with literalism (Schuon 2003, 204). The mythical creation was pulled back into time and space and the history of the world losing the animating power of awe and fascination in which the mystery of the divine overrides the senses pushing past the intellect. Is it logical for the trees to clap their hands and the rocks and hills to shout out and creation to realize an element of creation is missing; that of the manifested cosmic principle in the cosmos? No, but it is a fantastic mystery filling us with wonder, awe, and amazement as God moves from "a concept or an article of belief…become[ing] an element of experience (Borg 1995, 15)." Nature acknowledges the universal cosmic element that man has omitted from his story.

The restructure begins as man once again envisions the cosmos as continuously spiraling in God and God in it, not at rest but actively moving. The separation from God that man perceived portrayed man as alone but realization of the perennial perichoretic union of God, man, and creation resets all perceptions. This union, demonstrated in the universal and inclusive dance is the divine order, the cosmic glue, the action of the Logos of God, the all-encompassing rational order putting all as it should be mirroring the All in All.

Religion has omitted the mythical values of the cosmological beginnings which gave way to the catastrophic eschatological outcomes of the fate of the cosmos. As the value of the cosmos was lost it resulted in a failed cosmological outcome. Cosmogony includes the processes of cosmology and eschatology. Cosmology is the discourse or narrative of the origin or beginnings of the cosmos while eschatology is the ending or fate of that cosmos. Cosmology reveals the beginning processes of the universe in service to divinity and humanity and eschatology reveals the determined purpose of the divine intrusion. Eschatology took on fear because the purpose of cosmology was removed from religion. As religion lost the value of its cosmological purpose it resulted in a flawed perception of the eschatological outcome of the cosmos. In other words, the loss of mythicism in cosmology produced a catastrophic eschatology. The groanings of creation were not for the benefit of creation itself but was a refocus of the value and function of the all. Eschatology focused on death, judgment, and the final destination of humanity; but mythically, eschatology tells of the correct perception of realized being within the divine.

Ancient cosmologies convey the concept of the establishment and maintenance of order in the cosmos and in the process of calling forth order is the act of separating and extracting something from a previous element. Without these acts of differentiation, one would have chaos, but not in the traditional sense of the word. Chaos is not loss of order but amorphous-ness awaiting the command to become structured. Just as the devil is a faulty understanding of cause and effect enlivened by perception; it is from this misperception that evil was birthed. Duality then forced judgment through this misconception of good and evil which was attributed either to God or a devil. Chaos was conceived and termed evil and it represented the brooder or birthing place for all things perceived evil. Chaos is potential seed with latent energy, fully mythical as it seeks to explain the union of two worlds. This Hebraic cosmic energy was the Ruach and its Greek counterpart was the Logos. The Hebrew element, as Hebraic thought tends to do, goes to root cause; while the Greek concept goes to effect and outcomes. Remember the uncreated waters in the Genesis account? *Tehom* is the Hebrew equivalent of the Greek *chaos* and was representative of the brooding waters or latent energy awaiting activation.

Exiting the Matrix

The Matrix, a movie which stipulates the world in which we live is an altered perception of reality portrays a human who becomes aware of the reality he believes to be true is a false creation of perception, duality, exclusivity, and misconception. Early in the movie, Morpheus offers Thomas A. Anderson a choice between a red pill and a blue pill; the former which offers truth and reality and the later which maintains the current illusion of false reality. The red pill causes awareness of the matrix which is the illusive sphere of personal reality while the blue pill allows the illusion to continue living through the filters of perception.

The red pill arouses awareness, issues and challenges participation and creativity and encourages the journey while the blue pill is comfortable, easy, and unaware as it seeks and observes life as linear history. The blue pill ends the story and "you believe whatever you want to believe (Wachowski 1999)" but the red pill opens the mystery and magic as "deep calls unto deep" mentioned in Psalm 42:7 as the mystery of creation shares its experiences.

Exiting the matrix which is simply another contemporary concept of conscious awareness trades the competitiveness of duality for the singularity of differentiation as quality overrides quantity. As with Neo, time becomes meaningless as the power residing in the present moment overtakes the fears of the future and the regrets of history. Time is blurred as meaningless and profane time yields to the sacred, the moment of heightened awareness of Light, Life, and Love.

When one breaks from the status quo, your lens of perception, duality, exclusivity, and misconception will begin to radically change. Is perception reality? Everyone believes their perception to be real, so there are millions of realities as this ideology presents a reality that is fluid fitting the container it is held it as this view makes reality bendable and changeable. Our reality is based on our interpretation of input from our senses of the world around us. Our beliefs are based on perceived conclusions and our sub consciousness stamps them as truth. The subconscious mind uses these personal truths to constitute your personal version of the real world. Kant implies the human experience comes to humanity inside the framework of time and space and it is in these dimensions we perceive separation (Kant 1962, 13f, 177, 184, 237, 254, 335-36.).

Upon leaving the matrix of perception, what will the new lens allow us to see and hear? Will the declaring heavens, the cry of the rocks and hills, and the groanings of creation be heard; and finally, will our voice be joined to theirs? What is the new lens which allows the new vision of being awake, aware, and alive? The new lens will focus on singularity rather than duality, we will disdain exclusivity as we cleave to inclusivity and we will trade the illusion of reality for the truth of existence enlightening the being. The new lens reveals a whole and new holographic cosmos pointing to non-duality and total inclusion; unable to separate and perceive distance and a more than one. The holographic lens points to complete intimacy and relationship with God; All in All; and Light, Life, and Life or however your journey allows you to see Him. The relationship passes outside of the confines of time and space pointing to the present moment, the experience of mystery and magic with All Being. Giordano Bruno said: "all things are in the universe, and the universe is in all things; we in it, and it in us; in this way, everything concurs in a perfect unity (Bruno 2016)" referring to holographic perfection. You are not a piece of the cosmos, but you are the cosmos mirrored in one piece.

This non-separation proclaims the interconnectedness yet retaining the individuality which is perfection exhibited by differentiation. Does this dismiss the concept of "Thou art That" prevalent in Eastern concepts of unity and oneness? Not at all since you are not separated from "That" for which you are searching yet, you are seeking the discovery and mystery of who you really are. The differences are not dismissed nor obliterated but experienced in a mysterious way. Arthur Schopenhauer said, "my own true inner being actually exists in every living creature (Campbell 2001, xii)." John Crawford cited "the purpose of the glass is that it is refillable (John Crawford's Facebook page, accessed 2016, https://www.facebook.com/john.crawford.5496)" changing the focus of noun to verb. The focus on the glass changes from observing a degree of fullness to noting the purpose of the glass. The ultimate mystery of existence and being rises above duality, misconception, logic, and the delimiters of time and space. A myth awakens the heart as awareness of consciousness trumps perception every time heightening what Joseph Campbell refers to as *mysterium tremendum et fascinans:* (Campbell 1988, 38) a power or force before which man both trembles and holds a fascination and yet is repelled and attracted. It refers to the awe-inspiring mystery meaning the reality experienced in the present moment as entirely different from any other and yet an overwhelming power as the supernatural presence invades all as the mystery is experienced and awareness comes.

The holographic lens also presents an awesome mystery which resets cosmology and eschatology in the cosmos pointing to a present moment that is lost to time. Cosmogony includes the ideologies resident in cosmology and eschatology as the former looks at the beginning of the cosmos and the later considers the fate or outcome if it. The holographic view points to a beginning and rather than a completion resulting in destruction, foretells a fulfillment of an ever-deepening mystery. It is not that the journey ends in fulfillment but instead, the intent of the cosmic principle resident in the mind of God is manifested and continues without measurement in time. In Karen Starr's work, "The Cosmos" she says,

> Now take my hand and I'll show you earth's most
> coveted surprise. Just gaze into the mirror my love
> and see the cosmos in your eyes (Starr 2016).

The stanza is also reflected in the Hebraic idiom Paul referenced in 1 Corinthians 13:12 as looking into the mirror we see as an enigma, a ghostly incomplete figure but when perfection comes the image is clearer as the awakened consciousness sees face to face. The phrase face to face refers to what one sees looking directly into another's eyes. If you look very closely you will see yourself reflected in the eyes of the other and it is at this juncture, focus is absolute and it is no longer reflective but real. Now, reconsider Karen Starr's last stanza; humanity is the mirror of the cosmos and the cosmos reflects divinity in humanity. The cosmos, like humanity, is mythical, magical, and mysterious and waits to reveal its secrets hidden for us compliments of an awesome Creator.

-V-

DECRYPTING THE LOGOS ENIGMA

W hy do I use the word enigma in this chapter title? The Logos, or more correctly its principle, is demonstrated throughout all cultures and traditions. Enigma is a form that is imperfectly or incompletely seen. It is indistinctly reflected but never in the sense of non-existent. The concept is seen in Paul's words from 1 Corinthians 13:12 and I am using the *Jonathan Mitchell New Testament* which states:

> For, you see, at the present moment we continue seeing and observing through means of a metal mirror, within the midst of an enigma (the result of something obscurely expressed and intimated, giving a distinct image), but then [but then it will be] face to face. Right now, I am progressively coming to intimately and experientially know from out of a part (a piece; a portion of the whole), but then I shall fully and accurately know and recognize, from intimate experience, correspondingly as I am also

fully and accurately known, by intimate experience (Mitchell 2014).

The mirror is reflecting an indistinguishable image in the parts but each part is to reflect the whole. This is a hologram in which in each part the whole can be ascertained. Paul's point here is the holograph fully functions because of intimacy and relationship.

Word etymologies often point to a whole new side of a word or phrase giving a more complete understanding of its usage. For example, our English word "cool" has undergone huge etymological changes as an adjective it means not warm but usually not as severe as cold, yet, doesn't contain the full use of the word. Here are some examples in looking at the word more closely. In the sentence "That is a cool car," I mean the car is interesting, pleasing to the eye, and fun to drive. If I ask the question, "Are we cool?" I am not talking about temperature at all but I am asking are we without conflict. If I speak the command "Keep your cool man!" I am not telling you to stay temperate but to maintain poise and control.

Further examples can be seen in the word "pitch." In the sentence, "She was unable to maintain singing at such a high pitch" referring to a note or tone. Conversely if I say, "The roof really had a steep pitch," then I am discussing slope being a calculation of rise over run. In another case, if I shout from the softball stands "That was a lousy pitch," I am talking about ball delivery to the batter. Finally, if you declare "Present!" are you here or presenting me with a gift? If these few words completely change the concept of language, how can we not conceive that similar alterations occurred in the Bible and other historical books which have led to misconceptions and diluted meanings. As these words have migrated and cannot be locked down in a singular concept, it also follows our biblical words having been translated from Aramaic,

Hebrew, and Greek conveying a varied and multiple meaning from what is understood today. Many Christians become offended if the Bible is referred to as mythical and is solely because they consider myth to be a false story without truth and merit.

As we get into this chapter, we must look closely at myth and its uses through the past on our way to Logos. Myth, as a beginning definition, is generally accepted to be sacred stories generally locked in religious belief. If the story does not have a link to religion and the sacred, then it is not a myth but a folk tale such as Davy Crockett and it tends toward a more localized story. Also listed as myth is George Washington and the cherry tree. The story goes his father bought him a hatchet at six years old as a gift and he cut down his father's prized cherry tree. When asked, George is said to have replied: "I cannot tell a lie...I did cut it down with my hatchet." His father was so proud of his honesty and said that was worth more than "one thousand cherry trees." The story has no truth but is devised by his contemporaries to exaggerate his supposed honesty. When the central actor of a story is divine but the story trivial then it is a legend such as Hercules' strength and his "Twelve Labors." And again, when a story is about magical and imaginary beings and lands and the common beginning is "once upon a time..." it is a fairytale such as Snow White whose origins are supposedly Germanic (1823), Hansel and Gretel also from Germanic origins (1812), or The Three Little Pigs who has English origins. Myth contains truth and presents that truth in multiple layers infused with culture, tradition, and personal perception.

Myth, referring to the Greek mythos, is also related to the Greek word *myo* meaning to teach and was originally a word that depicted a true narrative but its truth element was forgotten as it was intermingled with the Greek arts and theater. The etymology of myth is linked to a speech, a thought, a story, or anything delivered by mouth. This was the meaning Homer intended when he wrote about the Trojan War in the 7th or 8th century BCE. Although modern culture considers the Iliad to be a myth (in the sense of a false story) the site of the city of Troy was found by German businessman Henrich Schliemann in 1868. So, regardless of a story's age, the lack of concrete evidence does not make the story a lie. Look through the layers.

The Metaphorical Logos

A metaphor is a language structure which applies a concept or action to a word or phrase in which it cannot be literal. An example is demonstrated in the following sentences about my son.

> "Matt runs very fast."

> "Some say he runs as fast as a deer."

> "Matt is a deer."

The metaphor is not "Some say he runs as fast as a deer," but the metaphor is "Matt is a deer" which is a literal impossibility.

The Logos is a cosmic force or principle which enlivens and forms the physical realm. It is that which sustains as above so below sourced in many ancient texts including *The Emerald Tablets* and the Bible. Logos is a term and principle found in grammar, logic, rhetoric, psychology, theology, and mathematics. Over 400 years before the birth of Jesus and the New Testament dates of writing the common usage was the means of communicating a concept, an idea, or an expression of thought. The Logos has been expressed by many metaphorical elements through the centuries as man, through myth, communicated his understanding of the cosmic journey.

The Perichoretic Movements of the Logos

The Greek term Perichoresis is a word meaning to dance (*chorea*) around (*peri*). Although it is often used in trinitarian explanations I find the richer meaning used in the operation of God in which He is the choreographer and simultaneously the lead dancer. When Jesus asserts his union with God in the Gospel of John saying he and the Father are one; we are also included in that union. This intricately orchestrated dance is inclusive of all of us. God is beautifully bringing about what He sees in His mind, in His Intent becomes physically manifested. This Incarnation mythically portrayed in Jesus and us, manifested and brought to reality the indwelling operation of God nullifying our false perception of separation. Also, this intent of the Incarnation was not a band-aid for a perceived fall of man but was God's intent all along and can be seen as Elohim says, "Let us make man in our image and after our likeness...(Gen 1:26-28)" We cannot be separated from God or He from us.

Choreography or dance writing is a dance that tells a story and as we realize God's story is ours we see the focus of the dance is concentrically centered in love, relationship, and union. In God's story, mankind is not a spectator, in observing the dance of God he is fully invited in or more correctly pulled into the dance writing because it is also our story. Man's steps may influence the outcomes of the scenes by either enhancing or detracting from the rhythm of God, but the overall beauty of the symphony is protected in God's plan held outside of time in the Divine Mind of God.

But what about sin or the appearance of death and destruction which seemingly opposes creation? What about the groans of creation in Romans chapter eight? When mankind steps out of the dance or experiences a miss-step it is simply a minor disruption of the beauty and rhythm of the dance story for a moment in time. It is not permanent because in the Christ, God enters and restores the rhythm again for us—the Rhythm of Grace. This restoration of the dance is permanent and universal and as we enter the dance we begin to see the choreography, the dance writing of His plan which unites us with Him so intensely that when we consider the Christ the mirror, and we see ourselves reflected in the Father's eyes. It is then our illusion gives way to reality realizing we all belong to Him.

The early meaning of Logos was to lay out or pick out in the sense of putting words together and therefore to speak effectively manifesting an intent. The Logos is dynamic thought in the mind which flows to reality as expression, or forced to manifestation by the power of the breath. The ideology signifies both the outward form (evidence) by which the inward thought (intent) is expressed or brought to fruition. Therefore, the functionary purpose of the Logos is to express the intent of God and it is this process that demonstrates interaction and it is the interpretation of this interaction that lies or rests in amazing potential through myth.

The Latin concept of this Greek word is a connected discourse, a rational principle, and a proportion which means a relationship or comparison between two. Stoicism considered the Logos to be evidence in nature's overall rational structure acting as the ordering principle or blueprint of the universe. The mathematical terms implied with Logos being rational and proportional reference numeric quantities. It may contain quantities that are expressible such as an ordered pair which are a set of two quantities that are then plotted on an "XY" coordinate plane expressing relationship. It is in this relationship sacred Geometry and the Logos are clearly evidenced. Sacred Geometry recognizes universally repeating patterns in the design of nature expounding the amazing relationship of geometry, mathematical ratios, harmonics, and proportion found in music, light, and confirming a grand designer of the universe. The Golden Ratio is a proportional unit repeatedly demonstrated in the array of numbers known as the Fibonacci sequence which are numbers expressed in relational sequence displaying a repeating rational limit, the Golden Ratio.

What has Perichoresis got to do with Logos in the above sense of proportion and ratios? Numbers are simply expressions of flux involving movement that can measure beyond the natural outcomes. The perichoretic variations of the Logos with our involvement are writing the story in every moment. Doctrine makes the details pre-arranged by pulling the dance back into time and in need of fulfillment losing the true meaning of relationship which is spontaneity—no script. The Logos has danced throughout ancient cultures as a people encountered the divine and sought the mystery of their origins. Perichoresis is the visibility of the Logos. Sacred Texts from all cultures beautifully declare the role of this organizing principle over all creation mediating both the cosmology which touches beginnings; and eschatology which references fulfillment of their world. For our discussion, I have used the Greek word Logos but this ordering principle, force, person is clearly visible in all cultures. In its Greek history, its first use was by Heraclitus who, more than a half millennium before Christ, connected the principle with the universal mind responsible for the harmony and order of the world. Plato added distance between humanity and this principle. The Stoic philosophers merged the concepts of Heraclitus and Neo-platonic views giving us the idea of the Logos as a divine entity that finds home in the New Testament period of the Bible which led a French exegete to state "Christ inasmuch as he is divine Wisdom, is the mirror in which God contemplated the plan of the cosmos (Feuillet 1966, 365)." The perichoretic Logos was distant and impersonal according to Greek view but was relational in the Hebrew concept. The Fourth Gospel went beyond personal to personification not intending a doctrinal stance but a universal oneness as the intent of God; but religion locked it in a man rather than seeing the archetype referencing all mankind. This will be expanded in this chapter as we consider the cosmic intent in ancient cultures too.

The interrelation of Logos and Logic according to The Metaphysical Bible Dictionary is "a rational relation or connection between idea and expression. Logic in its strictest sense is the only accurate method of arriving at Truth (Fillmore 2014, 412)." Fillmore goes on to imply that any philosophical premise or religious doctrine that is not derived through the "rules of perfect logic (Fillmore 2014, 412)" are then born of man-made dogma and do not contain truth. Logic and Logos represent synonymous terms in the expression of a rational relational connection between idea and its manifestation seen in the cosmos. Fillmore goes on to say that an understanding of the Logos reveals the law of creation from which all things are birthed functioning as "law of mind action (Fillmore 2014, 412)." The Divine Mind creates by thought sourced in ideas, concepts, and principles and their manifestation comes through an operation of the Logos bringing those ideas into reality. He goes on to say, "God is thinking the universe into manifestation right now (Fillmore 2014, 412)." The beginning [the Genesis] is always now since it must do with the active mind of God and not with time (Fillmore 2014, 412-413) therefore, the Logos maintains creational order and harmony is nothing less than the effect of the Ruach of God.

Logos has the following meanings according to David Fideler, as he identifies the Logos as an order or pattern, a ratio or proportion, a discourse as an articulation or account such as a reckoning, reason, principle or cause, and finally, a principle of mediation and harmony and it is to these concepts to which Jesus was personified in the fourth Gospel (Fideler 1993, 38). Charles Fillmore adds "the Logos is the Christ, the divine light, and the living Word, and in exemplifying that concept contains all potentiality as all things were made by it (Him) (Fillmore 2014, 412)." The doctrinal view holds this ideology in which man can appropriate all or a part of this potentially as he chooses yet with the understanding Jesus expressed it in its fullness in demonstration of what is possible becoming the Logos made flesh. In other words, Jesus so unified Himself in thought, word, and deed with this inner anointing (Christos) or creative principle of God, in which are all the ideas of the Divine Mind containing life, substance, intelligence, wisdom, love, strength, power, that even his physical body took on immortal transformation displaying the full glory of the Father. Those who follow Him can make this full attainment that He made, if they accept, as He did, the all-possibility of this Principle.

The Greek Logos is directly connected to the Hebrew Ruach being the wind or breath of God. It was the Ruach of God that moved over the waters in the Creation account in Genesis acting on the without form and void and through the breath of God his mind become formed and defined in space and time. This ongoing principle, the Ruach, brooded over these waters being the potential in me and acted on my "without form and void" and I became flesh in space and time. In the New Testament, this is carried by the Logos as the creating aspect of God, the initiating Principle which manifests thought into space and time and John made this process a man connecting this concept through the words "the life was the light of all men (Joh 1:4)" indicating divinity has invaded humanity. Logos then is the expression of God and not of one man but mankind and all creation. It is the Ruach—the breath or wind of

God defining his intent bringing that expression into time and space manifesting the cosmic structure and purpose reserved in his mind visualized as the immeasurable influence of God. Grady Brown's interpretation of the first view verses of John chapter 1 serve to join the Hebrew Ruach with the Greek Logos in an amazing perichoretic movement. John one of Grady's *Dayspring Bible* says,

> In the very beginning there existed the active reason pervading the universe and animating it. God and this rational structure were together and what God was that is what this animated principle was also. From the very beginning this principle which is always present was together with God. All things came into being through this principle of order and knowledge and apart from this principle nothing existed. Everything that has come into being received its life from this principle and that life became the light of humankind (Brown 2003).

The Historical Jesus & The Metaphorical Logos

The images of Jesus stemming from various cultures and religions are as varied as the cultures themselves. Does this mean they disagree with who Jesus was? No, not at all, for each saw him based on cultural and regional character and interpretation. It is said that each culture and generation sees Jesus as a reflection of itself. For example, Jewish writers separate Jesus the Jew from the Jesus produced by Christianity.

The recent past years have seen multiple quests to provide an accurate portrait of the mystery god-man. In the late 18th century the Enlightenment produced a Jesus who was rational and explained his miracles as purely natural phenomena and a teacher of timeless wisdom. The 19th century converted him to a man who did not exist or, at the very least, was irrelevant to theology. Going back a few decades the quest centers in Germany where we find Ernst Kasemann and Rudolph Bultmann who argues the accounts found in the Gospels sprang from the mythos of the early church stating in effect the modern view of Jesus cannot be removed from historical accounts and one must keep Jesus within the Judaism of the First Century. Now, springing to the last few years are books entitled *A New Christianity for A New World: Why Traditional Faith is Dying and What Should Take its Place* (Spong 2000), *Resurrection-Myth or Reality* (Spong 2001), *A Generous Orthodoxy* (McLaren 2004), *The Meaning of Jesus, Two Visions* (Borg & Wright 2007), *Meeting Jesus Again for the Very First Time; The Historical Jesus, the Heart of Contemporary Faith* (Borg 1995), and *Who Wrote the New Testament? The Making of the Christian Myth* (Mack 2015) are helping us to understand we must look first at the heritage of the man Jesus to understand what he became incarnated by the Logos of God and how this is universal affecting all of humanity.

These portraits offer amazing insights into Jesus and have emerged from authors such as those above. Borg, for example, portrays a Jesus who is focused on the present time and an amazing teacher and social prophet, while Mack images Jesus as a Jewish cynic or shock jock sage who encouraged the people to seek the heart of God. And yet, E. P. Sanders agrees with the heart of the others but shifts the time-frame to the future seeing Jesus as an eschatological prophet exhorting the kingdom rule of the Father. Just to note a few other points, Jesus did not preach himself as the answer but the coming kingdom of God being a Jew in the movement of the early Kingdom of God on earth. The historical Jesus and the Jesus of the early church bear little resemblance to each other as the historical man seemed to have never penned his words but was quoted by his hearers and documented as God said thus and so. He was abandoned by most of his followers at his death and his family did not seem to support his ministry versus the Jesus of the church exhibited great power and control. Just as tradition misapplied hell, it also seemingly misapplied Jesus as he became the sole image of Logos.

As stated previously, most civilizations develop myths to placate what they do not understand or cannot explain. When Jesus did not turn out to be the Messiah the Jews wished for, they turned his messiah-ship inward stating it was not of this world but a secret kingdom yet to come by placing it in time. This manufactured a reason for the Jews not being immediately released from Roman oppression according to the Jewish timetable by offering a yet to come agenda. The Jewish nation rejected the Jesus of History who not only did not save the Jews according to their vision but was yet coming to save the Gentiles too, a fully inclusive act.

In the Jesus Progression, which I use to describe the transformation of Jesus to the Christ, the Gospels demonstrate a growing or maturing of Jesus as he fulfilled his purpose. Did Jesus know what was written about him in Matthew 15? Jesus came to a woman from Canaan who cried out to him to have mercy on her and heal her daughter but Jesus ignored her completely. Does that sound like Christ or was he dealing with perception versus reality? The Disciples tell him to send her away and Jesus answers "I was not sent except to the lost sheep, the scattered people of the house of Israel" which was a narrowed and exclusive position he took by only including the lost sheep of Israel. He, later in this chapter, refers to her and her ethnicity as dogs which was a racial slur during this time period. But she is persistent and jolts Jesus out of his cultural comfort zone and touches the heart of God in him by awakening the Cosmic Christ/Messiah structure.

Now to a Samarian woman at a well in John 4:7-10. A Samarian woman came to draw water from a well and Jesus asked her to give him a drink. The woman responded "How is it that You, being a Jew, ask a drink from me, a Samaritan woman? For Jews have no dealings with Samaritans." Jesus responds, "If you knew the gift of God, and who it is who says to you, 'Give Me a drink,' you would have asked Him, and He would have given you living water." Hear her perception after their conversation in which she tells her village to "come see a man who told me all things that I ever did. Could this be the Christ"? They then believe because they heard for themselves and realize he is indeed "the Christ, the Savior of the World."

As Jesus progressed in his destiny, he came to realize that he was more than the savior of the lost sheep of Israel but he was the Savior of the World, the Christ of God. His language changed—first he astounded those in the synagogue when he was twelve to his exclusive purpose to Israel and finally to his inclusive purpose to the world. What was the purpose of the Christ—the Cosmic Structure of God? To reveal the *"Christic"* intent of the divine mind. The Christ is not one but All.

From where did universal Messiah-ship originate? Alvin Boyd Kuhn says the myth of God incarnate is a universal human concept but due to Constantine, Christianity left its origins and imposed creedal belief on the people (Kuhn 2015, 13). Then in the Epistles, Paul rekindles a faith that insinuates Christ is the name given to the presence of God within. The Christ is known by many names present in human history. It is a result of rituals and rules that have masked the inner light according to Kuhn. The Gospels are about the Christ and with Jesus as a symbolic personification implies every man can partake of birth, death, and resurrection. Our journey's purpose is to experience the Christ in our daily lives now and in every moment. It is the Christian personification of the Christ in the man Jesus which changed the goals of a Messiah from that of a universal principle to one man.

History of the Greek Logos

In Greek philosophy and theology, Logos was indicative of reasoning and planning and was strongly linked to the cosmos in that the Logos orders and gives form to it. It is not a past tense completed process but a continuous living process. Through this operation is defined in Greek terms for us today, it is also found in Sumerian, Persian, Indian, Egyptian, and most other philosophical systems pointing to a rational and living Perennial Philosophy. But it seemed to be hijacked by Christianity partly to show ownership and exclusivity to a non-exclusive principle, in assigning this role to Jesus who was infused with the Logos or Sophia indicated by Paul who said in Colossians 1:17 that he holds all things together and Paul's account of his anointing in Acts 10:38. Meister Eckhart says the Logos is "the eternal and unrestricted ratio which is prior to the manifestation of things... and which is identically the Logos (Kelly & Eckhart 1977, 68)."

Just as Jesus was given pre-existence in the New Testament Greek mindset, so too the Torah was given pre-existence in the Hebraic philosophy. The author of John embodies Jesus with the same substance and regards him as the personified source of life and light for mankind. John makes the Logos inseparable to Jesus losing the message he proclaimed. I do not think the Greek equivalent of Torah is *nomos* (law) but more accurately is Logos since the Hebrews enlivened the Torah, yet, not necessarily in the linguistic sense but more so philosophically. This Greek word was not necessarily the law but was a concept that existed in the law as laws were considered a human invention based on consensus to restrict certain natural freedoms for a common benefit of all. Therefore, could the product of the Logos/Torah be the Tree of Life while the product of nomos whose Greek meaning norm or normal way be the Tree of Knowledge of Good and Evil? As the Tree of Knowledge of Good and Evil emanates duality the Logos/Torah being emanations from the Tree of Life is singularity demonstrating no division or separation.

In considering Paul's use of nomos one must conceive a difference in this word and Torah. The word nomos has a connotation that law does not have in that for Judaism the law was monolithic (solid and possessing a single function) and unitary for the sake of societal goal of harmony with God and man. But the Greeks understood an additional idea of common or normal law as a law existed for the restoration of the victim while Judaism more so focused on relational restoration. So, if a law is broken in English understanding the next logical step is punishment as one is now a law-breaker. To the Greek and Hebraic mindset, one may not be a law breaker but one may have strayed from the principle of the law standing in an exception to law such as breaking with tradition exampled in getting the ox out of the ditch on the Sabbath. The Torah was the guiding authority of God as he directs the universe in rhythm with human inflection and interpenetration demonstrating the rhythm of the dance.

Using a syllogism which is a form of reasoning in which a conclusion is drawn whether valid or not, from two givens or assumed propositions or premises; each of which shares a term with the conclusion, and shares a common or middle term not present in the conclusion. An example of a syllogism would be a statement such as "all dogs are animals; all animals have four legs; therefore, all dogs have four legs." Its etymology means to bring together before the mind or to reason together and it demonstrates the mathematical transitive property which states if "a=b," and "b=c," then "a=c." One can trace John's conclusion from Jewish Rabbinic tradition who have argued that John is referencing the Torah in his prologue. The syllogism goes like this: The Torah equals the Wisdom (Sophia) of God. The Wisdom (Sophia) is the New Testament Logos. Therefore, the Torah is the Logos. The Logos/Torah, representing by the image of the Tree of Life demonstrates no separation or division and is that which the heavens are declaring being the decrees of God rather than judgments. In the decree of Torah is rest, yet, the nomos is the Tree of Knowledge emanating duality forcing judgment producing law requiring work which opposes rest.

The Greek New Testament followed the schematic of the Hebrew Old Testament when considering the Logos and Torah equivalency. It was the Hebrew concept which entombed the Torah in law enforcing judgment causing it to echo man's interpretation rather than the emanations of the intent of God. Torah served as a pointing out of the purposes of God to man and God writing them in their heart and placing them before their eyes appearing face to face. Interestingly, for the Greek and Hebrew mind to unite in the Logos the Greek would have to expand their concept as it being only a rational principle or divine power and the Hebrew would have to address their concept of a personal God. The Hebraic construct was that of a living Torah which became intimate with man while the Greek concept of Logos contains the ideology of reason and logic being transcendent as it propels the universe forward. The manmade law, in its attempts to point man to God, was instrumental in defining duality and literalizing the Logos. It was this law, not the Torah that marked the movements of Logos locking those movements in time. What were those movements?

The Incarnation, Crucifixion, and Resurrection. This law required a scapegoat and the personified Logos met the requirement paying for the sin of mankind becoming both intercessor and mediator between God and man repairing the perceived breach which the law enhanced. This manmade law proclaimed man's humanity while the heavens screamed the declaration of God. The manmade law (the nomos) was man's attempt at defining the Logos who proclaimed and demonstrated the declaration of God's creational intent.

In continuing the history of the Logos, one must consider the contrast of Philo and John who were both contemporaries of Jesus. The contrast of the two will also point out that John's word "Logos" was well known and understood by the cultures of his day. When he asserts that the Logos became flesh he is instituting a concept that was not circulating in his day in Greek thought but they did understand the concept of the cosmic Mediator who became the personification of God's Wisdom and Truth.

Philo's Logos was an emanation of God so far as he came out of hiding and this Logos that was revealed was God (Hillar 2015). However, to John it signified the Word of God becoming a person in Jesus while Philo's Logos was impersonal. Only John personalized the Logos in Jesus as Philo identified the Logos as upholding creation and did not connect it to a Messiah figure. John saw the Messiah/Christ as the Logos himself united with humanity and clothed with a body to save the world.

Philo's Logos was also an intermediary serving to link the imagined gulf between the infinite and the finite, or the spiritual and physical world (Hillar 2015). To fill this void Philo imagined a second god brought nearer to the finite as divinity (infinite) entering humanity (finite) the personified divine reason. John's concept was "the Logos was made flesh and dwelt among men" and named Jesus. His purpose was not to introduce reason but Jesus the Christ as the revelation of God through Christ to the world. Why did John equate Jesus to God? The region of Ephesus was the amalgamation of philosophical doctrines from Greece, Persia, and Egypt during that period of time there existed the God-Man in *Om* of the Indians (a creational vibration), the *Hom* (Homilies of Zoroaster) of the Persians, the *Logos* of the Greeks and the *Memra* (Angel of the Lord) of the Jews; and there John offered the New Testament God-man in Jesus.

The two concepts differ in origin as the impersonal Logos of Philo cannot enter creation without defilement of his divine essence while John's Logos is personal and desires interaction with creation. Philo did not subscribe to a God that was interactive with creation but God was an indirect influence through the Logos being a wholly independent being acting as an intermediary between the Creator and created. Remember, Philo lived at the time of Jesus and Paul and he was Jewish; so his philosophy was a combination of Greek philosophies and the Hebrew Creator he knew from his heritage. It was the nomos which originally functioned as the controlling principle in the Hebraic mind becoming the cultural custom making tradition law removing the relational heartbeat of God. The amalgamation of cultural law masked the expressive cosmic law which declared the heartbeat of the creator for the created. The cultural nomos removed the cosmic link while Torah and Logos fully express it.

As a final consideration, John Y. Campbell states there is considerable grounds to investigate the idea that the Prologue of John's Gospel was sourced in an existing hymn of the Greek Logos that may not have been of "Christian origin (Campbell, J. 1966, 285)." Another theologian who subscribes to this line of thought is Rudolph Bultmann who linked the Prologue to Gnostic concepts through a particular sect of John the Baptist's followers who directed the hymn to John himself and later adapted to Jesus (Bultmann 1955, 164-183).

The function and essence of the Logos has been thought to be the source of inspiration and intuition in humanity and it is from this source that Logos directs us on our journey prompting such things as creativity, discovery, and purpose. It is also the interpreter of our dreams and visions that are attune to God. The essence of the Logos is somewhat revealed in the concept of musical harmony. As individual notes of humanity are sounded the overall effect is a whole chord producing one sound. The Logos is effecting one sound in the human journey as the heavens and earth declare (sound) the glory of God. The movements of the Logos provided the music for the dance

The Divine Spark

The belief that man has a divine spark implanted by the Creator is traceable to ancient mystical religions. Is it truth or simply a hope? In the ancient mindset, this spark was the house of God in every human being. Although various religions have different names, Christianity posits the term incarnation and in this divine spark through the incarnation the perceived bridge between Creator and created is negated. The Bible is thought to support this concept in the idea of the breath of life. Does this mean that God gave man this life force or that this live force is inherently a part of him? Philo, who wrote in the beginning of the first century CE, was the first Jew as far as history records to teach that there was something divine in the human being. According to Philo, the human mind was incapable of knowing God if it were not for this implanting of the divine in man.

It is thus assumed this implantation sets man above all other creation but it is Solomon in Ecclesiastes 3:19 who says man does not have pre-eminence over the animal. Religious ideologies try to get around this statement by implying the soul of man has an animalistic component and a divine component. It separates the whole creating a carnal and spiritual aspect in man.

Was this divine spark the means of existence before our birth? John 16:28 indicates Jesus came from the Father and came into physical existence and is to return to the Father. Christianity can ascertain this means a pre-existence but it also supports the Hindu and Buddhist belief of reincarnation, a progression through many lives on a path to total spiritual awakening at which point a return is no longer necessary. Another portion of Scripture used to point to Jesus' pre-existence is John's Prologue which states the word was with God and was God and thus by implication included our preexistence. The idea of a preexistence is also shored up with an understanding of the terms Resurrection, Redemption, Reconciliation, Rebirth, all which indicate a previous condition that was experienced or enjoyed.

Early Christianity understood the myth of God incarnate as a concept encompassing the universal human and due, in part, to the dogmata of Constantine, Christianity left those origins and imposed creedal belief on the people enforcing rule and ritual. Then in the Epistles, Paul rekindles a faith that insinuates Christ is the name given to the presence of God within. The Christ is known by many names present in human history. It is a result of rituals and rules that have masked the inner light and humanity's awareness of its existence. The Gospels are about the Christ and with Jesus as symbolic personification implies every man can partake of birth, death, and resurrection. Our journey's purpose is to experience the Christ in our daily lives now and in every moment. It is the

Christian personification of the Christ in the man Jesus which changed the goals of a Messiah from that of a universal principle to one man.

Mythos and Logos

The Greeks have a clear distinction between mythos and logos yet their combination produces our English word mythology. Their Greek intent is a story or narrative vivifying beliefs relative to a specific culture versus an account or play by play of actual historical events. The logos is a scientific approach through logic, order, and purpose while the mythos is much less intuitive and historical. Logos is an observation of facts or the deductions of controlled experimentation arriving at objective truth that is impersonal, universal, and verifiable. Mythos might look at the poetic insights of a sunrise or look at birth metaphorically and arrive at subjective truth that is personal, and sense derived. Logos thinking has by far overtaken and all but removed mythical thinking losing the value of humanity and relationship.

A myth can be similar to a board game in that the meaning is not revealed until you play and the rich tapestry of its meaning is made clearer. Karen Armstrong, a comparative religion author, places mythos and logos in contrast yielding a composite result as she says myth and logic have different purposes and Plato used the strictest sense of emotion versus reason (Armstrong 2009). Armstrong reasons science has its place such as the knowledge to sharpen the hunter's arrow, to find the cure for disease, and to understand the laws of mathematics and the universe and yet myth will not nor cannot answer these (Armstrong 2005). Myth answers in the face of the limitations inherent in science and logic. In the presence of a natural disaster and the loss of life, a scientific explanation is not enough as humanity reaches for myth and ritual to fill the void replacing the grief with peace. In our modern culture, we have made myth and science antagonistic and never in agreement because we fail to realize their varied purpose. As humanity desires the what and how, we also must have the why answered and myth fills this missing piece but we made the myth impotent placing strict literalness to the story—our story.

In considering the Genesis creation story, the Western mindset cannot employ mythological thinking because it is dependent on literal interpretation. When this mind mixes mythology, history, and science through a literalness portal; it can only produce weak science, mind numbing religion, and a dying myth which has lost the ability to speak to the soul. In understanding the Genesis creation, it was never meant to be a detailed minute by minute account of our creation but is a beautiful representation of our creation as it occurs outside of time; in other words, mythically. In the retelling of myth, creation is a continuous process in all time.

As I have expressed before, a myth does not detail the what and how as much as it introduces a deeper level of why, overstepping the science and going straight to the mythos as there is more to it than an event but why did the event occur? It is enlivened as we understand the event is ongoing but because of our strict chronological concept of history we do not have an etymological understanding of myth which carries the event out of time and places it in the present moment. Karen Armstrong explains this concept as a myth is true not because it is factual but because it is effective (Armstrong 2005, 10). It must connect us to a deeper meaning of ourselves and bring us to a realization of infinite value as it forces a change of mind—a repentance and then gives a new hope and light, and in my opinion, that is the myth of the Gospel— not an untrue story but a story that causes a reconsideration of purpose and life, a story that causes a deep re-orientation of ourselves to the divine and voids the separation perceived or offered in religion precipitated in "The Fall" requiring a payment to play.

The mythos from the fall perspective arises following the sacrifice and acts as interpretation of the mimetic event. The interpretations are biased from the fallen society telling their side of the story in opposition to the victim. Society attempts to downplay the violence by blurring reality and as the myth develops the divinization of the victim is brought forward. What are the ritualistic tendencies found in myth? They are a symbolic imitation of the events in that ritual reenacts the mimetic crisis. As the ritual does not necessarily imitate the actual event it does entomb the meaning of the participants carried forward and expounds why the event occurred. Still, this explanation attempts to justify the sacrifice to a God who needed none. If no law is broken, then no sacrifice is necessary. In other words, a sacrifice requires a broken law to offer amends to the offended law giver. Was God ever offended or did man simply perceive the offence? The Logos is not mimetic, as mimesis produces scapegoating due to a fault. God declares no fault exists.

The Primordial Logos:
The Connection to Perennial Philosophy

I chose Primordial Logos as a sectional title because the term has been said to mean before the beginning of time but that is not the original intent of the word. Its etymological meaning is first or earliest form, or before the beginning as the first element referencing state of being without the linkage to time or measurement. It coincides with pre-existent and thus means first formed or first born.

The concept of the Logos for Christianity has its source in the Gospel of John. In generic terms Logos is a Greek noun and is usually translated word and more rarely reason. In our modern culture, it is best pictured from John 1:1 which states "In the beginning was the logos..." and resident in this sentence is a congruity of Hebrew and Greek thought from the mind of the writer and and his personal perceptions help construct our concepts becoming tenets of faith.

Greek origins take us to Heraclitus of Ephesus (5th century BC) who used the term to identify the fathering pattern of the universe which is partially hidden as an enigmatic apparition that is identified in the universe (Hillar 2012, 10). Between Heraclitus and other Greek philosophers who were proponents of the ceaseless movement of nature and who famously said, "one cannot step in the same river twice (Hillar 2012, 13)" because both the river and the one stepping have changed in time. They also likened this concept present in the universe to be found in the human soul and soul being a separate entity also a Greek origination. This concept of the Logos carries a sense of an imminent law of nature or cosmic law.

In the Hebraic mind, the Logos was not directly linked to knowledge as it was to experience. The word of God was not believed to be a principle but the voice of God bringing about that which was conceived in His mind or intent. In Genesis, God spoke commanding the light and light became and in this sense the words of God are verbs and bring about action. Philo of Alexandra who was a Jewish contemporary of Jesus and through Hellenization of Jewish thought links the Greek Logos with Hebraic Sophia supporting a portrait of the pre-existent Torah and speculates the

Logos is the emanation (Hillar 2012, 150) of God and is the means God is known.

In the New Testament, there are nuances of the Logos in Paul's writings and others (Phil. 2:5-11, Col. 1:15-20, Heb. 1:1-4, 1 John 1:1-3, Rev. 19:13). It is the words of John's Prologue that provide an enfleshment of the divine principle and at the same time a source for all of creation being derived from Hebrew and Hellenistic sources. Hillar postulates the term Logos was used extensively in the Greco-Roman and Judaic cultures and had several meanings including word, speech, statement, discourse, ratio, explanation, and reason (Hillar 2012, 6). The philosophical implications rest in two basic concepts and they are inward thought/reason/logic as an intuitive conception and an outward expression of thought and speech. The Greek philosophical schools added a rational and intelligent agent as a vivifying principle of the universe. It is this step that brought the Logos to a living creature. The ancient people did not have the active concept of function which is most often lost even in our etymologies therefore, every reality had an underlying factor or agent responsible for it to be and in the Greek mind this was the operational function of the Logos.

Is it found in other cultures? Of Course. The Chinese translation of the Prologue of John translates the first verse as "In the beginning was the *Tao* (Damascene 1999, 35)" and in using a word familiar to Taoism and the Chinese language provides a rich meaning as the Way of the universe. We can find this Perennial Philosophical principle as Jesus (100-200 AD Logos Christianized and personified), Logos (535-475 BCE and adopted into Jewish philosophy by Philo around 20 BCE to 50 AD), Torah (600-400 BCE, and according to Midrash the Torah was pre-existent to creation and was used as its blue-print), Memra (900-600 BC, early Hebrew and Semitic family languages of Syria), Tao (550 BCE), Rta (India

1500-1000 BC), Ma'at (2375 BC), Asha (2000-6000 BC) in the cultures of the West, Greek, Hebrew, Aramaic, Chinese, the Vedic language of India, Egypt, and the Avestan language of Iran and Persia respectfully. What does this mean? Does it mean there were multiple Jesus'? It simply means the principle—this powerful myth is of cosmological significance and this is even seen in our Bible which states the pre-existent light was also the light of the world acknowledging its universal scope.

The Logos of John's Prologue

In looking at the Perennial Philosophy and the flow of Logos we find this universal and timeless movement in all ancient cultures and philosophies. This fascinating aspect will offer a much fuller concept of this element in the human journey and mythology. "Mythology is not a lie, mythology is poetry, it is metaphorical. It has been said that mythology is the penultimate truth—penultimate because the ultimate cannot be put into words (Campbell 1988, 163)." Through the lens of our Christian based Western mind we trend to see it defined only in the 4th Gospel not realizing it is has been expressed many times assisting John with his concept found in the first chapter. John uses the Logos following Hebrew thought rather than Greek in which the word or wisdom of God is applied to God Himself as if it was God. Therefore, the intent of God was brought to life; the word became flesh not the incarnate son but the incarnate word or mind of God was en-fleshed, made alive, became visible, and existed as matter in the physical realm.

It is interesting to note the Logos first appears in the New Testament under the writings of the 4th Gospel attributed to John who appears to be a Gnostic Greek. His use of the term indicates his readers were familiar with his concept, but over time we seem to have lost the amazing meaning and said it was a man who became God or was God. It is John who first makes the Logos a fully personalized being. John also removes the intermediary of earlier understanding and gives him the status of mediator. He does not stand as a priest to god and man but is an example of their union in living form as the Christ. In the Hebraic mind, the Logos was linked to experience rather than knowledge. It was not an impersonal principle or law but was the steering voice of God. The Greek mind considered the Logos to be the fathering pattern of the universe. Philo's Logos was linked to Sophia or wisdom which was a portrait of the pre-existent Torah as an emanation or a method how God touches humanity. John gives the Logos transcendence adding a universal concept calling him the savior of the world.

Did the writer of John say that Jesus was the literal Logos or did he say Jesus was a representation of the Logos? According to Craig Lyons,

> Logos is designated as the power of reason, the pattern or order of things, the principle relationship, and an organized structure of something. Its meaning includes reason, relation, and harmony that exists in the universe and within the human mind so the concept is a cosmic and mystical one.
>
> Because of its abundant perfection, the Source [First Cause in the Realm of Being] unconditionally gives forth a secondary principle, the Logos, in the same way that the sun gives forth rays of light. The Logos is not the First Cause, any more than rays of light are the sun, but nonetheless the two are very intimately related. In this ancient teaching, the Logos is the first, harmonically differentiated image of the First

Cause. The Logos represents the first level of real manifestation or Being made visible in our realm of change through the actions of humanity, for it encompasses within itself all the laws and relations which are later articulated in the phenomenal universe. Since the Logos is the emanation of the Transcendent Absolute, it may be poetically and symbolically described as the Son of God, as we see in the works of Philo, the Hermetic writings of Egypt, and early Christianity. Underlying the source of all reality, the Logos is related to the principle of Nous or Universal Intellect, the repository of all the cosmic forms and principles on which creation is based. And as the rational image of Divine Intellect, humanity is itself the living, incarnate image of the Logos (Lyons 2013, 106).

Therefore, Logos is an expression of God, similar to the Love of God as an emanation or force seen in the universe yet resident in humanity. John describes the Logos as the blueprint of creation and then says Jesus represented the Logos as does everyman. We become the holographic universe. A very thought-provoking Facebook meme states, "You're not just one piece of the cosmos, you're the cosmos in one piece (Facebook Meme 2017)."

Martin Larson remarks the tremendous difference between the Synoptics and the Fourth Gospel is John, who being a Hellenized Jew, moves from Essene to Gnostic (Larson 1977, 492-497). John's Gospel gives us theological discourses which are not centered on the historical Jesus but more so on the awakened Christ. John moved beyond all historical accounts and made Jesus the mythical Christ as a portrait of the awakened human being the true soul. John makes this Christ a pre-existent son of God in the sense Christ was always in the heart of the Creator, and that being so, the Christ is the offspring of the activated mind of God. In my opinion, Christ is the action of the Logos effecting humanity.

The Johannine theology is dualistic but it operates very differently from the other Gospels. The duality of the Synoptic Gospels seems to exist on a horizontal plane and is time sensitive such as contrasting this age and the coming age (Ladd 2015). The dualism found in John as he brings forth the Hebrew yet Hellenized Logos is vertical between two worlds as in the world above and the world below (Ladd 2015). John's duality is cosmological and the Synoptics is eschatological. In the 4th Gospel, this world is evil ruled by a devil (16:11) while Jesus has been sent as the cosmic light-bearer (11:9). Even his authority to carry out his purpose is not of this world but from God (18:36) and upon its completion he departs this world for the world above with a promise of our joining him.

The Timeless Mirror of the Cosmos — The Logos

The Logos is a reflector of the movement of man.
One must look into the mirror to witness the change.
Author

Mirrors not only reflect but amplify light reflecting only what is placed in front of it. They are instruments that return light in such a way that the image is a replication of the original. Similarly, a mirror website is an exact duplicate or an image of the original website, although not the original; it is an exact representation. A mirror does not produce or duplicate the image because as you move away from the mirror the image is no longer generated whereas a photograph does represent a permanent image of the original. Psalms 39:5-6 uses the word shadow and Rotherham says our life is as an image in a mirror implying the image is temporary and is non-existent when you step away from it (Rotherham 1994).

Mechanically, light itself is invisible until it bounces off an object reflecting in our eyes. For instance, a beam of light traveling through space can't be seen from the side until it runs into something that scatters it. The process of diffuse reflection returns a light-print of the object by illuminating the object. The light-print is not the original but points to or mimics the original. The Greek word is *eikon*. Another trait of an image is that its dependence remains to the original in that the mirror image is not visible when one steps away from the mirror. An image also supplies proof of identity and kinship. How many times have we looked at family pictures and stated they look like their daddy or some other family member. It is a means of identification and not solely duplication.

The Mirrored Logos

Anytime one peers into a mirror, it is always with a purpose either to make an adjustment in appearance or to confirm one's appearance. Historically, mirrors were polished discs of plain metal that cost more than most people could afford. A citizen of less than a thousand years ago who wanted to see their reflection had to look in a pond of still water. Full-length mirrors are an even more recent invention being only about 400 years old. Mirrors were and still are an enigma to humans demonstrated by superstition and their place in science. They can represent truth and illusion often at the same time in that they show us as we are in time and can alter our image like the circus mirrors that do not reflect truth at all.

Matthew 16 is the account of Peter's awakening. Jesus asked the question, "Who do men say that I am?" The local perception was perhaps John the Baptist, Elijah, or some other prophet. This question is similar to the election of 2016 which brought us "fake news" and polling error. This question equals the inquiry of "What do the polls say?" It is the question of academia, not the question of knowing within. Then in Matthew 16 Jesus asked His disciples who he was. This was not from a man of doubt or heart of despair wondering about his identity because he knew at this time. It was a question of do you know me as God knows me. Simon Peter stepped up and said, "You are the Christ the Son of the Living God." What happened next? The Christ renamed him calling him Petra and upon the strength of right identity, this rock and strong foundation the church is based and not religion, not denomination, and not sect; but upon the fact of humanity's right identification the *ekklesia* was established. What is that about and what really happened? As each looked into the mirror, peering into each other recognition dawned; they saw themselves face to face, each in the other and their true identity was revealed and this is the purpose of the church which is to reveal everyone's true origin and identity not in judgment and religion but in love.

Ewert Cousins, in his concept of the universal Christ said, "For the first time since the appearance of human life on our planet, all of the tribes, all of the nations, all of the religions are beginning to share a common history. We can no longer think in terms of Christian history, or even Western history. When Christians raise questions about Christ, they must now ask: How is Christ related to Hindu history, to Buddhist history—to the common global history that religions are beginning to share (Cousins 1992, ix)?" This concept is totally missing from Western orthodox theology. The Christ Principle is purely metaphorical of the divine pattern of cosmic connection and Christ is the Western religious word for the "divine stream of life connecting one to all and all to one (Thompson 2017)." Cousins goes on to say this power is represented in Buddhism as the Buddha, Judaism it is described as Shekinah and is marked in all religions as they perceive this perennial power. Cousins adds, "The Christ power is the power to cross over into the consciousness of another" and to understand without criticism, to perceive without passing judgment, and to comprehend without analyzing (Thompson 2017)." It is the pristine ability to remove duality and see one.

It is this process, the renaming of Peter and the effect it caused in him demonstrates the process described in Romans 12:2. It states not to be conformed or bound by the senses but be transformed by the power of intent. As Peter looked into the Logos, the intent of God, a transformation occurred. Conform does not seem to be a physical operation but simply means to fashion into or make to function but transform does affect the physical makeup. It is the same word as transfigured used in Matthew 17. Philippians 3:21 demonstrates the difference in the two words as transformation allows conformation. We will be transformed (a radical physical change) so we can conform (make to function) like his body. When men were anointed they were commissioned and prepared to accomplish a task and it means to smear into or fully saturate by forcefully rubbing into. The picture is to rub or massage the oil into the muscles to saturate the sinews and cells into all depths of the living tissue. God smeared Himself, his nature, or His essence all over and in Jesus causing Him to function as a son, as His offspring. Can the concept of the anointing produce the effects of transformation and conformation? Jesus was smeared all over with God's essence and character and we are conformed which is made to resemble or pattern. Our likeness to His image is an accomplished fact in the mind of God but we are in the process of being manufactured into the fullness of the image for we are told in 1 John 3:2 that it does not yet appear what we shall be or we are not yet in the perfected state of our being: but we know that when he shall appear we shall be like him for we shall see him as he is looking in the mirror.

Parabolic Mirror

How does conformation and transformation occur? We have talked about the simple mirror and its reflection of the image before it but there is another type of mirror that also portrays the effects of our image in Christ. This type of mirror was known in the ancient classical era in the areas of Greece and Rome some 200 years before the birth of Jesus. The mathematician Diocles called them burning mirrors bringing another dimension of the mirror analogy found in the Bible and it is awesome to see how it parallels our looking to the Christ and see the true image of God in ourselves. The parabolic mirror is specifically constructed to concentrate the image reflected and as it does this a physical change occurs to what is peering into the mirror. Parabolic reflectors are used to collect light and sound energy bringing it to a common focal point such as satellite dishes, reflecting telescopes, spotlights, and car headlights.

It uses its shape to focus light in different degrees of intensity in proportion to the increasing nearness of the object being reflected. In other words, as the object reflected reaches the perfect center of the parabolic mirror the intensity of the light is markedly more powerful rendering change to the object reflected. This focusing in the perfect center of the mirror, where the light meets in absolute oneness, causes things to be visible that are normally not seen when the light is not as bright. The mirror, as the object nears the perfect center, causes physical change from simple reflection, to heat, to image permanence, and then to a strong magnetism. The simple reflection occurs as the object stands face to face with the mirror. As the object is positioned closer to the perfect center heat is generated; moving a little closer and the image of reflection is made permanent on the object much like a photographic print; and finally, in the perfect center magnetism is attained and the object is pulled into the mirror—becoming the mirror and now reflecting what it once saw. All in All, the completed hologram.

I want to convey those processes another way to reflect the Biblical mirror analogy differently. First, as we look in the mirror peering into the glory of God, we come to the light focus no longer seeing as Religion says through the lens of the fall, sin, duality, and judgment but we see the glory or the correct opinion and intent of God. Gazing into the mirror is not a damaging process but a transforming and conforming one. This is the revealing step of who we really are. Second, as we draw closer, we reach the heat focus. After we realize we are like Him then He provides the means for our cleansing process which corrects our perception realigning it to the conclusions of God and His intent. This step is never the first one because first the image reflected must be perceived correctly and then the heat of transformation and conformation yields intimacy through experience of the heat of His love. Third, as we draw closer still, we come to the photographic focus where the image of Christ is indelibly impressed within us realizing we are one and duality ceases. At this point, we come to realization we are made like Him because we see Him as He is. Fourth and finally, as we come to the perfect center we reach magnetic focus and we experience the magnetism of oneness where our character is so conformed to Christ, to God's intent, through transformation there is now perfect union resulting in All in All as we stand completely in Him and now becoming the mirror; we are no longer the reflected image but the mirror itself fully *Christed*.

Holograph versus Photograph

The word holograph has Greek origins meaning whole message. A holograph contains the intensity and amplitude of light while a photograph only contains light intensity — the contrast of light and dark. Any part of a holograph can produce the whole image but if a portion of a photograph is removed then a loss of information is evident. A photograph is 2-D while a holograph is 3-D. In other words, a holograph is visually indistinguishable from the actual object. The difference between a holograph and a hologram is the holograph is static while the hologram is dynamic usually in rotating motion. A holograph is produced by multiple laser beams splitting and reflecting the object. The Son, Logos, Torah, Memra, or Ma'at are holographic in that any remaining part can produce the whole and original intent.

The Hermetic Logos

The Corpus Hermeticum was compiled around 1460 CE from seventeen texts including principles of philosophy, astrology, alchemy, and magic and were translated from Greek into Latin by Marsilio Ficino. It was so named after the narrator, Hermes Trismegistus, or Thrice Great Hermes. These works were later adapted into various esoteric writings such as the alchemist movements in the 15th century, Rosicrucianism in the 16th and 17th centuries, Freemasonry in the 18th and 19th centuries, and finally the Theosophical and New Age movements of the 20th and 21st centuries. Yet, the theory of *Prisca Theologia* or Ancient Theology considers the *Corpus Hermeticum* substantiate proof for a common pagan origin of religions that followed including Judaism, Christianity, and Islam. The Hermetic Logos represents a sealing or protection from air and decay and is related to ancient occultic (hidden) traditions encompassing alchemy, astrology, and theosophy. Its etymology implies what is held inside is impervious to outside influence. Its structure was a combination of Egyptian and Greek mythology (Trismegistus, Sacred Texts 2015).

The Greek culture as well as others were very syncretistic and often incorporated another culture's gods into their own as that country's influence infiltrated their traditions and was a process that the Greeks called *interpretatio Graeca* being a comparative mythology which searched for equivalences and shared characteristics allowing identification between Greek and Egyptian gods. It was this process that equated the Egyptian god of wisdom Thoth with the Greek divine messenger Hermes who also presided over medicine and the realm of the dead. Often, their identity and character changed over time as Hermes later acquired the cosmic attributes of the native Egyptian god Toth who was the inventor of writing and divine mediation.

Hermes Trismegistos believed that all human beings had a divine nature and if the soul managed to develop the right relationship with the spiritual dimension of his logos (reason) then he could ascend a spiritual path that would climax in a connection with the gods and this process was the experience called *gnosis*. It was those on this path that produced the Hermetic literature in Egypt and it was often divided into two distinct classes one being the *Technica Hermetica* consisting of magical and occultic texts, and the other *Philosophia Hermetica* which had dealings in life and death and the spiritual aspect of man.

As Hermeticism became a type of Gnosticism the Greek language enabled the *Corpus Hermeticum* to be incorporated as Egyptian knowledge detailing Egyptian concepts of moral and spiritual virtues and in this, the Egyptian Ma'at was transformed into the Greek Hermetic Logos (Discourse). As the Greek concepts of Logos, Nous, and Gnosis intermingled with Egyptian concepts they altered the Greek view of Egyptian cosmogony forming a new Hermetic worldview producing a linear Egyptian spirituality rather than a cyclic mythology.

Hermetic cosmology places three participants in creation. The first was God as father and only true Creator and his first son the Cosmos who helped him organize and form life. God's second son, the third participant, was man who helped God rule the material world. Hermetic philosophy places God in all dimensions of existence and his emanations can be found in every aspect of being. *The Way of Hermes* says: "and God encompasses all and is through all, and Nous encompasses souls, and soul, air, and air, matter (Trismegistus, Corpus Hermeticum bk. 12.14, 62)." The physical creation emanated from his Nous which is his mind or will and sent these souls to created matter to interact with Nature. This creation was enhanced by the power of speech or logos. It was by the power of will that speech places sound (vibration and frequency) in air representing ideas. These ideas were born by will and the resulting action was creation portraying creation was only possible due to God's speech. In the Hermetica, God's Logos guided Cosmos' Nous (the mind of the crafter). *The Way of Hermes* indicates: "immediately the word of God leapt forth from the downward moving elements to the pure work of the Creator and was united with the Creator Nous (for he was of the same substance) and the downward moving elements of the creation were left behind, without the Word, to be matter alone (Trismegistus, *Corpus Hermeticum* bk. 1.10, 19)." It goes on to explain the instruments of creation were the combination of Logos and Nous when it says: "the Creator made the whole cosmos, not with hands but by the Word, understand that he is present and always is, creating all things, being one alone and by his will producing all beings (Trismegistus, *Corpus Hermeticum* bk. 4.1, 31)."

The Hermetic Logos offers the concept of the words uttered from the will of God to instill Cosmos to create what was vibrated through the air causing matter to be; implying air or breath to be the womb of matter. The will for the birthing of the Cosmos came from the Nous or mind of God empowering the Creator or Craftsman to act and it is the combination of the Nous of God and His Logos that produced life. As man was created to observe and interact with the works of God, it was his to also discover the divine arts God hid in the world. It is this Logos and mind of man that also creates in his realm as man is the only being with speech and is his instrument to exercise his dominion over the material world as he co-creates with the God of the Cosmos. The Hermetic Logos functioned as a divine gift assisting man to master the world and to connect with Creator and is thus an instigator in man to reach God and this gift operates in intelligence and moral discernment. The Hermetica also explains Nous as an emanation of God and corresponds to being in contact with God's will whose action is to grant man the gift of being one with God. In this concept, it is the Logos that helps man recognize and remember his divine nature and guide him toward the divine Nous. The Hermetical Logos provides man with the capacity to distinguish himself from other creatures and to have the conscience (moral awareness) of God and the conscious (spiritual awareness) of union. It is the journey of the Logos and Nous that is the focus of Hermetic literature.

In summary, Hermetica was a cultural phenomenon originating in Hellenistic Egypt and was a product of a culture that was constantly undergoing symbolic renegotiation. In this vein, Hermetic literature was not only written in Greek but was also reproduced in Latin, Coptic, Syriac, Aramaic, and Arabian cultures.

In view of this fact, it is evident that the Hermetica did not undergo any form of canonization as it was the product of wide cultural interaction and was instrumental in forming mental and spiritual concepts for many cultures to follow.

The Egyptian Logos in the Scales of Ma'at

As the concept of the Logos is traced back through Egypt, it rests in the Egyptian god Thoth in whom resides speech, writing, wisdom, astronomy, mathematics, music, medicine, and magic. It was often noted in Egyptian writing that Thoth was lord of Order, Lord of Divine Words, and Tongue of Re associating him with the speaking and ordering process of creation because in Egyptian cosmology, the Sun God Re spoke the divine names of the gods creating and setting the universe in motion.

Ma'at is literally rendered truth in Egyptian and she was the personification of truth, order, balance, and justice. She was also harmony and represented the cosmos as it should be and it was thought if Ma'at did not exist the universe would be *isfet* or chaos and turmoil. Egyptian cosmology understood the universe functioned as an ordered and rational place, stood in predictability and regularity, and was in perfect balance. It was because of Ma'at that everything in the universe worked in a pattern and it was later the Greeks called this pattern the universal Logos.

Ma'at has no direct English equivalent as its association includes measurement, balance, justice, truth, harmony, and she reached beyond these concepts to social and cosmic scale touching all the gods of Egypt as Ma'at provides her attributes to all of them. She makes the sun rise, the stars to shine, and gives mankind his ability to reason.

Craig Lyons offers insight into Ma'at regarding words by saying they are a vibrational complex element which is characterized by movement of variable frequency and intensity describing movement (Lyons 2013, 102). He goes on to further demonstrate this power of sound waves by discussing the infrasound waves, which are below 20hz and are the sound of volcanoes, avalanches, earthquakes and meteorites. Even though they can't be heard, they can shake buildings. Ultrasound waves, whose frequency is greater than 20,000hz and above audible hearing, are harnessed by medicine and used in knifeless microsurgery. On the other end of the spectrum, a soprano singer can shatter glass with her voice (Lyons 2013, 102). All of this indicates a relationship between frequency (sound) and form offering proof that frequency can alter physical form as every object has a resonant frequency at which it will begin to move or vibrate.

Egyptian hieroglyphs demonstrated this concept as they pictured their reality. Said another way, they understood words were an image and the image could come alive. In our time, it can be expressed as "a picture is worth a thousand words" and the hieroglyphs offered symbology to express a deeper metaphysical meaning. They recounted their stories not in past tense but by referencing that day when, effectively reliving the event.

Linking Memra to Myth: The Judaic Logos

The purpose of myth is not to convey information but mythical truths which are manifested as culture interacts in an ethical and moral manner. Armstrong remarks, "as soon as people become aware of their own mortality, they created stories that gave their lives meaning, explained their relationship to the spiritual world, and instructed them on how to live their lives (Armstrong 2005)."

As the myth is put into ritualistic practice it moves from a dead story to a living reality. Often science tends to simplify the concept of God and according to Armstrong, in the ancient civilizations the concept of god was not a deity living a separate existence because myth was not about theology but about the human journey's connection to the divine. As myth insisted not on what and how but rather why, it refocused the prime thought to what can I learn about myself. The Perennial Philosophy encases all religions through myth and is an instrument that man uses to express the inward sense indicating there is more to being human than the breath and heartbeat. It is to discover the source of the breath and heartbeat.

When ancient man perceived of God as an existence beyond the heartbeat and powers above and beneath, offering man duality in its extreme as man envisioned a gulf between two worlds; between physical and spiritual, and more so between God and man. It then became the chief objective in humanity to repair the breach whether by fear, hope, or myth. The point was this division was introduced in creation as spirit contacted matter manifesting in the relationship between God and the soul and the required return of the soul to its original place in the presence of the Creator. As this process in culture matured there became multiple methods of fixing the division between God and man and myth tells that story. As civilization created their gods in their image, they placed them so far above themselves and to escape the visible world, a bridge was needed to cross the gulf. This bridge or connecting link between humanity and divinity was, to Philo's mind, the Logos.

Rudolf Bultmann says the Prologue of John does not have its origin in the philosophical tradition of Hellenism but in the mythology of Oriental and gnostic mysticism. He purports the Hebraic Wisdom myth was not so much a living force in ancient

Judaism but was a mythological and poetic adorning of doctrinal law. Remember the encounter in *The Shack* when Mack was taken behind the waterfall and into the cave where he met Sophia? He was so awed he asks Jesus if there were four Gods rather than three. The encounter continues as Sophia demands Mack to become the judge and decide which of his kids he will send to hell (Young 2007, 151-161). Daniel Boyarin says Sophia (Wisdom) stands as the only authority to judge and according to Hebraic tradition this Wisdom was transferred to the pre-existent Torah. Sophia stood as God's instrument of creation and in some sense incarnated in the law as a dwelling prepared for her by God and he goes on to say the wisdom myth has its source not in Hebrew history but in pagan mythology. In addition, he says the Logos theology is not originally a Christian concept but is a common element in Jewish and Christian Jewish "religious imagination" as he compares Philo's Logos, the Memra of the Targum, and John's Prologue (Boyarin 2001).

Boyarin points to Philo's Logos as being a mediator and was a separate being God created in order to create everything else. This concept was based on his Greek philosophy and his Jewish background in Torah as the written text was the "eternal notion" of the Creator's mind and marked the image of his work in space and time essentially becoming a person (Boyarin 2001). The Torah/Logos was the expression/emanation/outflow of God in the physical realm reacting in time but not limited by it.

Memra carries the concept of a second God being the personified word equating to the Aramaic form which, according to Alfred Edersheim, is God's self-revelation. Rabbinic Judaism has attempted to suppress the Memra concept of the second god as heresy describing the "two powers in heaven." This self-revelation in Judaic thought was to express the theology of a transcendent God who gives himself permission to contact humanity. Memra as the en-fleshed word (*logos ensarkos*) is distant and difficult to relate to while the Torah as the pre-existent word (*logos asarkos*) and mediator of God's law as he relates to humanity (Boyarin 2001).

The Greek metaphysical concept of the Logos is in distinct contrast of a personal God of the anthropomorphic mind of the Hebrew. What happened when the Greek philosophical mind met the Hebraic mythical one? Philo of Alexandria, a Hellenized Jew happened, providing a synthesis of both as they flowed to mold the messianic apocalyptic Logos being the basis for Christian doctrine today.

Why do we use the term Logos? We must first realize that the Early Christians adopted a Greek word, and this word carried foreign concepts and terminology and most of the time these concepts were not adequately translated or carried forth to the new language. This thought is locked to the Prologue of John and has lost the fuller concepts that were meant to migrate with the word. We have a transliteration of Logos because there is not a word that adequately carries the meaning. Do we use other transliterations? We have many such as Christ, baptism, angel, and manna. To grasp this point, consider a culture who has numbers that only correspond from one to four. Afterwards, they adopt the numerals of their neighboring civilization who has a number five. How can they borrow a word for five without adopting the concept of five? This is what has happened in Western religion.

The Greek Metamorphosis to John's Logos

The Greeks simple explanation for Logos was word, reason, or plan yet in Greek philosophical and theological concepts it carried a richer and mythical meaning as the absolute reason of the cosmos giving it form and meaning. Even though this idea is present in

Greek, Indian, Egyptian, and Persian theological systems it has been hijacked by Christian theology as another means of describing Jesus Christ as the principle of God active in creation and functioning as he who maintains cosmic order revealing the divine plan of salvation to a lost world.

Logos in the Greek mind seems to have its source in Heraclitus (600 BCE) who ascertained the cosmic structure was analogous to the reasoning power of man. It continued to develop in the mind of Zeno of Citium (400-300 BCE) who categorized the Logos to be "the active rational and spiritual principle that permeated all reality (Encyclopedia Britannica "Logos, Philosophy, and Theology." www.britannia.com/topic/logos.)" and called it providence, nature, and the soul of the universe. Moving to approximately 100 CE, Philo of Alexandria said the Logos was the intermediary between God and the cosmos being both the agent of creation and the agent through which the mind comprehends God. In the 4th century, Plato says the Logos was both immanent in the world and at the same time the transcendent divine mind.

As we migrate to John's Gospel we find the same Logos concept but noticed it is living and en-fleshed. Is there a basis for John to incarnate the Logos in one man? The concept of identifying Jesus with the Logos does stem from the Old Testament concepts of the phrase "word of the Lord" which carries the idea of God's active power and comingled with the Jewish view that Wisdom or Sophia is the divine agent that draws man to God and is too identified with the word of God. John uses expressions and concepts familiar with his Hellenized readers to convey the redemptive character of the Christ in the same way as the Old Testament Jews viewed the Torah as pre-existent with God. Why did the author convey this concept? Divine inspiration alone or in conjunction with tradition and culture to present a superior God to the world steeped in pagan philosophy?

The metaphysical concept of the Logos has its origins in Pythagoras and the cosmological triad being the monad, dyad, and harmony. The principle of harmony which represented the dynamic universe was responsible for proportional (*analogia*) relationship (*logos*) between the components of creation (Hillar 2012, 7). Anaxagoras said this concept can be explained as the "cosmic fire (Hillar 2012, 28)" being an impersonal natural force that creates the world from itself and itself from the world representing the early transcendent concepts of God in Greek thought. Plato was the first to promote a dualistic view of reality by introducing the real world of Forms thereby presenting the Demiurge, the pure Mind, the fashioner of the world. Next, Xenocrates elaborates on the function of the cosmic principles found in Plato's philosophy who projected the Logos as reason or ideas to being thoughts of the divine intellect. It was Aristotle who introduced the duality of the Prime Mover (Hillar 2012, 27) being the pure mind, in contrast to the Prime Matter (Hillar 2012, 218) being one substance. Finally, moving to Stoic philosophy, the Logos is perceived as a natural dynamic principle, rational and immanent whose function is to animate creation and is described by the names of Logos, Nature, Fate, Providence, and the idea of ideas (Hillar 2012, 49) as the pattern or blueprint for all things.

The Law of Operations: The Cosmic Logos

Cosmology seems to have lost its place in mythical time as humanity seeks his origin. Cosmology must be restored because it too points to us. Biblical cosmology is not scientific nor was it intended to be; but it is mythic and cannot be taken literally. Psalm

19 proclaims the realms above us are speaking and declaring the glory of God and each day and night (period of time) is filled with their sayings without words and yet the entire creation hears what they say.

> 4 God stretched out in these heavens a tent for the sun, 5 And the sun is like a groom who, after leaving his room, arrives at the wedding in splendor; He is the strong runner who, favored to win in his race, is eager to face his challenge. He rises at one end of the skies and runs in an arc overhead; nothing can hide from his heat, from the swelter of his daily tread (The Voice 2011).

This talks about the amazing zodiacal footprint in the heavens above us. Remember Job 9:9 which proclaims:

> Who made [the constellations] the Bear, Orion, and the Pleiades, And the [vast starry] spaces of the south (Job 9:9 AMP).

They continuously decree to creation below them. All components of the heavens are declaring something and it is not the demise of humanity. The suns and stars are talking, is that strange? More so, is it literal? If strict literalness yields to the mythical, then amazing insights and mystery of worth our Creator places on us becomes hugely apparent. Upon leaving the heavens in Psalms 19, God's Law is brought up in verses 7-10 of that chapter.

> The Eternal's law is perfect, turning lives around. His words are reliable and true, instilling wisdom to open minds. The Eternal's directions are correct, giving satisfaction to the heart. God's commandments are clear, lending clarity to the eyes. The awe of the Eternal is clean, sustaining for all of

eternity. The Eternal's decisions are sound; they are right through and through (The Voice 2011).

The heaven's declarations and God's decrees reassure all creation of the goodness of God. Two voices with the same message, the Cosmological Law (the Law of Operations) sounded by the cosmos and resound the decrees of the Principle of God. They are not declaring a broken creation and separation of man from his Creator like religion is declaring. Religion has repurposed law to allay guilt but the decrees of the Lord instill wisdom and open the mind and his commandments bring clarity to the eyes removing duality and division. They are not citing a dying god on a cross but what is happening to humanity symbolized in the cross being an intersection of divinity and humanity functioning as a movement of the Logos. The Cosmic Law is not forcing comparison in judgment but issuing a proclamation of union.

Man often sees a deficit in myth and fulfillment in Logos. The Logos proclaims peace with nothing broken and nothing missing while myth which speaks through perception, often sees a fall and sin explaining perceived distance and separation. This does not make myth totally erroneous but does fully reflect the human concept of himself as the myth attempts to lift him to his proper place through a risen savior. The decrees are not as loud as judgments in the Bible when it is read literally in linear time rather than mythically which produces mystical realities. In other words, literalism sees one cross and one incarnation which occurred over two thousand years ago; while mythical time too sees them, yet occurring and effective in all time. The Logos mirrors Cosmological Law reflecting the Principle of Operations in all civilizations, yet called by different names and possessing various nuances of meaning. The Logos becomes noticeable as one consciously watches for its movements. This expression of God is not human yet invades humanity as the Ruach of God expressing the mind of God and manifesting that expression into space and time, our spatial universe.

Sophia — Wisdom

Is there a relationship between the personification of Wisdom in Proverbs 8:22-30 and the Word in John 1:1-18? Proverbs indicates Wisdom was with God from the beginning and long before creation stating: "Then I (Wisdom) was by Him (God) as one brought up with Him and I was daily His delight, rejoicing always before Him..." It seems that what early Judaism says of Wisdom John and Paul say of the Word. It is interesting to note the Jewish philosopher Philo considers wisdom which he also refers to as the logos the "eikon" or image of God. There are three instances where the phrase "image of God" is used in the Bible and in two of those instances it refers to man (Gen 1:27, 9:6) and the third is found in 2 Corinthians 4:4 and refers to Christ. Philo goes on to describe Wisdom as bringing forth the universe and as God's son. Matthew 12:42 says "The queen of the South will rise up in judgment with this generation and condemn it, for she came from the ends of the earth to hear the wisdom of Solomon; and indeed, a greater than Solomon is here" (1 Kgs 10:1). Why did Jesus compare Himself to the wisdom of Solomon? Is He saying that now Wisdom has come in person?

An image or icon is a reflection, a light print, or an expression of the original. It is important to note that it is not the original but points to or mimics the original. Another trait of an image is that its dependence remains to the original demonstrated when you step away from the mirror, the image no longer exists. Greek concepts pulled the historical Jewish relationship of Wisdom to the Greek

Logos equating them to the Intent of God representing His image. If God steps away or no longer intends then there is no Logos, no principle, no reason, or no power holding the universe together.

In the theology of the Eastern Orthodox Church, Holy Wisdom is equivalent to the Divine Logos. Philo is accepted as one of the first philosophers to link Logos and Sophia in the Greek and Hebrew mind. It was not Jesus who pre-existed, but the Logos concept equating to the Hebraic *Chokmah* (Greek *Sophia*) being the breath of the Divine. Throughout the New Testament there is evidence the writers linked Jesus with certain eternal concepts such as divine wisdom (1 Cor. 1:17-18, 24-25); saying Jesus is the radiance of God's glory (Heb. 1:3); and the true light giving light to everyone (John 1:3).

Consider the identity of the speakers in the two passages in Matthew 23:34-36 and Luke 11:49. The sections of Scripture are listed below.

> Matthew 23:34-36 9
> 34 "Therefore, indeed, I send you prophets, wise men, and scribes: some of them you will kill and crucify, and some of them you will scourge in your synagogues and persecute from city to city,
> 35 "that on you may come all the righteous blood shed on the earth, from the blood of righteous Abel to the blood of Zechariah, son of Berechiah, whom you murdered between the temple and the altar.
> 36 "Assuredly, I say to you, all these things will come upon this generation.
>
> Luke 11:49-51
> 49 "Therefore the wisdom of God also said, 'I will send them prophets and apostles, and some of them they will kill and persecute,'
> 50 "that the blood of all the prophets which was shed

from the foundation of the world may be required
of this generation,
51 "from the blood of Abel to the blood of Zechariah
who perished between the altar and the temple. Yes,
I say to you, it shall be required of this generation.

Matthew indicates that Jesus is speaking and in the account in Luke he identifies the speaker as "the Wisdom of God". Several books of the wisdom literature (the Wisdom of Solomon, Book of Enoch, and Proverbs) parallel John's Prologue in linking Wisdom and the Word. For example, John 1:1 states that "in the beginning was the word and the word was with God" while the Wisdom of Solomon (9:9) states "with you (God) is wisdom, who knows your works and was present when you made the world". John 1:4 states "in him was life and this life was the light of men" while Proverbs 8:35 says "for whoever finds wisdom finds life". Paul carries on the correlation in 1 Cor 1:24 and 30 by stating that Christ is the power and wisdom of God. Wisdom and Logos seem to be equivalent in ancient concepts as each enacts similar principles of God. The link was problematic linguistically however as Logos was masculine and Sophia was feminine in language, yet posed no problem in their philosophical meanings.

The Logos Protraction

David Fideler said the Prologue in John's Gospel reflects the ideas of the then current Hellenistic Logos teaching as the early Christians personified the Logos in Jesus while the Greeks represented the concept in Apollo who was the God of geometry and music (Fideler 1993, 63). Another impartation was found in the Egyptian teachings of Hermes as Fideler indicates E. A. Wallis Burge, a renowned Egyptologist, points out the Logos principle was identified in the Egyptian divinity Thoth (the Moon god) along with his wife Ma'at (Truth) who were the personification of the order of the universe being the heart and tongue of the sun god Ra (Fideler 1993, 226).

Jaraslov Pelikan, a Lutheran Church historian and professor at Yale, said Christian philosophers in naming the Logos Jesus were trying to give structure to the works of the Logos by providing the first concept of the now known term Cosmic Christ illustrating a universal expression as one that is not locked in time (Pelikan 1999, 57-70). The mystical side of Paul is demonstrated when He presents the Logos/Christ as being the image of the invisible God, the first-born of all Creation, and He who holds all things together (Col. 1: 15-1). Has the concept of the Cosmic Christ been gleaned from Orthodox Religion? It seems each religious branch claims Christ for their own faith alone even to the exclusion of all others who believe differently. Yet there remains a light that causes the believer to see, to hope, and to dream for a God greater and far reaching than religion presents. Incidentally, the ancients believed when the pupil was ready the teacher would appear (Buddha Siddhartha Guatama Shakyamuni). Meister Eckhart says, "all of existence was an expression of the Word of God (Eckhart 2016)" as all of creation are words of God—thoughts that have become manifest in matter. He goes on to say that Christ, the incarnate Logos, was the word of God and this caused man to realize they too were words of God and as we come to realize this cosmic truth effectively birthing the Logos, we also become reborn as sons of God (Eckhart 2016).

A protraction is a forward movement at a joint or juncture through angular motion and all movement is connected and dependent on the preceding action to accomplish the next. Physically, it is the action of rolling the shoulders forward and all the required responses to initiate the action. This principle is seen in the movement or flow of the Logos; God, by His breath, is the cause and Logos is the effect. The Great Meme which is an element of a culture or system of behavior that may be passed down not through genetics but through language and imitation throughout past civilizations is the incarnational concept of God upholding the Cosmos. The philosophical aspect of the Logos entered Christianity, and as it protracted, it remolds itself into new forms out of necessity of shifting circumstances as it comes down through history caught in time. But what if it were removed from the capsule of time, what would the Logos impart?

Is the Logos an emanation of God which is an abstract yet perceptible something that outflows from a source? It is thought the Absolute God is surrounded by his powers and according to the Greek concepts they are ideas yet in Platonic thought they are language. The Logos appears as immanent reason residing in the mind of God and this concept was propagated by the Alexandrian Christians (home of Philo) while the other aspect is the breathed out or uttered Logos and this aspect was sourced in Palestine where the word appears as the Angel of God in the Pentateuch. The Alexandrian viewpoint is based in God's hidden being while the Palestinian aspect of the Logos is active in the world and is upholding that which was spoken and filling all things with Light and Life ruling them wisely and beneficently. How did the community of Alexandria become so far removed from their Hebraic roots? Recall it was here where the Septuagint originated being a community of Jews not fluent in Hebrew because of their cultural Hellenization. It was the Essenes in the region of Palestine who contributed the pre-existence of the soul and linked the sun to the son—the Logos. John in his Prologue carried the meme of the incarnation of the Logos as Life and Light and projected its creativity to a man who progressed to godhood.

I mentioned earlier the movement of the Logos. These movements of which we are more familiar are Incarnation, Crucifixion, and Resurrection and others such as Transfiguration and the Prayer in Gethsemane are seen through our culture and geography and in religion they are literally locked in time while in mythical reality they are new every morning so to speak. They exist perpetually in the present moment as the Logos fluidly maintains purpose. Just as creation is ever expanding as the Logos manifests God's intent so too these movements are ever living and active regardless of time. Another word is logistics meaning the overall management of the way resources are obtained, stored, and moved to the locations where they are required. It is the protraction of the Logos, the ever-moving and rolling forward expression, the breathing of a creative God that frees them from time. His breathing is an expression of His mind as words require breath to be articulated. God breathed and potentiality exploded and forced the image held in His mind to materialize. The Logos is effective in all of us freeing us from time and it is from this perspective that the son of God is not a historical figure but an eternal philosophical principle that infuses into us by the breath of God our identity.

The Gnostic Logos

The Gnostics were Greek intellectuals who wanted to live in the realm of divinity and yet maintained the concept of participation as divinity intersected humanity. Their influence was seen in the writings of Philo of Alexandria, Roman law, and even Christian theology. It was the writings of Marcion which brought Gnostic dualism forward as he explained, according to Gnosticism, the creation was bad and therefore the god who created it was bad also. He identified this god as the god of the Old Testament. He taught salvation was liberation from the physical world freeing the soul. As the soul ascended, it identified the demonic powers by name causing them to lose their influence becoming unable to imprison the soul any longer (Wikipedia. "Marcionism." 2016).

In the Gnostic myth of creation, Sophia was the feminine creative force and desiring to procreate a being liker herself, she does so without her partner utilizing her own emanation. Producing an imperfect being, through her shame she hides him in the clouds away from the other gods. She later expels him from heaven to physical matter. This Demiurge, meaning a skilled worker or craftsman, then creates man. Gnosticism posits this is the god of the Old Testament who differs greatly from the God of the New Testament. His act of creating beings out of himself trapped spirit in matter—hence the Gnostic dilemma.

Gnosticism considered the Greek Logos to be equal with the Gnostic *Aeons* which were entities or cosmic powers who were emanations of God. It was these aeons or saviors who entered the physical realm to deliver human souls and in this vein of thought, the Christ was made the Logos and the trinity doctrine was wombed.

According to the Gnostic view of humanity, man is asleep and forgetful of his origin and true nature. It is through gnosis the soul of man is awakened and recalls his past union with God. Jesus is personified as one of many Gnostic revealers and this is proclaimed in the Gospel of John. Yet the Gnostic Logos is the source of all knowledge and it exists without yet also within, permeating all space; therefore, space we have considered empty and void may not be so. Humanity has never been separated from his Creator but man has perceived so. Craig Lyons said, "we can never be separated from the harmony of the universe because we are its living reflection, even if in our slumber, this recognition has been temporarily obscured (Lyons 2013, 111)."

The Chinese Logos

Tao is a Chinese concept which signifies way, path, route, or more loosely doctrine and principle. It includes the intuitive knowing of life or the gaining of wisdom and experience through living. In Taoism and according to the *Tao Te Ching*, Tao is not a name for a thing, in English concepts then, it is not a noun; but is the natural order of the universe or more so the activity of maintaining the order functioning as a verb. The Tao is an active and holistic concept of nature rather than a static one. Perhaps better stated it is the flow of the universe.

There is a remarkable similarity between the concept found in the Chinese Tao and the Greek Logos. Chinese translations interpret John1:1 as "in the beginning was Tao... (Joh 1:1 The Canton Ed. China 1911)." Tao is employed in Chinese philosophy to signify the way of the heavens and the way of humans indicating a cosmological meaning as well as anthropological. The Lao-tzu states:

> Something is formed in the chaos, which existed before heaven and earth. It is quite and profound. It stands alone and alters not. It revolves eternally without exhaustion. It is regarded as the Mother of all beings. I do not know its name, except to call it Tao. When forced to give It a name, I would call It 'Great' (Tao Te Ching, Ch. 25).

It is in this quote that the Taoist cosmology is clearly outlined as the "something undifferentiated" is the source or first cause of all things. Tao is considered the creative power and the cosmic principle, again, that maintains order; and like Philo and John, Lao Tzu recognizes the need for mediation between the transcendent Tao and its physical manifestation in the universe.

The Logos and Kabbalah

As there were varied meanings in the Greek flow of language for Logos including order, pattern, ratio, mediation, and harmony; Kabbalah placed the word "Word" in the traditional act of cosmology. It was readily seen in the magical properties of the spoken divine names of the Hebrew Kabbalah. The Kabbalah concept was seen in the word *Abracadabra* whose origin was in the Aramaic language and means "I create as I speak." In Hebrew, it was "I will create as spoken (Wikipedia. "Abracadabra." 2015)." The concept was seen in the "Name it and claim it" or "You have what you say" doctrine of the faith movement (Wikipedia. "Prosperity Theology, Wikipedia 2015). Was it possible that key ministers and evangelists of the faith movement saw a link through Kabbalah and Aramaic concepts. Word of Faith circles were strong in first the spirit then the physical concepts which is the ancient concept of as above so below.

In the Harry Potter novels, the incantation *Avada Kedavra* was known as the "killing curse" and during an interview in Edinburgh in 2004, J. K. Rowling said the etymology of the Killing Curse was an ancient spell in Aramaic and it was Abracadabra originally meaning "let the thing be destroyed" and altered to be "what has been said has been done (Rowling 2004)." It was an ancient display of the power of words or more precisely letters as the Hebrew language bore out in its mythology which is the root of Kabbalah.

The God Particle and the Logos

The Higgs Boson also referred to as the God Particle was considered to be the instant of creation. This concept of time at the Big Bang was outside of standard particle theory of physics. As the universe was rewound approaching the instance of creation the universe becomes increasingly dense and hot until standard models in physics no longer apply. It became so hot that the three basic forces (strong, electromagnetic, weak) of physics could not exist separately and thus became unified in one force. As the exact moment of creation approached, the temperature and density increased so that gravity, the forth fundamental force, could not exist as a separate force and in the Quantum Physics realm this union of fundamental forces into a single force or particle was the Higgs Boson.

In Christian theology, God not only created the universe but He upholds it moment by moment and depicted in mythological aspects as Atlas, supporting the world in his shoulder. If God withdrew His Logos, would the universe cease to exist? The particle is not visible but its effects are universal. Paul says in Colossians 1:16-17 that the Christ, the Son of God, the Firstborn of all creation, holds all things together. In Hebrews 1:3 it is the perfect imprint of the Father "upholding, maintaining, and propelling all things" which would include the entire physical and spiritual cosmos by his word carrying the cosmos along to its predetermined goal (Hebrews 1:3 AMP). In Colossians, Paul says the Logos pre-existed creation as he is the "controlling cohesive force of the universe" (Colossians 1:17 AMP). Even in the Old Testament there are indications of an active Word in action in Psalm 75:3 says the earth and its inhabitants are distressed in rough times but it is "I [God] who will steady its pillars" (Psalm 75:3 AMP). Job describes

God as the one who shakes the pillars of the earth and has full command of the sun and all celestial elements and it is He who made the constellations and he does unbelievable things too amazing to number. So, according to these statements it is apparent that if God silenced His Logos the cosmos would cease to be. This is borne out by the Higgs Boson principle as without the origination of the Higgs Boson nothing would have mass, the universe would be matter-less. The Higgs Boson is a contingent particle. It exists only when the union of all forces reach an excited state and as soon as it is formed it decays (in sacrifice) losing existence. The particle is not visible but effects are universal. It is the Logos that maintains the elevated level of energy.

The Logos Consciousness

What causes our awareness of the Logos? Is it simply a principle transcendent to us, or is it active and working in us? How do we see it? To consider the consciousness of the Logos I want to explore an article by Charles Johnston who wrote for the Theosophical Society in the late 1800's. He presents his case of the Logos by simply looking at a piece of paper and peeling back layers of what is actually occurring in operation from many perspectives.

On the table is a piece of white paper and as our eyes focus on it the wheels of consciousness begin to turn. Out of my awareness of the white paper I suddenly find myself beginning to explore possibilities. Perhaps I am going to write on it with a red ink pen or maybe I am going to fold it making a paper airplane. Consciousness has brought reality of what is seen, the act of perceiving, and the one who sees which is the trinity of perception. Our world is alive to us because of these three elements held in our being, processed through the senses, and contemplated by the mind. As more awareness develops, I become acutely conscious that sight/perception is only one sense through only one of our many receptors. It is through these powers of perception that we gain sense of color and beauty seen in the sun and stars and the snow-covered mountains and hearing the river flow over the rocks. Through the action receptors we gain the sense of space and form. Reaching out to touch a rock we get the sense of firmness and stability. As we walk across the field we get a sense of distance and proportion and we see the outcome of order and lines. Through the hearing of sound we can understand frequency, intensity, pitch, and harmony; all based on mathematical principles (Johnston 1923).

"Your perception of the world is a reflection of your state of consciousness. You are not separate from it and there is no objective world out there. Every moment your consciousness creates the world that you inhabit (Tolle 2016)." It is this process that gives Logos conscious application in humanity and all aspects of our being are employed. It is the Logos that empowers the creation of our universe in our consciousness. Our world consists, for each of us, the sum of our perceptions coming to birth through the activity of the mind and manifested out of the action of consciousness. The Logos touches our consciousness and imparts creativity, inspiration, and freedom as the ego allows interchange and the entire picture shifts as the soul is awakened to the Logos within as well as without. It is the Logos that empowers our consciousness to now rightly perceive without duality. We are not billions but one. God is not a trinity but one, and we are not body, soul, and spirit, but we are a soul—one.

The Purpose of Decrypting the Logos Enigma

Logos ideology developed into a living reality but first was simply a factor or cause as to why something happened or why change exists. The difficulty arose because ancient philosophy lacked the functional concept of the principle. Aristotle put forth the fuller meaning of the Greek *rhema* and *logos* which in Christianity simply meant Christ's utterance and Logos as Christ Himself. Aristotle used them very differently. He paired the word *onoma* as the subject of logic and in grammar, it functioned as the noun and was descriptive. He then paired the word rhema as the predicate and in grammar functioned as the verb describing action. And finally, he paired logos as the proposition and in grammar it functioned as the entire sentence providing a full idea. It was the act, the actor, and the acted upon. The Logos must be set free from the entombment of religion and realize it is metaphysical, historical, and personal and in this way, it transcends time. It is logically prior to the laws which govern the universe as the Logos is the one who establishes those laws, who enforces them, and finally, receives their effects.

Decrypting the Logos Enigma, for me has been a true unlocking and ever deepening understanding of our mystical (an awareness of reality not derived by the senses), mysterious (causes or inspires awe which is a realization of a face to face encounter with reality, it is to comprehend you are not alone but connected to all, it is that moment you realize there are not two), and magical (the ability to control or influence natural forces) God. God is not hiding from us but for us and he has amazing truths that are in Him as we come to understand and deepen the relationship of the divine and human. He invites us into the hiding place to enter his mystery and live in the mystical realities of Himself. I said earlier, the mystical is ascertaining spiritual reality without the senses and that is but one of the functions of the Logos of God. The mystery of God is not an unknowable aspect of Him but it is an aspect of Him that arouses wonder and awe by looking through the literal for the mythical.

Many consider man to be spirit having a human experience but that does not flow with my understanding of who and what we are. I do not simply possess a soul for I am one. I am not in an earth suit trapped away from my primordial existence seeking release and return. I am a soul formed from the union of God's Breath (an uncreated element, a wave) and dust (a created particle). I have the privilege of standing at the intersection of divinity and humanity and out of that union, I AM conscious. The Logos is many things and in this case the action on the awakening soul of humanity producing the Christ. I am a soul experiencing something new that has never occurred before. I am a new creation of spirit and flesh. I am a union of the Ruach of God and the dust of matter and I, a soul, am proof of animation at the hand of the great Animator and the Animator's Logos marches on.

-VI-

THE COSMOGONICAL KEY

"There is no religion that is not both a cosmology and
a speculation about the Divine."
David Émile Durkheim (Campion 2012, 1)

osmology cannot be defined exclusive of the human journey. Having said that, our cosmological view shapes our world view and affects our concept of origin and purpose. Inclusive of our perception of origin and purpose are the abstract notions offered by myth. It is part of our journey to mold our views encompassing myth not by deconstruction or separation but rather enfolding mythic aspects; thereby creating a distinct unity realizing an enriched drama of the mystery encircling our journey.

A narrow and restricted cosmological view dismisses myth, relationship, mystery, and the magic of God; while an open and flowing cosmological view welcomes the mysterious and magical interaction of a Creator who invites humanity to tell the story. What opens the cosmological view to consider the possibility of an exposed, intrusive, and invasive Creator? There are three key points that move one's worldview to entertain the concept. First, becoming aware of the function of myth in ancient cultures to telling man's story of divinity and humanity. Second, an altered view of time flowing from linear perspective which entombs the myth to a cyclical awareness of the eternal now that enlivens the myth. Third, recognizing there is an ever-present cosmic process acknowledged throughout ancient cultures as a continuous becoming which has been manifested throughout time.

Cosmology is principled in time while cosmogony is timeless. Is the account in Genesis a cosmology or a cosmogony? Cosmology (Cosmo-logos) is a study concerned with structural order and logic. Cosmogony (cosmo-gonia) is an endeavor to derive a purpose of becoming or coming into being which is concerned with function. Cosmology, now deviating from the scientific aspect a little, is a narrative written to a specific people in a specific time inclusive of cultural traditions. Cosmogony is generally poetic and flowing alluding to a purpose of those created. Cosmology conveys dynamic motion and that motion is described as a quantity. Cosmogony, having the same root as genesis, seeks to convey the purpose of beginnings and the becoming of the cosmos as quality expressing the value of the motion. Cosmology is the Greek expression while Cosmogony contains Hebrew assertions. Cosmology builds the house while Cosmogony makes it a home.

Cosmogony, focuses on the functional motive or intention of the cosmos instead of the mechanical process and is steered by perennial, philosophical, and theological concerns arising from mythologized creation accounts. Myth is a mysterious and integral part of both cosmology and cosmogony, yet religion seems to push the mythical insights to the periphery or omit them altogether.

Ancient cultures saw the cosmos as a beautiful order or an adornment and they also considered the sky a theatrical component or a stage on which the cosmic drama was displayed. Throughout history most human cultures, somehow and in some form, related their fears, concerns, and even their hopes and dreams to the sky or more so to the organizing principle displayed throughout the cosmos. This was evidenced by the expression of the heavens and its mysteries found in myth including the Bible. Our cosmology will not fit if our cosmogony is not first centered and open allowing myth to provide abstract insights into the why's of our journey.

Creation

God's first creative act was not order but the potential of His intent hoovering, brooding, over chaos — the waters of potentiality, ready to receive the force of His breath; then God breathed."
(Author, 2016)

Hermann Gunkel portrays Genesis as a myth in which "it is not the free composition of an author but is rather the deposit of a tradition (Gunkel 2006, 11)." Immanuel Kant conveys creation is never finished or complete by implying it had a genesis but will not have an ending. "Creation is not the work of a moment (Weinert 2013, 21)." The model of the cosmos contains two aspects: an ethos and a mythos. An ethos conveys the spirit of a culture through their myths, folklore, and traditions. The mythos of a people contains their concepts of God in relation to their origins and of God's perceived intervention in their affairs. Brown, an associate professor of the Old Testament says, "throughout the Biblical cosmologies, as in ancient Near Eastern lore, creation was both the locus [meaning point of singularity with the One] of transcendence and the habitation of chaos (Brown 1999, 22)." These cosmologies drew both from their cultures, myths, and traditions and yet, there was no firm separation of the imaginative world of myth and the immediate world of perception. Also, the sky was part of the sensory input offering insights and apprehensions of transcendence evidenced by the perceived divergence of the human and divine (Brown 1999, 22).

What does it mean to be created? What does it mean to exist? John Walton said existence is anchored in the authority and relationship to the one governing existence (Walton 2009, 22). In other words, function defines existence. This was a trait of understanding in the ancient world as they believed the virtue of existence was not tied to its material makeup but to its function in the cosmic order. Existence then, was fulfilling a purpose in the ordered system of their cosmic structure portraying a cosmogony rather than cosmology. This process can be pictured as something could be manufactured physically but not exist because it was not functional. In building a computer one collects the hardware, connects the cables, and installs the software; but it does not function as a computer until it is powered up and the software utilized. Unless humanity benefits from function then true existence is not achieved. According to Walton, "unless something is integrated into a working ordered system it does not exist" adding "create is the English word for bringing something into existence. It does no good to know what create literally means—we have to know what bara literally means (Walton 2009, 23-25, 37)."

What does it mean to functionally exist? One tenet in a house may use one of the rooms as a dining room. But you move in and decide it should be a library. After you have named it now you separate it, not tearing it from the structure but forming it to function differently according to your intent. You repaint it and furnish it, not with a dining room set but a comfortable chair, a reading lamp, and bookshelves full of books. Now you have created a library. You call it good because it now functions after what you named it, a library. Now you rest; sit in the chair reading a good book enjoying the library you formed. You changed the condition of the room, seeing a room full of potential and seizing that potential, you created a room according to your intent.

To get another dimensional grasp of the meaning of create, consider Genesis 2:2 which says, "By the seventh day God had finished the work he had been doing; so, on the seventh day he rested from all His work (Gen 2:2 NIV)." Was the Seventh Day of rest a period of inactivity as religion seems to indicate? What did you do in the chair when you rested in your library? Maybe you took a nap. Maybe you read a book. Or perhaps you just enjoyed your library. A deity rests in his temple and rest is what occurs after a crisis has been resolved and stability is achieved. Rest is proof of normal operations in the cosmos as God takes his rest from ordering and begins to maintain his created order.

Returning to the computer analogy, one has spent time installing the components, connecting the cables, and installing the software and when you are done you cease building and move to function when it is powered up and its capabilities are utilized. In other words, it functions according to its created purpose as the computer operates in its assigned role. To further see how tradition has interpreted the rest, consider your answer to the question of "What did God do on day eight?"

The temple is a sacred place where deity is at home. We are a temple and the cosmos functions as a temple as well. What is the fractal practicality of the rest? The temple is very different from creation in naming and separating. It is not a product of creation but is ushered into existence as God rests. It is not spoken into existence but it becomes. It comes into being as a process in response to the rest of God. The account of creation is the functional ordering and preparation for a divine intrusion as God sustains and maintains the cosmos. Maintaining the cosmos relates to material and physical existence while sustaining the cosmos relates to functional and operational aspects or more importantly relationship. God did not just create the cosmos but named, separated, and ordered it to function in a certain way and he called it good meaning it works the way he saw in his mind. He then rests, enjoying the cosmos he fashioned from the womb of creativity. He rested, not meaning inactive but the structure and function ceased and he began to enjoy the fruits of his intent; like you, sitting in your chair in the library. The library, I mean the cosmos, became sacred space; a dwelling place for interaction, reflection, and relationship.

In considering the difference between a house and home, as one purchases a structure one may look at the physical aspect. What is it made of? Is it made of bricks or aluminum siding? How many rooms are there? Is the electrical and plumbing suitable and in good condition? While others begin to see how the rooms are to be used. Is the family room comfortable? Will this be a good bedroom for Tori and this one for Matt? How will the furniture be placed in the Living Room? And in later years, is there a place for Nia, Zach, Aleah, Olivia, Breanna, Alexis, and Brooklyn; the amazing grandkids to play? What is the difference in the aspect of the structure? One is considering the house while the other is considering the home.

In the Ancient Near East accounts of creation, there was little concern for how the house (cosmos) was built but for what purpose was it built. Of much more interest was how the house had become a home for humanity. In this concept, the Genesis account is not a house story but a home story. It is the presence of God in the Cosmos that is important and because of his presence the cosmos becomes sacred space, a temple, a glorious place of relationship.

The Old Testament does not refer to the Genesis three account as the fall of man as tradition has done. It does not portray a world that is no longer functioning as good. Walton implies the fall was an invasion of disorder that entered the sacred space setting up a perception of distance or alienation in the minds of humanity. The concept of sin and its accompanying perception of alienation readily came from Augustine and not the writings of Paul. The purpose of cosmogony from any culture is not to recover but to discover.

Catherine Keller said the Hebrew word *tehom* was translated as the deep or the abyss and was basically the site of creative energy (Keller 2003, 163, 169, 239n). Keller indicates tehom is not nothing nor emptiness but far from it, as it means potential activity. Tehom seems to have preexisted the heavens and the earth as all of creation stems from it. She said rather than understanding tehom as a place before beginning, instead see it as simply beginning. According to Keller, it was a between space of all other spaces loaded with potentiality and possibility. The unfolding of this non-space produced time, space, spirit, and matter. This creativity, according to Keller, did not become but it makes becoming possible as the "matrix of possibilities (Keller 2003, 161, 184)" or an environment from which development can occur. She added tehom was the "ocean of divinity (Keller 2003, 217)," the womb and place holder of beginnings and God was the effect through whom all causes arise (Keller 2003, 161, 169, 213-228).

The Hebrew word *bara* whose English equivalent has been translated as create is used in the Old Testament and it does not necessarily mean to make a thing but is more abstract as if in English one said, "I created a masterpiece." The Hebraic concept is not that God made something out of nothing but it reveals the role and function assigned to it. One can create a piece of art but that does not imply you constructed the canvas or made the pigments. Yet maybe you did, but that is not the point in the Hebraic implication. The point is you are the one who gave the art piece its value. It can also be pictured in the English statement "I created havoc in the store" meaning a disruptive situation or "I created an atmosphere of cooperation between the two rivals" meaning a condition of peace. It is describing role, function, or purpose. The point the Genesis account is making is God brought the cosmos into function defining existence by separating, naming, and assigning purpose and intent. When differentiating, naming, and purpose are ordered—one is valued.

Time & Creation

This quote was on a piece of wall art in which Ruth Graham said, "Fear not tomorrow...God is already there (Graham, R. 2010)." Is there a tomorrow with God? A Yesterday? Or today? Or are these divisions of time for our purposes only? These divisions are enumerators or methods of defining change yet change is only relevant in time. Do yesterday, today, and tomorrow occupy space or are they only mental markers that exist only in our perception?

What about sacred and profane time? Are they also only mental markers that exist in our perception? Sacred and profane time are not periods of time but are aspects of time relating to God and man. We use such terms as present moment in which the markers of time are absent. Time seems to be a tightrope we walk from birth to death as linear notions of time impales our senses with a dimensional reality from subjective perception. Our reality comes from our senses as we go from heartbeat to heartbeat. Can man subjectively ascertain absolute truth? Perception does not offer a pure representation of the physical world because all sensory input must pass through neurological and cognitive filters causing different people to have varied subjective views. Therefore, can science claim objective findings which have been processed through subjective lens? As such, can people know the physical world through human perception?

Modern historians separate the accounts of Genesis indicating they were written in different times. The first account found in chapter one is the Elohistic text which says the world was created in six days by Elohim who then rested from creation on day seven. Genesis two is the Jehovistic text in which the God of Israel creates man to inhabit an earthly paradise. The Elohistic account is similar to the Babylonian epic "The Enuma Elish" in the 18th Century BC which told the story of a struggle of the Creator whom the Babylonians called Marduk and Chaos which has now become personified and describes the creation as a progressive sequence of developments between them.

If creation is regarded as an event, then it is assumed to have taken place at a point in times past on a specific day based on the western mind's concept of linear time. This forces another question as to what existed before creation? In the 4th Century, the Bishop of Milan, St Ambrose wrote in his work *Hexameron (Six Day*

Creation): "In the beginning of time, therefore, God created heaven and earth. Time proceeds from this world, not before the world (Ambrose, Hexaemeron, I, 6:20)." Rather than exploring "Time minus X" western religion says it does not nor cannot exist. Can we explore creation from other than a temporal viewpoint? Is it possible to envision "zero time"? The closest to the Big Bang as time approaches zero is Planck's constant which is time of zero plus 10^{-43} seconds later. It is scientifically accepted that the universe began approximately 13.8 billion years ago. The extreme conditions out of which space, time, light, and matter developed seem to be beyond the reach of current science. In the Big Bang, at "Time=0," an explosion occurred but could not have occurred in the absence of matter in the concept propagated by creation out of nothing. Since the closest one can come to "Time = 0" is 10^{-43} seconds from zero, which is one preceded by forty-three zeros, the first milliseconds of life are more appropriately described in terms of energy and temperature rather than time. Interestingly, to see backward scientists look forward. The Big Bang does not necessarily tell us the age of the universe but more correctly the duration of cosmic evolution which is the length of time since the end of the Planck era which is between 10^{-43} and 10^{-32} seconds after the big bang in which the cosmos consisted of early particles bound by a primordial force. Next, gravity separated from itself and the infinite temperature fell 10^{27} degrees. Another separation of forces occurred revealing the elusive Higgs boson—the God particle. Looking forward to see backward is graphed as one accurately measures the expansion of the universe which is the speed at which galaxies are moving away from each other. Did God call the explosion to occur when he declared "Let there be light" which were not the luminaries but a cosmic reaction that is still reacting billions of years later?

In considering the metric of time, how is time measured? Like the tree falling in the forest, if no one sees it fall does it make a sound? In the same analogical concept, if no human is around does time pass? John Alexander Gunn said, "time does not create events, but events create time (Weinert 2013, 111)." Said another way, time is the measurement between experiences, events, or some stimulus to the senses. My premise then, is time was not created but simply began to be marked. The passage of time is a product of human consciousness and would cease being marked if humanity were not present. In other words, the sole metric of time is the mind.

Mystic Views of Creation and Time

Rabbi Lawrence Kushner's novel, *Kabbalah A Love Story*, is an excellent book that introduces several premises of Kabbalah in story form. He weaves the plot around ancient documents such as the *Zohar* and other writings in which he describes the Kabbalah concepts of creation in modern occurrences. In the beginning of the story, Rabbi Kalman and his high school astronomy teacher were having a discussion in cosmology and the teacher remarks if one could take a trip to the event horizon one would not see a sphere of earth but as time reverses, as one exceeds the speed of light one would only see a point of light.

This point of light is considered a spark of infinite density containing everything yet to come including galaxies, planets, civilizations, centuries, and people; everything from this single point outside of time. The Kabbalah reiterates the spark was a dimensionless point, a pin prick of light reflecting the world that is yet to come indicating creation is now and in the very moment. This infinite density is the beginning or formation of God's intent. Kushner offers one of the greatest teachings of the Zohar indicating creation is ubiquitous and continuous meaning ever present, found everywhere, and in all times (Kushner 2006, 24, 40-41, 112-113, 156-160).

Through Kabbalah eyes, a wide view of the Greek Logos is also displayed. Midrash speaks of the light that is hidden throughout creation. In Hebrew, it is called *Ohr Ha-Ganuz* or hidden light. This light is conveyed in Genesis One as the light God called into being days before the creation of the natural light of the luminaries. This light created before the sun was said to be some seventy times brighter than the sun. When Adam and Eve were created on day six they never even noticed the sun in the heavens. The light was so bright that in its radiance they could see from one end of creation to the other end of time and in this light, nothing was concealed from them. The Midrash says of this light: "The light the Holy One created during the work of creation shone from one end of space to the other end of time" but it was hidden away. Midrash goes on to say it is "through this light the world endures. Every single day a ray issues from that hidden light and sustains the entire world. Through it the Holy One nourishes creation (Kushner 2006, 71)."

Cosmology and Time: Cosmogony and No Time

Aristotle said matter cannot be created nor destroyed. There can be no absolute beginning of motion as it was *nous* (mind) that set the universe in motion. Time is intimately related to motion and does not have a beginning yet Plato says time came about at the same instance as the heavens. Aristotle's "now" excludes a beginning for time as the present moment was a midpoint of beginning and end. It was the beginning of future time and the end of past time.

Augustine believed an omnipotent God creates everything in heaven and earth out of nothing. It is God who generates time and motion where there was none before. God created all things simultaneously and if so creation is static and finished rather than dynamic and living. It is from the early Christian thinkers that we get the notion that God created time when He created space and matter. Augustine says "The world was generated with time, but not in time. What is generated in time is generated both before and after other times. Before is past time, after is future time. No time passed though before the world (Gregory 2013, 212)."

Walton considers the creation of day and night or the ordering of day and night is the creation of time and it is functional creation rather than a material creation (Walton 2009, 55). He explains the sun is not a function of creation but rather has function in the creative process. Creation is an act of separating or differentiating for functional purposes not dividing which is making more than one (Walton 2009, 55). Incidentally, separating and differentiating is a qualitative process while dividing is a quantitative process. The Human body a perfect analogy as each cell divides and becomes differentiated to function as an organ and a system, from a single cell. Walton's primary premise in the purpose of the Creator is simply not to bring forth materials but forming and ordering them to function in such a way that they work. But to whose standard? The Creator (Potter) or the created (clay)? It is the task of the Creator who establishes the functionality to effectively keep the operation going. The celestial bodies are to serve humanity as the Creator purposed them to reveal signs, seasons, days, and years in governing the day and night as seen in the psalmist's announcement of the heavens declaring the glory of God.

One of the most important imprints from Greek philosophy is the recovered link between time and cosmology. Augustine said, and it seems a weak point but is really profound when deeply considered, we can be aware of time and measure it only when it is passing and once it is passed; it no longer is and therefore cannot be measured. Greek philosophy gave us the concept that time is coming out of what no longer exists, passing through what has no duration, and moving into what does not yet exist. The mind functions as the sole metric of time as it measures and notes the flow of time. It was Ian Barbour who said, "Time is truly nothing but a measure of intrinsic change (Weinert 2013, 165)."

Creation, then, is not an occurrence in space and time but is potentially everywhere at all times. There is no single point of beginning. Ayn Sof procreated or called into being a spark that was not yet light and a womb which was to contain all possibilities of a world that was yet to come. Did the Greeks rename it chaos?

Tohu wa Bohu

"The Heavens Declare the Glory of God;
The Skies Proclaim the Work of His Hands."
Psalm 19:1

When did *tohu wa-bohu* or the primordial elements become the chaos of Hellenistic thought? Chaos has come to mean lost, desolate, without hope, and evil. Tohu wa-bohu was a description or condition of existent matter; a condition of the earth (*aretz*) and the deep (*tehom*). Chaos was paired with tohu wa-bohu in the early Greek Ophitic writings according to Irenaeus, who portrayed the elements separated from each other as each element sought primacy and from this battle of elemental supremacy spirit was borne according to Irenaeus' *Against Heresies*. Quintus Aurelius Symmachus (c. 345 – 402 AD), who translated the Hebrew text into Greek, indicated the phrase was linked to Hellenistic chaos as the earth became "unwrought and indiscriminate (Kister 2007, 12)" as found in his work *Symmachus in the Pentateuch* which Origen later used when he did a comparison of works with the Septuagint in his work titled *Hexapla* meaning Six Translations (Jewish Encyclopedia 2016).

Tohu wa-bohu, the primordial elements, and creatio ex nihilo are three ideas of the creation of the cosmos which carry a very different conceptual trail as each provides a divergent portrait of the Creator. In this triplet, it is generally assumed that tohu wa-bohu describes the condition before God commanded "Let there be..." The phrase tohu wa-bohu translated in the Septuagint is rendered unseen because it was covered by water according to Josephus in *Antiquities of the Jews*, and darkness and unconstructed (Kister 2007, 24) offered by Basil in *Hexameron*. The *Jewish Aramaic Tagumim* translates the expression as "the land was desolate and empty (Kister 2007, 3)." In extra biblical literature tohu wa-bohu as well as other primordial elements existed outside the boundaries of the universe. Jewish Mysticism indicates tohu wa-bohu was not replaced by the creation but was simply pushed by creation carving out a space as the *Sepher Yetzirah* indicates (Kaplan 1997, 75). The *Qumran Scrolls*, in particular the War Scroll, indicated the phrase tohu wa-bohu along with the ancient concept of darkness was a matrix or birthing chamber pushing against creation. Most ancient civilizations equated evil to be an echo of chaos and it was believed evil spirits originated when the breath of God met the primordial elements and they resisted. *The Dead Sea Scrolls* also carried the idea tohu wa-bohu was associated with evil. The concept is seen in Isaiah 45:7 as the writer recorded God saying, "He makes peace and creates evil" and the following phrase as "He forms light and he creates darkness." The Hebrew and Aramaic flow indicate these words describe the state of the earth or "her mood (Kister 2007, 4)" and further imply the earth was "bewildered, amazed, and frightened (Kister 2007, 4)" as expressed by Origen who renders bohu as having an element of fear (Kister 2007, 4). This element of fear arose in translations through mysticism and Gnosticism in response to the action of the Logos on the elements. Also, because evil was thought to be an echo of chaos, it refused the effects of the breath of God. Tohu wa-bohu seemed to be a figurative description of the condition of tehom/deep before the constructive Ruach/Logos of God. In other words, it was the condition before God orders and structures.

Does Genesis one describe the primordial elements such as the darkness and the abyss as existent before creation? Were they eternal, coexistent with God? The belief that the primordial elements out of which the cosmos emerged was pre-existent is shared by many ancient cultures as shown in their cosmology. In consideration of their existence with God in such that God was not the only eternal being is contrary to monotheistic thought. Yet the idea that the primordial elements being created by God was not sourced in traditional Judaic doctrine for several centuries either. A Samaritan writing found in the work *Literary and Oral Tradition of Hebrew and Aramaic Amongst the Samaritans* by Z. Ben-Hayyim reads, "You created the world without any partner. You drew from it creatures from where there was nothing" setting up "creatio ex nihilo (Kister 2007, 18)."

David T. Tsumura said the expression tohu wa-bohu was usually translated without form and void and was considered the direct opposite of creation. Tsumura indicated the phrase had nothing to do with primeval chaos but simply meant emptiness referring to the earth in a bare state without vegetation, animals, and humans. Early in the development of Christianity, the interpretation for tohu wa-bohu was generally understood as formlessness and was generally translated as confusion, unreality, emptiness, or nothingness (Tsumura 1989, 20). William Foxwell Albright in 1924 published a work that indicated the Hebrew account in Genesis was in opposition to the Mesopotamian myth and concluded that tohu wa-bohu meant chaos equating it with watery deep or tehom (Tsumura 1989, 20). Levenson implied the Genesis account indicated tohu wa-bohu meant disorder or disorganization being antithetical to creation (Levenson 1988, 53-65). The word bohu was always paired with tohu and appeared to be a Semitic term, meaning from the Hebrew, Arabic, Aramaic, and Akkadian languages, based on the root *bhw* and linked to the Arabic *bahiya* whose concrete meaning was an empty tent rather than the abstract meaning of nothingness or void (Tsumura 1989, 18). The Akkadian equivalent word *nabalkutu* was referenced to the earth and spoke of the earth's womb in the sense of the earth being out of functional order, barren and unproductive rather than in disarray (Tsumura 1989, 92, 135).

Etymological traces indicate it meaning to be a waste or desert (waterless) in Arabic. Because of its meaning of formlessness, confusion, unreality, emptiness, and nothingness; the assertion became chaos—without order. The Mesopotamian cosmic structure carries a sense of an undifferentiated, unorganized, confused lifeless agglomeration which later came to be chaos being an opposition to creation. The Ancient Hebrew concepts offer a different perception of tohu wa-bohu in that it refers to emptiness or vacancy such as a tent or house that does not contain furniture or household goods necessary to make the tent or house function as a home. How could historically defined words change in meaning? Compare them to our current vernacular of the following pairs of words. If I said I needed some bread do I mean the stuff a sandwich is made with or money. When granny asks for sugar did she mean a kiss on the cheek or something to sweeten her tea. And now, when the usually well-dressed lady said her hair is a hot mess she means chaotic and disheveled. Therefore, using a summary of Hebrew, Ugatic, Arabic, and Akkadian semantics it points to a fuller meaning of tohu wa-bohu being "the dysfunction of the earth's womb (Tsumura 1989, 27)" as being barren and unproductive and non-functional rather than a place of chaos and disorder.

Tsumura also asserts these ancient concepts were far removed from the meaning of chaos as generally accepted in orthodox descriptions. Tohu wa-bohu was a description of tehom. The implication from ancient languages was the earth was unable to produce, being barren in the womb. Chaos was not loss of order but rather no order standing as a receptacle of potential awaiting the command of God to be. Chaos was a condition not substance or matter.

Creatio Ex Nihilo stood as the prevailing doctrine in church history in support of a God who was omnipotent, omnipresent, and omniscient. In the idea of creation coming from nothing, or no matter; if it can be named such as tehom, or the deep then it was not no-thing. Vail tied the doctrine of creatio ex nihilo to Judaism who were trying to protect God's omnipotence which became prominent after the second century in response to gnostic philosophers. The doctrine was sealed in orthodoxy by the pens of Basilides, Theophilus, and Irenaeus who maintained God's creative activity is free from any pre-existent substance (Vail 2009). It strongest supporter was perhaps Augustine who fathered many of the long-standing tenets in the Christian faith. Augustine also said "You did not work as a human craftsman does, making one thing out of something else as his mind directs. Your Word alone created [heaven and earth] (Augustine, Confessions XI,5)." In contemporary thought this statement can be translated as before

"Time equals 0" in which the singularity of space, time, matter, and motion did not exist. There was simply nothing which is another term for infinite density. Nothing is not an empty space or an area of non-existence nor can it be a place void of God.

Vail says Gerhard May's work declared the doctrine arose from Christianity's own ideas locked in God's sovereignty and unlimited freedom using the Greek concept of world formation (Vail 2009, 5). Levenson rejects the claims of a clear notion of creation out of nothing (Levenson 1988, xiii) which was supported by a modern translation of Genesis 1:1 as "In the beginning God created the heavens and the earth" which he said has been doubted since the Middle Ages and has fallen out of favor with scholars. He deemed a more accurate translation was sourced from E. A. Speiser in his 1964 commentary who favors the grammatical concepts of the second millennium interpretation of Rashi who was Rabbi Shlomo Yitzhaki or Solomon ben Isaac (1040-1105) and lived, like many Jews, in Northern France. He translated Genesis 1:1 as "When God set about to create heaven and earth—the world being a formless waste, with darkness over the seas and only an awesome wind sweeping over the water—God said, 'Let there be light' (Levenson 1988, 157n)"

Levenson says the waters were a symbol of chaos having no beginning and the waters stand as "the ancient and enduring opposition to the full realization of God's mastery whose opposition is destined to be eliminated at the turn of the aeon (Levenson 1988, 38)." He posits chaos was an anarchical entity challenging God's supremacy and was a real power presenting a continuous possibility adding that chaos was dark, ungodly, and evil. Levenson goes on to say that creation was a defeat of the forces which interrupted order thus forming chaos into order (Levenson 1988, 22). Yet God did not defeat these forces in creation but confined them (Levenson 1988, 17). They persisted as chaos or evil and sought expression in any available portal including humanity thus indicating chaos or evil was persistent in the cosmos. In Levenson's view, the created world was a safe and secure world indicating God's creative act was not a once upon a time idea but an ongoing operation of maintenance as creation in process.

The Jewish concept of creation was different from the Greek idea. The Hebrew mind was focused on the God of the cosmos rather than the cosmos itself. The Old Testament saw natural phenomena primarily as pointers to God who created them and whose glory was revealed through them as the psalmist declared in chapter 19. Yet in contrast to other ancient cosmogonies and according to most contemporary pastors and teachers, the book of Genesis points to an absolute beginning or a definitive starting point of creation.

The doctrine of creatio ex nihilo has no real etymological support from the Bible. In scrutiny of the cosmological order and as considered earlier, it was necessary for the early church to support the biblical view of divine omnipotence and was accepted by Judaism in the late middle ages. This doctrine found footing as 2nd century church theologians who rejected creation out of chaos due in part as a gnostic counter response to Marcion who propagated the concept of matter as being below spirit and inherently evil. Joseph Brown said, "Evil takes on many faces however, like divinity, its only reflection is in the mirror of humanity. The manifestation and acts of both are played out in the affairs of men rather than in some ethereal realm (Mark Eaton, e-mail message to author, November 20, 2011)". Evil is only evidenced as a reflection and is only seen in man. This concept removes evil from anything spiritual or divinely instigated and places it in the realm of creation of or by mankind: in the same arena in which chaos was entombed by an evil connotation. Creation out of nothing offered God an out in handling evil and restoring his goodness in the affairs of humanity. The explanation of evil required the creation out of nothing doctrine to segregate God from evil alleviating Him as its cause but it did not succeed.

Chaos

"Cosmos is a Greek word for the order of the universe.
It is, in a way, the opposite of Chaos. It implies the deep interconnectedness of all
things. It conveys awe for the intricate and subtle way in which the universe is
put together."
(Carl Sagan 2016)

The Greek term for order was *cosmos* while *chaos* generally meant disorder. But the Greek concept of cosmos also references a rising of something new by adding quality suggesting formation, ordering, and an organizing element. Pythagoras used cosmos as the wholeness of the universe as he recognized an order which governed the whole. Yet, the idea of mathematical order is much older coming from ancient Egypt and older civilizations. This view suggests cosmos is the ordering of the initial state of chaos and later the concept was amended to include the ordering agent identified by the Greek word nous being thought or reason of the divine mind.

Various views of chaos exist but are built on a rather unbalanced foundation of the word as it passed from Hellenistic sources which added a darker and sinister representation. Depending on whether chaos is a created element or exists autonomously will support or destroy a supposed relationship between chaos and God. There are other views that consider chaos neutral being neither negative nor evil and neither positive nor good. Still more concepts consider it an anticreative anarchical force that resists order and stands in opposition to creation, and coming to the Greek biblical context in which it is a void, a nothingness, an abyss where God is absent. In the biblical concept, God begins calling chaos to order, resulting in the structure and establishment of its boundaries. Does God conquer it or work with it separating, dividing, and differentiating matter?

The Greek poet Hesiod believed chaos was the first thing to have existed and according to etymology means "the yawning and void receptacle for created matter (Pember 1971, 19)." Incidentally, a receptacle functions as a receiver or container, a placeholder. Did chaos pre-exist or come into being? Is it a primordial agent that God orders? Or is chaos an anarchical force that resists order and opposes creation? Theologically, chaos was defined as a formless and void state rather than a place. Yet it was a place that preceded creation of the cosmos in the Greek creation myths. Pember says chaos lost its etymological meaning and was replaced by without form and void as the crude shapeless disorder from which the universe was born (Pember 1971, 19). This idea hints at God taming chaos forcing it into obedience and the changing of this word pointing to chaos as evil and disobedient promoting the notion of evil being ever present waiting for a breach to rise and exert diabolic influence in the affairs of humanity.

Susan Niditch indicated chaos is to be understood not as disorder but as no order (Niditch 1985, 17). Disorder is a loss of order which was once possessed while no order means never having experienced order. Her precepts support the validity of myths expressing experience rather than strict creation myths as a means of information sharing. She says, "creation is not only the act of causing to be but also a process of ordering and maintaining that which has become (Niditch 1985, 13)." In this idea, Genesis tells of a progression from chaos to cosmos if read from a linear, historical, and literal standpoint. This linear path traces a pattern of violence and repeated disobedience giving civilizations a sense of separation of humanity from humanity and humanity from divinity (Niditch 1985, 63) and the focus becomes repairing the perceived breach that marred relationship rather than seeking to further understand the Creator and purpose of being. She says the creation after this pattern was not a paradise, but a creation of "potentially good reality (Niditch 1985, 71)," man now sought to build relationships rather than knowing one was always present; offering man a good creation rather than a perfect one.

The receptacle was empty awaiting a filling up, an expressive act of purpose and function. What is the missing etymological piece? The earliest Greek concepts (before 700 BC) portray chaos as the container for all matter. Later Greek translations removed the Hebraic concept of chaos and tohu wa-bohu as a state of being to a state of physical matter. Chaos and its descriptor tohu wa-bohu were the primordial state of unfulfilled potential that births or morphs physical matter. In this sense then, chaos which was not purposed and functional held a positive connotation as order residing *in potentia* awaiting the command to be.

Law & Chaos

While the Greek meaning of Logos carries the concept of words it is more than that. It also refers to the inherent power or energy in those words to produce an effect. In this concept, language is a tool of law functioning as an enforcer. If language is ill-used or misunderstood then it inadvertently enforces a law which destroys by falsely distancing the parties. How? If myth is utilized to enhance language then law is emasculated, or in other words judgment is moot. In traditional concepts of chaos, it is the law which must order and align chaos to establish order and this idea arises because the law fails to be differentiated as cosmic (declarative) or manmade (judgmental). It is the law that always points back to perceived separation and portrays duality between divinity and humanity. In the midst of law, language instills fear and guilt arising from judgment. In order to calm the fear and allay the guilt the law is formulated and judges enforcing punishment rather than correction. How? By being obedient to the law, formulated to appease the law giver. When myth enhances language, man hears decrees rather than judgment. In judgment chaos loses potential and sinks to disorder.

Chaos is not an enemy of the cosmos for out of it a higher order appears and this result is not a onetime event at "the beginning" but an ongoing process or continuously beginning. This process is all inclusive of all systems from the tiniest atom to the largest galaxy. The cosmos is not a clock or closed process but a game in which there are multiple paths to a universal goal. In this game, a multitude of random processes of chance and serendipity allow room for human choices, individuality, and unpredictable creativity.

There is no detailed blueprint or rulebook for the universe which allows for a creation of continuous beginning in process influenced by a multifaceted humanity nor can there be. This idea is reiterated by physicist Paul Davies who states:

> There is no detailed blueprint, only a set of laws with an inbuilt facility for making interesting things happen. The universe is then free to create itself as it goes along. The general pattern of development is predestined, but the details are not. Thus, the

existence of intelligent life at some stage is inevitable; it is, so to speak, written into the laws of nature. But man, as such, is far from preordained (Davies 1988, 202).

This concept of cosmic creation represents a fractal order that welcomes an open process in a creation where all is not determined. Enjoy the game.

The law governing the cosmos was considered static or unchangeable due in part to Newton's Laws of Relativity which has stood for over 300 years, but now enter Quantum Theory. What is the source of Cosmic Law? There are more than twenty plus universal constants pointing to an ordered universe appearing out of chaos. But we see complete order on one dimension, but in fractal reality, there is a dimensional change and as you focus closely, another level/dimension appears; out of focus at first, in disarray, but potential is present. This is Quantum Theory. These numbers are givens and will not change and their values were assigned some 10^{-32} seconds after "Time = 0." Even though their value is unchangeable their functionality in the cosmos continuously produces a dynamic effect. What do I mean? These values do not change but their relationship in the cosmos is dynamic, living, and explorable. Chaos is unfulfilled potential awaiting to be and is filled with wonder and awe. For example, if you exceed the speed limit, you most likely will get a ticket. If you exceed the speed of light, time reverses, and you might see your birthday. Your first one! The constants are fundamental parameters functioning as pillars yet leaving infinite room for creativity and maintaining a high degree of order. Order does not mean a static unchanging cosmos but a structured one. Stable yet flexible in response to creativity and discovery.

The process governed by cosmological law is a declaration while the law of Moses, as any manmade law, is judgmental. In the operation of cosmic law, it calls order out of potential while the Law of Moses judges why chaos exists. Chaos does not contain negativity but simply a place or condition of potential and that potential is realized in the declaring yet is lost in the judging. The Logos causes the chaos to rise up and retain order becoming productive and functional. Cosmic law functions outside and regardless of time, while Moses' law only operates in time where judgment resides.

Chaos is not lawlessness or absence of law. Chaos is simply without purpose or dysfunction in line with understood law. Chaos may not follow a set of laws in the way that we perceive them, maybe because the law is unknown or not understood. Cosmic law did not arise from chaos but lets us know it exists or more correctly Cosmic law defines chaos. The law of Moses makes chaos a void of God (the earth was without form and void) but Cosmic Law sees it as a place cut out inside God (Sepher Yetzirah – God carved out a place to form creation.) Chaos is potential purpose while Cosmic law is realized purpose. Cosmic law is the visible and discoverable effects of the Logos exerted on chaos, while the law of Moses cannot see potential. Before God orders purpose and intention, chaos is neither good nor evil but full of potential. What God called "good" was not a reference to quality but that which he called good was about its ability to fulfill its purpose; its ability to function as so designed. Cosmic law points and defines purpose and function while the law of Moses highlights a perceived loss of purpose by causing an awareness of guilt and then establishing a path of repentance to return to order. Cosmic law affirms the Logos while the law of Moses imprisons and forces conditions on the Logos by manmade restrictions to explain man's perceived condition.

Double Chaos: Chaos Theory and Theology

Sjoerd Bonting believes scientific chaos is equal to primeval chaos which he says is uncreated and morally neutral yet acts as a source of creativity and evil. He suggests God is the one who established order from this chaos but some of it remains and continues to threaten creation in the form of natural evil which arises from the chaotic behavior of complex systems (Bonting 2005, 101, 136). Bonting acknowledges that God can act through chaotic events and in this view evil is sourced in chaos.

Chaos Theory has its origins in 1963 in the work of Edward Lorenz, a meteorologist from the Massachusetts Institute of Technology who posited the mathematical model of flow of atmospheric patterns and their sensitivity to various phenomena. Lorenz concluded that for weather forecasting, "...prediction of the sufficiently distant future is impossible by any method (Lorenz 1963)." In view of this inevitable incompleteness of weather observations, "...precise very-long-range weather forecasting would seem to be non-existent (Lorenz 1963)." As his results became known, others came to agree that the human ability to control the weather or even forecast it over the long term "was scientifically unfounded." It was his research in weather forecasting that birthed a similar concept in chaos theory known as the Butterfly Effect. The Butterfly Effect is a metaphorical expression of a general characteristic found in complex chaotic systems. The analogy is founded in an example of the fluttering of a butterfly's wing in Peking and as its effects cascade unpredictably through complicated systems will have a very large effect later in time perhaps producing a thunderstorm in New York. It is a concept that shows the effects of the "sensitive dependence of initial conditions (Lorenz 1963)" on events in a complex system.

This effect is also visible in the flow of gases and liquids through the atmosphere, the behavior of certain chemical equations, electronic circuits, the human heartbeat, the spread of diseases through a population, the formation of patterns and fractures in metallic and crystalline surfaces, the stock market, and the formation of snowflakes. The formation of snow and its predictability in Arkansas is perhaps the most difficult for meteorologists to forecast as specific initial conditions must be met and maintained. In each of these examples, very small changes early in the system can produce dramatic and erratic unpredictable behavior at some point later in time.

Another avenue of research in chaos ideologies is seen in the 1970's by Bernard Mandelbrot, an IBM employee in New York. He is credited with forging the new field of mathematics that he called fractal geometry. He used the term fractal in reference to the highly specific and varied patterns of natural forms such as that seen in snowflakes, clouds, the coastline, and the jagged pattern of lightening. He expressed traditional Euclidean geometry had forced the eyes to measure in straight lines and gentle curves and fractal geometry offered mathematicians a new perspective allowing him to see nature in its highly complex yet orderly forms (Davis, 2002, 75-76). It was these concepts which revoked the Newtonian ideas of the predictable "clockwork universe" that has driven research for the last 300 years. His premises add a level of knowledge indicating there is chaos in order and more surprisingly there is order in chaos.

Bonting links Chaos Theory with the Butterfly Effect and Mandelbrot's principle with Theology and offers Chaos Theology (Bonting 2005, ix). He posits his ideology on two worldviews which he labels the theological and scientific. The scientific worldview seeks to answer the how questions while the theological aspect answers the why. In this picture, creation resides on the side of theology while cosmic evolution finds its place in the scientific aspect. Bonting projects two worldviews of a single reality describing the cosmos in a multifaceted methodology. Both worldviews have their limitations in that the scientific model does not deal with the beyond but it deals with the mechanisms foregoing purpose. Theology offers very little about the mechanics of the universe but fully responds to purpose. Bonting suggests the universe is "not the rational order of the Greek cosmos but a divinely decreed harmony in which each creature fulfills the will of the Creator (Bonting 2005, 55)." Greek Cosmology sees the celestial bodies as independent deities who influence human life but Bonting points out that these bodies are the servants of God who function for man. He goes on to say that God did not create by destroying chaos but by ordering it; by pushing back chaos in three separations, differentiations, or dimensions; those being light from darkness, the heavens from the waters, and the land from the sea as seen in Genesis Gen 1:3-10 (Bonting 2005, 53).

This concept of separation is paralleled in current cosmology as seen in time and space, the four fundamental forces In these comparisons, we see a stage set for the ordering process leading to the appearance of the heavenly bodies including galaxies, stars, and planets; and on earth living things such as plants, animals, and humans. Bonting sees this as "initial creation (Bonting 2005, 58-60, 96)" for the separation phase and the term 'continuing creation' for the ordering phase. Continuing Creation implies that the universe is good (functional) but not yet perfect. He goes on to surmise in theological terms the primordial chaos is diminished but not obliterated during the creation process. The prospect of an initially perfect creation that was damaged by a human fall which will be later restored by a merciful God on the last day is both theologically and scientifically untenable according to Bonting (Bonting 2005, 166-172).

Dr. Bonting fully rejects the creatio ex nihilo doctrine based on compatibility with today's scientific discoveries and a re-evaluation of scriptural interpretation. He points out the Big Bang Theory describes an initial explosion at "Time = 0" which required pre-existing energy and various physical laws, or all combined which in no way represents nihil or nothingness as usually perceived (Bonting 2005, 71). He stresses the doctrine is not included in the Apostles Creed, the Nicene Creed, the Athanasian Creed, nor in any texts of the Councils from Nicaea (325) to Chalcedon (451). He goes on to say it was Theophilus who introduced the concept to early Christianity. Bonting's Logos is God's creative agent (Bonting 2005, 57-58, 145) and not a person as Justin Martyr nor created as Arius believed but an energized expression of God. F. J. Mayers paints a beautiful Hebraic concept of the condition of nihil in the presence of creativity. He says:

> In the infinite 'nothingness' which preceded the manifest universe, there must have existed in potentiality some causal entity or form that is by nature unknowable, and perhaps not readily distinguishable from Eternity. All that is, or ever was, or will be. It did not exist materially, therefore, it must have existed in Spiritual Being. That Spirit Being in whom lay the potentiality of All things was, by ancient Hebrew philosophy denominated 'Ayn Soph;' the as yet un-manifested and, therefore, the 'Unknown God' (Mayers 1948, 11).

John Walton surmises "in the beginning" was not a point in time but a period of time (Walton 2009, 43). The creative process according to the ancient world was invoked by naming, separating, and assigning functions and roles in an ordered system (Walton

2009, 46-49). He says the beginning state of Genesis one was non-functional and it's the starting point of being tohu wa-bohu; it was unproductive rather than without physical form (Walton 2009, 47) or evil. Then, why was tohu wa-bohu translated as absence of material form? Walton says it is because religion considers Genesis one to be an account of material creation rather than functional creation (Walton 2009, 120) seeing a creation of how rather than why. A cosmological image rather than a cosmogonical one. The cosmos was functionless, there was potential energy—there was the quantum Logos but God had not yet breathed. Then tohu wa-bohu responded to Ruach of God as He said, "Let there be..."

A fractal is an element in a set whose parts have the same character as the whole. The part reproduces the whole. In a funhouse of mirrors, you see yourself reflected over and over in the mirrors in an endlessly smaller scale. The mirrors are repeating a reflection of your image across multiple dimensions or scale. As the image dimensions change they remain identical in a mathematical term called "self-similar."

In similar fashion to the Mandelbrot Set, if you look at the earth from space, you see the round orb called earth, then you focus on North America, the East coast, New York, Manhattan, and finally Wall Street. As the magnification or dimension changes you see in finer detail and each dimension is ordered and logical. The lines, curves, and shapes become more detailed on each magnification yet beneath that particular dimension lies another one. Fractals have implications in math, logic, music, as well as metaphysics, cosmology, and theology. Paul said, "now you are Christ's body and individually parts of it (1 Cor. 12:27)." Good theology then is a fractal. It will maintain perennial principles throughout its parts and in all dimensions. Fractal theology removes the concept of "a beginning" for the deeper dimension of continuous beginnings.

Chaotic Evil & Creation Out of Chaos

According to Janet Warren, chaos has three meanings. Chaos, in common usage is complete disorder. In ancient literature including the Bible, chaos is set opposite to cosmos and because it stands as a paradox to order it carries the connotation of evil as evil is symbolized by darkness, the abyss, and of course chaos. In science, chaos describes that which on the surface seems to be unordered but is actuality under the control of established universal constants (Warren 2011).

Paul Ricoeur offers his definition of myth by saying it is not an explanation by means of images and fables, but a traditional narration of events that happened at the beginning of time whose purpose is to provide a basis for the ritual actions of man. Also, the myth is a form of thought by which man understands himself in his world as he describes his perception and experience of evil in cosmogenic, Adamic, tragic, and the exiled soul seeking return (Ricoeur 1967, 5). Ricoeur describes four mythical types found in ancient societies as they understand the problem of evil. The first one he calls "the drama of creation and the ritual vision of the world (Ricoeur 1967, 175-179)" which is the traditional dualistic view of the age-old conflict between good and evil. Creation is the work of the good god struggling with evil chaos. In this vein, humanity cannot be blamed for the origin of evil but entertaining it and propagating it by not exercising control. He awaits the good god to overcome evil at the end of the world. This type of myth serves to retell the demise of evil in creation. The second vein he titles "the Adamic myth and the eschatological vision of history (Ricoeur 1967, 232-235, 173)" which is an anthropological account of the human fault, the classical fall narrative. There are three characteristics linked to this type. First, the origin of evil rests with a human ancestor. Second, it serves to set up an origin of evil distinct from primordial matter. Third, though there are other agents in the story such as the serpent and the tree, the central theme is to order all humanity in a central figure, Adam, who becomes the federal head for humanity. Salvation in this view comes not by ritual but through a linear history. Creation is completed and recedes to a cosmological background as the drama of sin and restoration takes the lead role and are played out in the world with the final work of salvation reserved for the last day. Here, creation is complete, but realized salvation is yet in the future. The third vein he calls "the wicked god and the tragic vision of existence (Ricoeur 1967, 173, 211-214, 216)" and this view is the world of Greek tragedy in which the fate of humanity rests by the initiated first cause as mankind is at the whim of the puppet master. The fourth vein of Ricouer's myth is "the myth of the exiled soul and salvation through knowledge (Ricoeur 1967, 279-305)." This type is a dualistic anthropological type which divides the human into soul and body. Evil is an inheritance infecting all and suffering comes through the soul, being the true self trapped in the physical body. The soul, not being from this realm, leads an occultic existence in the body of an exiled being longing for a return to origin and liberated from death in the body. Salvation is through knowledge or awakening that is applied freeing the imprisoned soul.

Did these mythical types affect our concepts of chaos? Of course. Vail discusses the various frameworks from which definitions of chaos have risen. In the first frame, he says chaos lacks a precise definition in theological studies as it tends to be used to designate various pre-creation conditions and is often linked to evil (Vail 2009, 210). He goes on to say most theological circles reject any suggestion of anything that pre-exists God's creative activity adding there is no pre-existent form, force, power, or matter or even another part of God that is called chaos; setting up the necessary parameters for creation out of nothing. The second frame is offered by Catherine Keller who says creation sprang from tehom or the watery deep. Her view of chaos is neither before or after creation nor existent or non-existent but rather "of-creation (Vail 2009, 212)." Her vein of thought implies chaos is inclusive of the process of creativity as that which was created springs from it. Framework three links chaos with disorder requiring God's creative activity. This realignment points to the work of creating as achieving and sustaining a "comprehensible structural arrangement (Vail 2009, 212)." This creative process indicates ordering and structuring are the telos (purpose) of God's creative activity. Bound within chaos are all aspects of good and evil. It is God who establishes order out of chaos such as light from the dark and sets bounds to the boundless simply by His word. Therefore, creation is a correction or reset of chaos resulting in the redemption of chaos.

What about chaos and evil in day to day experience? Can we experientially say that God is a God of order? Do our life's experiences reflect complete order? Or put another way, can we say that order reigns in the Christian description of an overcomers life? These questions pose a difficulty in answering them due to the fabricated link with chaos and evil, and because of this paradigm we cannot see beauty in chaos from the standpoint of the traditional definition because we tend to link evil with disorder. Our concepts of God are effected by our environment pointing to the fact that derived theology tends to be localized and to have a more accurate view of God we need to make a distinction between God and our understanding of God. The instant we make our concepts of God an absolute, we have fashioned an idol in a box.

The Old Testament writers perceived God's breath as not always good as found in Psalm 18:13-15 (ESV) where a rebuke issued from the "blast of the breath" of God's nostrils. Also, it does not always provide peace as seen in Joel 2:28-31 (ESV) as it causes cosmic terrors in the sky. According to the Old Testament authors, God could create a perfect chaos or an imperfect one or so it seems. Is this perhaps the contemporary concept of the insurance industry as an act of God when describing natural disasters? One must remember the Biblical myths are related to us through their lens as they understood God's intrusion in physical space, time, and matter.

The concept of creation ex nihilo places the source of evil on God's shoulders threatening the goodness of God. The oldest concept even in early Christianity is creation out of chaos being the matter from which the cosmos was structured. Process Theism proclaims chaos was not passive matter resisting the divine will but was creative activity—potential energy. This cosmic view proposes that from small life to the movement of the celestial bodies, all are related to each other in such ways that all movements and experiences propel the process onward.

The Cosmogonical Principle: Cosmic Harmony

"The Logos is God's likeness, by whom the whole cosmos was fashioned."
Philo of Alexandria

Lee Smolin said, "whether the talk is of God or of an eternal and universal Law of Nature, the idea that dominates is that the rationality responsible for the coherence we see around us is not in the world but behind it (Smolin 1997, 194)." Interestingly, when discussing such a principle there are two schools of thought. One lacking interest of distant galaxies with a sole concern for that which brings comfort and hope now versus the idea that cosmology effects the entire physical realm of our existence and the thought of the distant star being part of us. I think the aspect that must diminish is the idea of a casual external observer and become aware of the story of the heavenly declaration found in Psalm 19 as inclusive of us and for us.

Astrology functioned as the language of the cosmos as man tells his story (history) while Astronomy was man's response to astrological measurements and identification. Its meaning across cultures testify to this as in Greek astrology (*astron-logos*) means "star words." In India, it means "science of light," in Japan it is the "yin yang way," and in China it is "sky patterns." Astrology, as a language, also encompasses the idea the stars are messengers, revelators of long ago mysteries while astronomy is location of the storytellers. In these ancient cultures, the stars and the heavens were divine and could convey messages or omens on behalf of deity in the heavens. It was noted the stars operated in exact mathematical order indicating the Holder of that order was initiating the message to reach across the cosmos.

The key fundamental premise of astrology is that the cosmos is reflective of the earth acting as a mirror of heaven. The Chinese historian Xiaochun Sun said, "The Universe was conceived not as an object independent of man, but as a counterpart of and a mirror of human society (Campion 2012, 13)." This is carried through the occult or hidden science texts called the *Emerald Tablets* (Trismegistus 2013) and is conveyed in the Hermetic phrase "as above so below." It was from this concept that Egypt introduced the idea of conflict or cosmic struggle that existed between light and dark and other dualistic operational pairs. Egyptian cosmology says the cosmos is alive and endowed with personality and its counterpart, the human soul, being immortal would travel the stars. The journey to the stars was a central feature in Hellenistic cosmology and ultimately saw parallel support in the Christian belief of a journey to a celestial paradise. The purpose of the cosmos according to Chinese thought was "to explore the boundaries between heaven and man (Campion 2012, 99)."

Judaism sees a once only creation of a single cosmos by a patriarchal God whose Judaic purpose involved the cyclic themes of oppression, lawlessness, alienation, punishment, and redemption which produced regret, return, and forgiveness. Creation possessed a repetitive order that manifested relationally to God and Creation. This birthed the need for observation of laws and Sabbath rests stressing the observance of patterns in time marked by the celestial bodies which closely followed the cyclic themes. These laws, allowing for the achievement of certain goals by obedience, were tied to the flow of time. Importance was attached to the celebration of festivals in the Hebrew calendar measured by the sun-moon cycle as each week represented a complete cycle from birth to maturity.

It was the Greek mind that gave us the idea of a cosmos as a portrait of beautiful order. Plato viewed the cosmos as emanating from a single Creator, a supreme consciousness or mind rather than a personal God; thus, the entire cosmos was intelligent, divine, and conscious. It was a single living creature and all physical forms emerge from this soul. This world soul was the organizing principle of the cosmos and is the source of each individual soul according to ancient Greek worldviews.

In early Greek culture, Anaxagoras (497-428 BC) was the first Pre-Socratic Philosopher to give a cosmic intelligence or independent existence a role in cosmogony. It was his concepts that served as the precursor to Aristotle's nous which he said was the reason for the arrangement and order of everything (Stanford Encyclopedia of Philosophy 2015). Plato then adds the condition if nous withdraws its influence then there is no framework in place to maintain cosmic order (Campion 2012, 107) unable to sustain cohesiveness and function.

What is this Cosmic Principle, this cosmic glue that maintains order and function? I believe it is seen in the notion of Cosmic Harmony. Basil of Caesarea said:

> Before all those things which now attract our notice existed, God, after casting about in his mind and determining to bring into being that which had no being, imagined the world such as it ought to be, and created matter in harmony with the form which he wished to give it...He welded all the diverse parts of the Cosmos by levels of indissoluble attachment and established between them so perfect a fellowship and harmony that the most distant, in spite of their distance, appeared united in one universal sympathy (The Hexaemeron).

The harmony holding together the atom and the galaxy is visible in the cosmic system and brought about and maintained by "the magnificence of the Creator-Logos" according to Gregory of Nazianzus. The harmonic concept expressed in the Greek world finds a place in our Bible through Paul who said it is the Christ who holds all things together according to Colossians 1:17 and the Message translation adds "right up to this moment" indicating a continuous need of action. The Logos as cosmic harmony morphs all of creation into a functional whole. The cosmos reflects this harmony instituted by the Logos as the expressed act of the Ruach of God. Cosmic harmony is the operational balance of the scales of the universe.

Miriam Hillar conveys the intent of the Logos as carrying the meanings of philosophical thought as inward reason or intuitive perception and then projects that thought outwardly into manifestation (Hillar 2012, 6). The home of Logos in the Greek world of philosophy rests in the use as a rational, intelligent, and vivifying principle of the universe and was analogous to a living creature as the universe in Greek cosmology was a living reality requiring an infusion of life provided by the Logos (Hillar 2012, 6).

The Greek notion of harmony finds its origin in the monad,  dyad, and triad out of the understanding that more than two are required for harmony to manifest. These concepts represent the metaphysical trinity which is not personified but purposeful and functional. The monad's emanation is the initiation of the cosmos and source of order. The dyad represents diversity and opposing powers, duality of subject and object which when balanced produced harmony. The triad is the actual dynamic process in cosmogony. The triad represents the silencing of duality and when balanced the harmonic chord is produced. It silences the division, the more than one, by enhancing differentiation and varied functionality. The one is unification of all. The two is diversification and differentiation of the one. The three represented the harmonious chord struck by the Logos uniting the one and two thus demonstrating the functional power of Logos. In the above diagram through mathematical lens, unity is a set without elements, a null or void set yet waiting to be ordered and filled. It is the womb of creativity from which all manifests. The second structure is duality and is a set with two elements indicating not division but differentiation. The third structure is harmony and is a set with three elements functioning or harmonizing as one. Unity is not split increasing quantity but is specialized emanating quality.

The Logos' origin as God's thought and intent is eternal for all generations and not limited by time. It existed before the physical manifestation of all which is simply the secondary product of God's intent and therefore the Logos is called the firstborn of God. Philo says the Logos is more than a quality, power, or characteristic of God; it is also an entity and an eternally generated extension to which he ascribes various names and functions such as "the first-begotten Son of the uncreated Father (Hillar 2012, 58)." Philo also adds thoughts to the expression in the Old Testament of the Ruach of God as he says there is one that breathes, the breath itself, and finally, that which receives the breath. He says He who breathes is God, that which receives what is breathed is the mind, and the breath is spirit resulting in functional union of the three (Hillar 2012, 61). This is a prime example of the monad, dyad, and triad and the resulting harmonic function of the Logos as the bond of the universe stated in Colossians 1:17 when Paul says Christ is the glue holding all things together. The monad, dyad, and triad are representations of formation, separation, and naming that was accomplished in the creative process all stemming from the universal monadic set. The monad is the initiation of the cosmos as it proceeds to functionality through differentiation rather than the misapplied view of plurality focusing on quantity. The dynamics of differentiation is best portrayed in the maturation of the human cell. The human is produced from one cell which is maturated through differentiation and specialization to fully perform the intricate operations of the human being. The human possesses organs for site, hearing, taste, the heartbeat, and the lungs as each are specialized for a very specific function to sustain the body. Therefore, the division that occurred was not solely numeric in purpose, but even as one cell it possessed the internal potential of very specific yet diverse function. The triad silences duality and competition as balance is achieved and differentiation is enhanced as all parts function in a harmonic whole. The triad exhibits the dynamic process of cosmogony, while the dyad demonstrates cosmology as function not yet achieved, and the monad awaiting the command to be.

How did God begin ordering in Genesis chapter one? First, He breathed expressing intent then He separated, and then named thereby placing what was separated and named to its purpose. He placed elements in the monadic set and the dyad was formed. As it was energized by the Ruach they harmonized with their Creator, reaching the triad, becoming fully functional. An example is naming a room in a house and then going about separating it to begin to function what you named it. Remember our dining room turned into a library.

According to Hillar, it was Paul who sought to fuse the metaphysical Logos of the Greeks with the Hebraic Messiah and out of this union came the deification of the God-man resulting in a revelation on a cosmic level becoming the problem of the origins of Christianity (Hillar 2012, 151). It was this mingling of two worlds which led to an earthly political figure becoming a deity. To counteract the Gnostic and Philonic perceptions in the messianic community, John, the author of the 4th Gospel, introduced a dialogue which demonstrates Jesus was a human messenger and who became the embodiment of God's Logos.

The Voice Translation (Thomas Nelson 2012) places pronouns in Colossians 1:17 personifying the power that maintains the cosmos. The Logos or Christic origin was not a single personification. The Logos premise pre-existed physical creation, yet not in a natural sense but a metaphorical one. The physical creation is a by-product, the effect of a first cause in Greek thought. The cause was God breathed and the effect was physical creation. That moment which caused the draw of Breath was Logos—His thoughts and intents hit a crescendo and erupts into words, "Let there be." He thought and creation became and in this sense Logos preexisted creation being the firstborn of God. Thoughts have been long considered the firstborn of their originator. Here is an example from Moby Dick (Melville 1851, Ch. 17) in which Melville's Ishmael remarks "...hell is an idea first born on an undigested apple-dumpling." The telephone was considered the firstborn of Alexander Graham Bell. Philo, applying this ageless comparison, said the Logos is more than a quality or power of God it is also an entity and an eternally generated extension that he calls the first-begotten of God.

The first mention of the deification of Jesus is generally attributed to Ignatius, the bishop of Antioch in writings to the Roman Emperor Trajan around 98 CE often using the expression Jesus Christ our God or Jesus the Christ indicating Jesus was God. These expressions reinforced the prologue of the Fourth Gospel interpreted in a Hellenistic slant identified Jesus as the Son of God converting the Logos from a source or emanation to a person. The concept of the Logos of God becoming human as divinity intruded humanity is John's point but tradition accepts one man rather than humankind. According to Hillar, it was the melding in the first century of Messianic and Greek philosophical concepts of the Logos transforming Jesus into an intermediary between deity and humanity. In the next sequence of events it was this mediator being fully human who then was crucified for humanity. Hillar goes on to say, "John's theology is a creative living Christology which is still explored, formulated, and not an established set of theological tenets (Hillar 2012, 119)." John, without knowing what he defined, introduced the Fractal Logos. The cosmos is an infinite multidimensional system of fractal patterns.

One must entertain the concept of fractals before developing one's views of chaos in conjunction with the Logos. As the concept of the Logos migrated through religion and tradition it became more and more a static principle rather than a living fractal whose mythic aspects were enlivened. The Logos became separated from its cosmic element being entrapped in tradition, religion, and tenets losing its vivifying properties. It was this Logos that became imprisoned in flesh (Religion and Law) and not a soul. When the Logos is fractalized, then its many multifacets are seen. A fractal concept is found in William Paul Young's *The Shack* as Sarayu said "A fractal...is something considered simple and orderly that is actually composed of repeating patterns no matter how magnified. A fractal is almost infinitely complex. I love fractals, so I placed them everywhere (Young 2007, 128)."

Not only are fractals found in the world around us they are also found inside of us. Fractals appear in human physiology and are seen in the respiratory, circulatory, and nervous systems and are amazing instances of fractal architecture through their branching and subdividing signatures. The lungs display fractal scaling and if turned upside down they resemble the same branching pattern found in trees. Interestingly, both trees and lungs carry on the process of respiration but in reverse. As the lungs take in oxygen and expire CO_2; trees intake CO_2 and expire oxygen. They perform a similar function as well as share a similar structure. The branching pattern in the human lung contains eleven orders of branching from the trachea to the alveoli at the tips of the branches in the lungs. The heart and circulatory system are filled with fractal networking through the coronary arteries and veins. The blood vessels also carry on the gas exchange on a cellular level throughout the skeletal system. The redundancy of the system also strengthens the body against injury. Brain function is a print of the Fibonacci process in that the golden mean is a clock cycle of brain waves according to Harald Weiss (Weiss 2003, 6). The algorithm that generates the similarity in infinite diversity is not a specific number but a range of Fibonacci ratios characterized by the number phi. Phi is not a magic number but an average of all such ratios that is essentially the same number over the infinite Fibonacci process. Incidentally, the Golden Ratio is beautifully found in the human face. One of its strongest connections of phi to the human form is what the eye perceives as beautiful. What is all this saying about the cosmos? It is simply displaying order through chaos. But what is chaos?

The cosmos seems to be screaming chance is managed by a principle outside of itself and this algorithmic governance is such that infinite variety is never precluded but rather enabled. This allowance of all possibilities follows the voice of open theologians offering a God of fractals, of sacred and secret numbers which reveal mystery, magic, and awe to creation. Benoit Mandelbrot expressed his thoughts in fractal geometry when he considered himself an explorer rather than inventor adding his imagination was not vivid enough to invent what he was seeing. He said "I was discovering them; they were there although no one had ever seen them before. It's marvelous! A very simple formula describes these very complicated things. Who could have dreamed that such an incredibly simple equation could have generated images of literally infinite complexity? We've all read stories of maps that revealed the location of some hidden treasure. In this case, the map is the treasure (Clarke 1995)!" All compliments of our mystical, magical, and fractal God.

The Law of Operations –The Cosmic Logos

Cosmology has lost its place in mythical time. Even though it is the study of universal origins; it also encompasses our role in the universe. Looking cosmologically at the Bible through mythical lens rather than literal, one might turn to Psalm 19 and see an amazing zodiacal footprint in creation. The worship leader says:

> 1 The celestial realms announce God's glory; the skies testify of His hands' great work.
>
> 2 Each day pours out more of their sayings; each night, more to hear and more to learn.
>
> 3 Inaudible words are their manner of speech and silence, their means to convey.
>
> 4 Yet from here to the ends of the earth, their voices[a] have gone out; the whole world can hear what they say. God stretched out in these heavens a tent for the sun,
>
> 5 And the sun is like a groom who, after leaving his room, arrives at the wedding in splendor; He is the strong runner who, favored to win in his race, is eager to face his challenge.
>
> 6 He rises at one end of the skies and runs in an arc overhead; nothing can hide from his heat, from the swelter of his daily tread.
>
> 7 The Eternal's law is perfect, turning lives around. His words are reliable and true, instilling wisdom to open minds.
>
> 8 The Eternal's directions are correct, giving satisfaction to the heart. God's commandments are clear, lending clarity to the eyes.
>
> 9 The awe of the Eternal is clean, sustaining for all of eternity. The Eternal's decisions are sound; they are right through and through.
>
> 10 They are worth more than gold even more than

abundant, pure gold. They are sweeter to the tongue
than honey or the drippings of the honeycomb.
(Psalms 19. The VOICE, Bible Gateway.com)

It is not two witnesses telling their own story rather one testifying to a single truth. The law that man instituted indicates a restitution is needed but the law/decree declared from the heavens says nothing is broken and no separation exists. This Psalm flowing from Hebrew thought is to see God in the universe as well as his declarations and understand they function as one story. The two witness which are the celestial heavens and the eternal law declare identical messages. They both focus on humanity and divinity.

Verse 8 from the Voice says: "The Eternal's directions are correct, giving satisfaction to the heart. God's commandments are clear, lending clarity to the eyes." In considering the Law, religion has placed upon man, does it satisfy the heart and clear the eyes? The precepts or directions (*mesammehe*) of God satisfies the heart being a sign of peace while the commandments are clear giving wisdom and light. They do not tear down, divide, and pursue death. In essence, the law or decrees of God are not declaring what you did wrong but are declaring rightly who you are. Job 38 references the "Law of the Heavens" and this is not rules like the speed limit sign but definitive statements, decrees, or assurances; like the law of gravity. The declaration is not citing a dying god and what happened on a cross but is proclaiming what is happening to you symbolized in the cross a movement of the Logos. The Law or declaration of God is not forcing a comparison in judgment but issuing a proclamation of union.

Mimesis concepts influenced the mythos rather than the logos. As man sought a remedy for his guilt, he found it in mimesis by offering release, his freedom from guilt came through the scapegoat. In emotion versus reason which also can be expressed as myth versus logic, a sacrifice was required out of emotion and man provided himself a lamb as an offering to heal his emotions but logic decrees more loudly one was never needed. The decrees are not as loud as the judgments in our Bible because the Bible is read as a literal book rather than a mythical book where we can seek mystical realities. Creation did not spring from nothingness or void but a much richer beginning. We did not spring from disorder but from an alternate order through a process of unfolding and differentiation as God named and declared function. It is the concept of the Ruach pulsing over this creative matrix awaiting restructuring not from an unruly mess but from non-purpose to purposeful beauty because of an en-fleshment caused by the breath of God. The breath effects tohu wa-bohu, the womb of potential creativity and we were there.

Is the book of Genesis the only account of creation? Of course not. Did it evolve by chance? By evolution? Or a divine Orchestra Leader, a director of the symphony who choreographs the dance offering a perichoretic interpretation of the interaction of divinity and humanity? Digging deeper in Cosmology and Cosmogony reveals valuable insights in the drama of our journey.

Cosmology seeks to answer the how it was formed using scientific and mechanical principles. It looks at the cosmos and sees a very structured and logical process detailing the cosmos in terms of quantity. Cosmogony is also the study of the cosmos but is not concerned with how it was made but why it functions the way that it does. It employs metaphysical, philosophical, and theological approaches exploring functionality. What is the cosmological and cosmogonical purpose of the cosmos? So divinity and humanity can dance!

-VII-

QUANTUM PERICHORESIS

The universe is a symphony of wonder and beauty, simplicity and complexity, elegance and extravagance. Yet those of us living here in the miniscule sector we call home wrestle with fear and survival, discontinuity and incompleteness, life and death. We feebly reach for something beyond this small space but remain firmly entrenched. We humans live for what we do not see and die for what we do. We fight for what we want to believe rather than live into this strange, dimensional, and fractal nature of the cosmos and the symphonic entities we were intended to be (Augsburger 2013, 9).

The Stage, the Music, the Dance

Quantum Perichoresis communicates my view of the cosmos in universal vibrational harmony. Although Perichoresis has been used as a theological term expressing the Western view of the Godhead; its meaning runs deeper as a demonstration of their interaction and harmonic existence as one. It was first used in 5th Century Greek ideas as rotation or spinning and is pictured in the stanzas below by Ian Mobsby.

Perichoresis - The Divine Dance of God

Heads bowing, hands sharing, hearts racing
Feet poised suspended in the support of the other.
Holy Three yet one, laugh, cry, celebrate and lament their co-creativity.

Time burst out as the by-product of a hurling helix
of mystical presence
swaying through the dance.
Life and all things became real
Out of the dynamic of joy and love expressed in movement.

The Creator led the dance from summation to incarnation,
The Redeemer led the dance from incarnation to Pentecost,
The Companion leads the dance now from the time of the church
to the consummation.
But Holy dance,
don't slow down,
don't wait on us inattentive humanity.

Free us Holy Three in one to learn the dance,
Teach us to be free from our selfishness and greed.
Let us relearn how to dance spiritually
And be a blessing to the Cosmos
And be the spiritual community
The dancing God calls us to be.
Amen

(Ian Mobsby, "Perichoresis-The Divine Dance of God," Mobsby's Creative Space, August 13, 2007, http://mobsbyscreativespace.blogspot.com/ 2007/08/Perichoresis-divine-dance-of-god.html.)

Perichoresis, which has been hijacked to singularly mean the aspects of the Trinity, also portrays an interaction revealing the fully realized myth unbound and free as the dance itself and ever deepening. It depicts an entanglement of all components connecting everything and is intricately displayed in the concept of quantum physics and more especially in quantum entanglement. Its etymological meaning includes the concept of making room for in order to be enveloped or contained and looking back further still it carries the concept of coherence or interpenetration to the point of being unable to differentiate the components involved. It points to the concept of non-duality as demonstrated in quantum entanglement. It displays an action of cyclic movement that is both a static dwelling as well as a dynamic interweaving exemplifying potential and kinetic energies and is suggestive of the partnership of movement seen in dancing. Diarmuid O'Murchu said, "Energy is the substance of life, the unrelenting wellspring of pure possibility, escalating and undulating as in a great cosmic dance (O'Murchu 2004, 45)" suggesting a graphical movement or story embedded in the perichoretic flow.

The Matrix: Womb of Potentialities

It is in the perichoretic dance we uncover the cosmogonical key of the creational process of becoming. God's breath brooded over the tehom, the deep, which was in a condition of tohu wa-bohu translated as without form and empty. Tradition presupposes this was a state of stagnate disarray and lack of order but is better understood to be a matrix, a womb of potentialities within potentialities. F. J. Mayers considered this matrix to be a spiritual place of development which fully contained "all the Divine purposes and their fulfilment (Mayers 1948, 59)." The first manifestation of God was to energize his intent, the inward light, the divine mind, and with the expulsion of the Ruach of God; Light crossed the barriers of the unseen to the seen. As He again proceeded to breathe he divided the waters. One aspect of the waters rose to form the heavens, the *shamaim*, whose richer meaning is the "glorified waters (Mayers 1948, 59)" while the other portion descended condensing to mass forming the *aretz* (earth) or in metaphorical thought solid water. Everything conceived in the mind of God was physically manifested at the out flow of His breath. The cosmos mirrors, the Intent of God, and the stars reflecting that intent influence the soul of man as they declared God's glory. The manifestation of God's mind in the seen realm was the act of conception producing the offspring of God; that which was unseen became seen and we call it creation.

A discourse by Kabbalist Rabbi Simeon ben Jochai confirms creation as the intent of God functioning as a cosmic rhythm in which he says,

> Tune [tone, resonance] had begun. Its great pendulum, whose beats are the ages, commenced to vibrate. The era of creation or manifestation had at last arrived. The *nekuda reshima*, primal point or nucleus, appeared. From it emanated and expanded the primary substance, the illimitable phosphorescent ether, of the nature of light, formless, colorless, being neither black nor green nor red. In it, latent yet potentially as in a mighty womb, lay the myriad prototypes and numberless forms of all created things as yet indiscernible, indistinguishable. By the secret and silent action of the divine will, from this primal luminous point radiated forth the vital life-giving spark which, pervading and operating in the great, enteric ocean of forms, became the soul of the universe, the fount

and origin of all mundane life and motion and terrestrial existence, and in its nature and essence and secret operation remains ineffable, incomprehensible and indefinable. It has been conceived of as the divine *Logos*, the Word, and called *Barashith*, for the same was in the beginning with God (ben Jochai 2014).

We fail to entertain these amazing and mystical concepts because of a disjunction of cosmogony, religion, and myth. Religious concepts force literalness rather than mystical stopping the flow of the beauty of potential. The literalness of religion implants fear in potentiality rather than inspiring mystery and awe.

Reunion of Cosmogony, Religion, and Myth

What would the reunion of cosmogony, religion, and myth look like? As we apprehend new concepts of the cosmos, including the microcosm of ourselves, expanding previous perceptions we process these concepts in our own unique creative way and from these new impressions our worldview will be adjusted and rebuilt time and again. This is the process of becoming; a progressive awareness and heightened state of being awake. We acknowledge responsibility for the reaction we create and for those reactions others put back into the living cosmos. God is processing our actions forming Himself in us and our perception of Him is in constant rearrangement, becoming more descriptive, intimate, and living. God offers back our interpretation of this soulical experience providing value from the divine perspective. Then, we process this new intrusion again altering our worldview through the *phronema*, the spirit of the mind, and divine intrusions reoccur and reform in never ending dialogue of divinity and humanity. It is good, functional to be alive as God continues to breathe. Why did

Western religion divorce itself from cosmological elements even though cosmological concepts are implanted into its theologies? There has always been a relationship of interdependence and interpenetration between God, man, and the cosmos. It was lost in the religious dogma of current orthodox thought as Judaism sought to enforce manmade laws as God's. The illusive God of the East was non-relational, impersonal and the distant God of the Greeks was beyond touch and in these aspects, religion lost the rhythm of the dance.

It is said to study the history of any faith is to see how faith flows in culture and tradition of a people in a particular time. Tradition is symbolized by a flowing river like the Colorado in the Grand Canyon carving new paths in past time yet endures through time. The Mississippi river has changed course in history even running backwards (This Day in History 2009) as it floods and carves tributaries like tentacles on its way to the ocean. The river's inherent purpose is to flow to the ocean and it will but how it gets there is the story of tradition but why it flows the way it does is conveyed through myth. If we could look at a single point in time it would tell a unique story or path in that time. Yet looking at multiple points we begin to understand how time affects the tradition as tradition stands still. Myth seeks to unify tradition into a cohesive whole offering a multifaceted view of the journey. Tradition is much richer than any one specific point in time. We can look at Nicaea in the 4th century and the other Early Church Councils and see a notable story. With Aquinas in the 13th century another new story emerges; or Martin Luther in the 16th century and Wesley in the 18th; as each offers a distinct part of the story in time but tradition is much richer than any singular period and like the rivers, it is constantly moving, stretching, and flowing; continuing to tell a story through time. It is myth which removes the restriction of time causing the story to reach outside of all time. The drama is not depicting universal salvation for a lost world as recently thought but is telling the story of divine relationship, the union of divinity and humanity; and myth offers interpretation of the intrusion.

The Stage: Sacred Space

Traditional religion conceived a God who created heaven and earth to provide a stage for the drama of salvation, a composition that spans from creation to annihilation of the cosmos and birth to death of humanity. If Biblical cosmology is invalid, does that also invalidate the Bible? Not if the Bible is comprehended as a mythical narrative rather than a literal one. The Bible originated in an age when man interpreted the forces of nature and the events of their lives according to their mythologized and super-naturalistic beliefs. The Bible is like other literature of its time and is also a collection of myths, folklore, embellished histories, superstitions, assumptions, and speculations. Paul expressed the concept of a cosmic drama in Romans 8:22 when he says the whole creation groans indicating a redemption of not only humanity but also a cosmic release based on the actions of humanity is forthcoming.

Walton points out Eden was a reflection of the cosmic temple (Walton 2009, 82). In ancient Near East writings, almost all cultures incorporate the concept of the cosmic temple and in doing so convey their belief that the cosmos is complete and functional. Also, gardens were standard features in temples in this region and the image of a river watering the garden flowing from the temple indicated the belief that life issued from the temple and outflowed to sustain life and support the community. In the Old Testament, the Israelites had a temple or tent where the high priest met God acting as a sacred yet movable space for a nomadic people (Walton 2009, 77-85). The sacred space was that which sustained life, gave peace, and threatened death by holding death at bay.

Levenson united the temple and the cosmos in a most significant way by implying the temple functioned as a microcosm of the greater cosmos (Levenson 1988, 78-99). The temple reflected the world as it should be, holographically reflecting the cosmic sanctuary of all things being ordered and energized while the world viewed the temple as the resting place of a God who was unchallenged by his creation. Because the temple was symbolic of the meeting point of heaven and earth, it was designated as a microcosm, an encapsulation in miniature of the qualities or features of something much larger as temple architecture reflected the cosmology of the people who constructed them. Many ancient religions celebrated annual festivals through temple ritual usually at the new year. It portrayed the ritualization of the fall of the cosmos once again into chaos and the process of the people to assist the gods in resurrecting the cosmos out of death. In that space and time were so connected to the cosmos and the new year, the end of one meant the end of the other; time was circular as each ritualization renewed the earth.

Mircea Eliade, a Romanian theologian in the early 20th Century who later taught at the University of Chicago, expressed a strong interest in eastern meditation and comparative mythology seeing a unique yet divergent relationship between the sacred and profane parameters of space and time. He cited this separation occurs despite religion and secular ideologies. He noted profane time is experienced in the linear or arrow of time while sacred time is cyclical and re-actualizable or relivable by means of myths and rituals. Sacred time also propels the participant into a mythic experience of a past event such as creation or crucifixion. This sacred time, although continuously present in all times, is accessed via myth and ritual. Profane time is the reality of daily life while on the other hand sacred time is the re-actualization of myth as God encountered humanity. Cultures considered the cosmos as experiencing newness and rebirth at each new year. In ancient Babylon when their creation myth was recounted during the new year festivals, the perceived the creation of the cosmos out of chaos occurred at that time again (Eliade 1987, 77-78). The universe actually experienced a rebirth according to the festival goers. This was the power of myth which is so lost in our understanding at the expense of Western views making them untruthful because they were taken as literal accounts rather than realizing myth incorporated the purpose of origins as understood in a time attempting to convey what was difficult to comprehend. When time is viewed as cyclical, an event in history maintains sacred value but when time is linear; history becomes non-specific, powerless, lost, equating to profane and that is what occurred in most religions.

Elaide considered the sacred a structure of human consciousness and manifested to the mind in hierophanies or physical representations of the holy. A more contemporary term used is a divine intrusion or incarnation. The purpose of the sacred is to experience the mysterious, the awesome, and the beautiful. Inside the experience of the hierophany is the excitement of the ontophany or the experience of being expressed as the manifestation of reality. The location of the hierophany becomes the *axis mundi,* the center of the cosmos. It is this location that became the temple and the source of law and order were decreed giving credence to sacred space as religious man sought to live as close as possible to the center of the world being perceived as the place where heaven meets earth (Eliade 1991, 12). As consecration of this location occurs it becomes a temple of the Divine as God resides with man. The temple symbolizes or reflects the cosmos and the cosmos itself is sacred as the Divine established order. Once humanity entered the temple, man interacted with Deity, re-igniting the desire to return to the beginning of time and space, to origin or singularity and touch the Former again. Interestingly, the concept of being born again is rooted in the ritual aspect of touching the beginning. This is one of the key aspects or purposes of ritual being a symbolic returning to the primordial when all was sacred; all was a single unit entering the womb once more or being born again.

The Music: Sacred Time
Symbology Revived in Myth

Eliade suggests symbols in the ritual process appeal to the imagination rather than reason. Any object can become symbolic of ritual when infused with the supernatural such as Aaron's Rod or Moses' Staff, and any symbol can be both sacred and profane often at the same time. As cultures diversified by adopting various symbologies; those things which were identified as symbols deepened and solidified later becoming in some cultures the primal elements of earth, water, air, and fire. Earth represented stability and solidity enforcing order and offering security. Water became the cosmic representative of the flow of chaos to order and from barrenness to renewal and productivity. Water also was figurative of formlessness and the need for boundaries or limits. As rising out of water symbolized the awareness of form and structure and the ability to function; immersion in water was the dissolution of form and functionality, loss of differentiation. Elaide contends the early church fathers touched early aquatic symbology and added

Christian concepts to justify it (Eliade 1987, 129-136). Air was analogous to the breath of life and speech, which issued from the breath offered harmony. Fire symbolized the transformation or restoration to purity and encouraged life by metaphorically pointing to light and energy.

Eliade's sacred and profane space finds expression in the cosmos as energy is called into the physical dimension (Eliade 1987, 20-29). "$E=mc^2$" is the equation of calling what you cannot see into matter which can be seen. Quantum physics expands this equation a bit by explaining the cosmos is brought into existence by the energized vibrations of sound. Sacred space is the potentially real part of the universe, unseen but fully ordered. Profane space is ambiguous and non-specific which has taken on the contemporary meaning of chaos lacking specialization. The Sacred is the solid fixed point from which all originates while the profane is the vast formless expanse of time without essence or meaning. Sacred is ordered, distinct, and moral. Profane is characterized by lack of structure, amorphousness, homogeneity, and the absence of rules or governance. Sacred space also functions as a portal of return, a door to the beginning of creation while profane space masks the door (Eliade 1987, 20-115). The Sacred does not provide an escape from reality but is a portal to once again touch the beginning of time or sacred reality. Sacred time is time outside of time in the sense the sacred interrupts ordinary experiences of time. Sacred time might be experienced during intimate worship in which time is lost or when God is revealing a mystery and all senses are muted. Sacred time is non-measurable while profane time is paralleled in historical time in which there is a time for everything as proclaimed in Ecclesiastes three therefore marked.

A recall of an event can be either ritual or mythical. A rite is copied or imitated to remember while a myth serves to tell the significance of what is remembered. Ritual tells us what to remember but a myth tells us why we remember it. It is this significance that is lost in ritual which tends to become a repetitive event. For example, I remember taking the Lord's Supper at church every 4th or 5th Sunday, but if I enter sacred time then I understand the mythical significance causing it not to be a repetitive ritual but life giving and mystical. I don't think a ritual can be sustained and enlivened in the present moment but myth thrives in it. Rituals are lifeless in historical time while myth is ever flowing in cosmic time thereby enlivening the ritual.

As stated above, a ritual can be revived in myth. The Passover is a Jewish ritual of deliverance which is the base of the Protestant Lord's Supper. A ritual must re-focus on the above the natural intervention or intrusion of divinity to be enlivened in myth. When it does, the symbolism is dramatic and time moves to muteness and the ritual is alive because of the symbology the myth provided. Sacred time is the rest of the cosmos, the time of dancing, the experience of the seventh day. Remember sitting in the chair in the library. Time is rhythm and motion. Sacred time which is oblivious to the clock cycle moves the ritual from duality to the harmonic triad and the enjoyment of the dance. The created and the Creator in relationship and all of creation fully conscious of it providing the perfect present moment. It is in sacred time and sacred space the music is heard and its resonance felt.

The Dance: The Pulsing Breath of Union and En-fleshment

It was the Ruach of God which was implanted in man and this same breath hoovered over the waters the womb of the earth. The Ruach pulsed with life awaiting the forceful push caused by the words from the Creator. This pulsing dancing breath was productive and vivifying. Catherine Keller offers an amazing image of the dance in which she paints a portrait of God as the composer who then calls on the orchestra.

> Elohim calls forth art, like the music of a jazz ensemble, with multiple solos and constant reintegration, with ever more complex riffs on the elemental themes, sounded in the depths. Primal themes, like E=mc^2 and the law of gravity, seem to express the law or Logos of the universe. Then when biology happens, ACGT—the letters representing the four nucleic acids comprising the gene—sound the primal theme. The variations on these four will branch out into thirty-thousand genes making up the human genome and account for unfathomable diversity of life. The Logos of John 1:1, echoing the Elohimic utterance of Genesis becomes a metaphor for genes. If ACGT is itself a primal theme upon which we creatures riff at a collective level way beneath consciousness, is it not also a possible metaphor of the divine word? Here genesis and genetics are one (Keller 2008, 60).

Process theologians have a very interesting concept of the creative event of the cosmos. Their primary assumption views God as open who knows all there is to know but He does not know the future until it is actualized. For example, considering Shakespeare's *Hamlet*, did the literary work exist before the birth of its author? Process Theology allows for human creativity as God did not pre-know *Hamlet* which was birthed in the mind of Shakespeare who was not born but whose mind was in the divine yet not functioning as Shakespeare. Process Theology has its roots in Grecian philosopher Heraclitus who viewed reality in terms of becoming rather than being. He saw creation as a process of continued creative events, a dance between creator and created. In opposition to his view was Parmenides, a contemporary of Heraclitus, who stressed the concept of cause and effect saying any change was the result of some eternal fundamental reality. In other words, anything that occurred had a higher cause for it to be and was thus known to the instigator of the cause. It was his principle that prevailed in the Western world becoming orthodox as everything that happens does so under the direction of God.

The process of becoming views chaos as a potential creative matrix in agreement with older languages indicating chaos was simply an original creative state that was neither good nor evil. In this vein of thought, order was a realized creative process as chaos and order operated in perichoretic harmony as one served the other being activated, energized, and enlivened by Logos. The Logos, being the effective dynamic power of breath, the Ruach of God, called the universe to full functionality according to the intent of the Orchestra Leader. Chaos was a birthing chamber full of potential from which all things developed into a distinct entity, the true matrix. The Encyclopedia Mythica says chaos was the "gaping void" out of which all things develop or became a distinct entity (The Encyclopedia Mythica 2016). In this scenario, the beginning was not an origin but an opening up, an outflow, or unfolding. In chaos, all things existed in an unstructured non-functional state and amorphous shape before separation into a functional unit as they entered the process of becoming, a living dynamic process of discovery.

The idea of tohu meaning formlessness syncs well with the description of the cosmos being probability waves which have not collapsed into a physical state through the interference of observation. String theorists posit immediately following the explosion of the Big Bang bringing potentiality into actuality there was an expanding network of invisible connections of energy that existed in all dimensions. It is the book of Hebrews which posits God did not make things from things that were visible but from things invisible. In other words, God made the visible world of matter from an invisible energy that collapsed into matter at His command. It then seems God, in the initial stages of creation, created all things in an invisible field of energy which was the "primordial building blocks or the sub-strata of the material universe (Mason 2010, 126)."

The Quantum Cosmos

The classical physics model employs several modalities. The first major modality is cause-and-effect and is exemplified when one pushes the power on the TV remote and it comes on indicating everything happened because something caused it to happen. The second modal element is the concept of determinism which states it was predictable that the TV set would come on when the power button was pushed based on the assumption that both the remote and the TV set were in working order. Everything in the universe is assumed to work in this predetermined, predictable fashion. Modal element three is reductionism which observes the wholes comprising a certain number of parts; for example, the TV is a whole machine and the remote too is whole both consisting of many parts. If the TV did not turn on then it must be the result of faulty parts in the TV or the remote and reductionism further states simply repair or replace the broken part and all will be functional again. The fourth modal element is rationalism and is demonstrated as the TV should work because it has the correct electronic components needed and should function as designed. The fifth modality is objectivity which is demonstrated in the scientific process; other TV's are operational so this particular TV should function also.

The quantum physics model utilizes other modalities with the first being the wave property which states a quantum object can exist at more than one locale simultaneously. The second quantum modal element is the collapse of the wave which implies a quantum object does not exist until it is observed and measured. The collapse of the wave function is a difficult operation to grasp in which before observation a myriad of possibilities exists, yet when observation commences only one of these possibilities will materialize. The wave is said to have collapsed into the single possibility that has now become surety. The third modal element of quantum physics is called the quantum jump describing a quantum object which ceases to exist in one locale yet simultaneously appearing in existence at another location without traveling through the intervening space. The fourth modal element of quantum physics is described using Einstein's terms "spooky action at a distance (Einstein 1964)" in which the manifestation of one quantum object under observation simultaneously influences its correlated twin object no matter how far apart they are. The effect is connected due to sharing identical origins.

A quantum is a mathematical term specifying an amount, portion, or a packet of energy. It is a description of energy that cannot be reduced to a smaller unit. With this understanding, quantum physics is the study of the near physical world using the quanta scale. The non-local (something that is not part of the dimensional world of space time) quantum world seems to be the interface between energy and physical matter. It is the smallest whole part of the hologram. Newtonian cosmology presents a cosmos that is mechanical and spatial being related to space and locked in time. His universe was very predictable and linear garnering the name clockwork universe. Quantum cosmology offers a cosmos that is holistic, unpredictable, open, interconnected, and rather than linear is spiral and flowing bidirectionally. The quantum cosmos negates distance offering insights into cosmic reality which is the significance of oneness and the negation of duality.

Sociologist Albert Bergesen suggested three stages of alienation predominate in religion which seemed to enforce duality with the outcome being distance from the divine however perceived in cultures (Rosado 2000). These three stages although solely processed in man's perception impact the entire realm of creation. The first stage is division from the Divine, then humanity from humanity; and lastly, separation from nature. The stages represent the concepts of I am God, I am self -sufficient and I need no one, and finally, all I experience is for me alone; therefore I am. The Quantum cosmos ideology negates this and instead offers an amazing image of the whole in every part. The dance of the cosmos remains intact and all parts are connected. There is the story of a dialogue between a Yaqui Indian Sorcerer named Don Juan who was teaching Carlos Castenada, his pupil, about the subtle realities of the invisible world. It was at this time Castenada felt a strong gust of wind on his cheek and simply commented to his teacher it made his eyes burn. He looked from where the wind came from and stated further stated, "there was absolutely nothing out of the ordinary. I cannot see a thing" It was at this point the teacher took the opportunity to teach.

"You felt it," he (Don Juan) replied.

"What?" "The Wind?" (said Castenada)

"Not just the wind," he said sternly.

"It may seem to be wind to you, because wind is all you know." (Don Juan) (Braden 2007, 142)

We cannot fully rely on the filters of perception because the world is alive and energized on both seen and unseen levels. Quantum cosmos removes the perception of duality and separation and instead offers interconnectedness and specialization.

The removal of duality unmasks an entangled reality. Diarmuid O'Murchu said, "At the heart of the quantum vision is the conviction that all life forces are interdependent and interrelated. In fact, we experience life, not in isolated entities, not in separate units, but in bundles of experience (quanta) (O'Murchu 2004, 71)." German physicist, Werner Heisenberg adds the idea that the cosmos is really an "interconnected web of relationships" (O'Murchu 2004, 85). It is this view that destroys the human aspect of social alienation and the spiritually fragmented world of generalized religion. Quantum interests penetrate through the parts focusing on the most minute particle in search of understanding to discover the union of the part reflected in the whole which is the cosmic hologram. It is this force, this Logos, the intent of Source which governs and upholds all. To truly live is to see the amazing power of non-dual relationship, to comprehend that all life is interconnected, interrelated, and interdependent. This is lost in the perceived alienation and isolation of humanity and divinity. Max Planck, who coined the term *quanta* made a statement that penetrates the heart of Quantum Physics in which he says, "Science cannot solve the ultimate mystery of nature. And it is because, in the last analysis, we ourselves are part of the mystery we are trying to solve (O'Murchu 2004, 85).

This universal interconnectedness of the cosmos, or quantum holism understands the universe is a seamless indivisible whole. It was the EPR (Einstein, Podolsky, & Rosen) experiment which determined the phenomena seen in quantum entanglement in which the particle was effected by observation without regard to distance occurs because the part is not really a part but is holographically integrated into the holistic system. David Bohm, an American physicist, explains the parts are not really separated parts but represent an "unbroken wholeness" affirming the "interconnectedness of the whole universe (Rosado 2000)." This phenomenon of nonlocality picturing holistic interconnectedness goes beyond the stand-alone mechanics of the Newtonian universe projecting the hologram through all possible dimensions.

Divine Matrix

All matter originates and exists only by virtue of a force...
We must assume behind this force the existence
of a conscious and intelligent mind.
This mind is the matrix of all matter."
Max Planck (1944)

Did creation evolve from a matrix of potential energy awaiting the command to move, to be brought into functionality? Creation presents us with the possibility that the actual process did not solely occur in the past but the potential creative energy is continuously moving and interacting. Conversely, a pre-creation implies the energy was dormant, motionless yet ready to act. Graham says in metaphysical concepts it is called the Absolute but in Scripture, it is the condition of being without form and void. This place or space is the "field of cosmic manifestation" or "congealed energy" (Graham, L. 1975, 15). Energy in its potential state is functionless but contains all that is necessary to become functional and is the beginning state of the creation process. Graham says the earth is "a precipitate of primordial substance and a congelation of cosmic energy. But energy of itself is neither constructive nor purposive. For it to become such it must have a guiding directing intelligence, and as that intelligence here on earth is genetic, so is it in heaven, space—as below so above (Graham, L. 1975, 15)."

Graham goes on to say this condition of being was "one vast nothing materially, [yet] all things potentially (Graham, L. 1975, 15)." This concept of no-thing was the *chaos* of the Greeks, the *nox* or night of the Romans, the *nur* or nothing of the Egyptians, the *po* of the Polynesians, the *parabrahm* of the Hindus, and the *tao* of the Chinese fully demonstrating for divinity to become fractal and holographic on the physical plane, it must first become functional in humanity (Graham, L. 1975, 16). This act of functional becoming is perichoretic, enfolding, and alive. The Vedic hymn entitled "The Song of Creation" discusses the condition of pre-creation in the following stanzas:

> There was not non-existent nor existent; there was no realm of air, no sky beyond it. What covered in, and where? And what gave shelter? Was water there, unfathomed depth of water? Death was not then, nor was there ought immortal; no sign was there, the day's and night's divider. That one thing, breathless, breathed by its own nature: apart from it was nothing whatsoever. Darkness there was: at first concealed in darkness, this All was un-discriminated chaos. All that existed then was void and formless: by the great power of warmth was born that Unity (Pascual 2010, 126).

Graham postulates an atom is not attracted to another atom because of a particular law but because of its energy content (Graham, L. 1975, 20). Because of its energy, it acts, or metaphorically expresses itself in a world where it is not alone forming subatomic relationships and experiencing expressions of interaction. These expressions and relationships endured by these particles are constant in the quantum realm and man perceiving and documenting their constancy calls it law. Because these natural laws are so ancient and antedate man; he then ascertains they pre-existed all things when in fact before the particles existed the laws were mute; they were non-functional. Laws, however, are neither causative, coming into being out of self will or creative and neither do they pre-exist matter. They simply came into being with being and are pillars arising out of the matrix of God's intent.

A matrix is potentiality from which something develops or forms. Its etymology in Latin is womb and its French counterpart is *matrices* meaning pregnant animal or *mater* which is mother. In Biology, a matrix is the tissue in which more specialized structures are embedded. A matrix is the mold from which something is fashioned or extracted; this mold is referred to as the master. The Latin base, mater, references the symbology of the earth as mother in the emblematic process of man being taken from the earth. A common practice of early man was laying a new born on the ground or the actual birth occurring on the ground as a testament to the earth mother who supplied Adam with dust becoming his body (Eliade 1987, 141-144). In considering the aspect of the matrix, it does not detract from God to acknowledge the source of humanity's flesh being mother earth.

Is the cosmos a hologram? A location in a hologram reflects all locations and a property in existence anywhere exists everywhere. "In the non-local hologram of our universe, the underlying energy that links all things instantly connects them as well (Braden. 2007, 106)." Ervin Laszlo, a Hungarian philosopher and advocate for quantum consciousness, describes the perichoretic pattern as he says, "life evolves, as does the universe itself, in a 'sacred dance' with an underlying field (Braden 2007, 106, end notes)." An ancient description of holographic concept is seen in *The Sutra*, Sanskrit for string or thread and references philosophical life knowledge and experiences which holds things together, describes an infinite number of jewels serving as cosmic eyes. Through the eyes all things are visible to all other things. The Sutra goes on to say each jewel has the power to effect change. "Each of the jewels reflected in this one jewel is also reflecting all the other jewels so that there is an infinite reflecting process occurring (Braden 2007, 107)." This description represents an infinite interrelationship of all the parts reflecting the whole (Braden 2007, 107). As the hologram is unable to be divided or partitioned by its nature, religion attempts to dissect the hologram

The whole in every part aspect of the holographic principle was first demonstrated in 1982 by a research team from the University of Paris led by physicist Alain Aspect. Due to their research, they realized on the subatomic level electrons could "instantaneously communicate with each other regardless of the distance separating them (Matai 2011)" violating Einstein's concept that nothing can travel faster than the speed of light which would equate to breaking the time barrier. This possibility offers the concept of the holographic universe essentially implying that "objective reality does not exist" that "despite its apparent solidity the universe is a heart a phantasm, a gigantic and splendidly detailed hologram (Matai 2011)." This whole in every part displayed in the hologram offers an amazingly new and exciting portrait of the order of the cosmos. Matai goes on to imply the Western world of exploration was to cut and dissect in order to study and evaluate for the purpose of gaining understanding in a living specimen; in other words, to understand the whole one must dissect and study the parts. He says, "A hologram teaches us that some things in the universe may not lend themselves to this approach. If we try to take apart something constructed holographically, we will not get the pieces of which it is made, we will only get smaller wholes (Matai 2011)." Religion has sought to dissect the hologram, and when observed, continues to see the whole not realizing it. God cannot be sliced and dissected to be comprehended; He is the unified field, the container of all that was, is, and will be; the holographic God. As our concepts of God bend to light we begin to see the cosmos as a holographical and unified field of energy, of movement, a dance; and is a fully functional whole.

Quantum Entanglement

Quantum entanglement supports the long-held concept of another dimension of reality outside the dimensions of space and time. The concept of non-locality is its principle characteristic as seen in quantum theory supporting the great premise of quantum thought which is there is no "over there" or "out there." Quantum theory is a now and present moment response to the human being as Quantum Perichoresis acknowledges the mystical, the mysterious, and the magical God. In describing the phenomenon of quantum entanglement author Brian Clegg referred to it as "the God Effect (Clegg 2006, 1)."

Irish physicist John Bell and Alain Aspect proved the cosmos to its most primal element is non-local meaning there is no distance from point "A" to point "B." On the quantum level, the cosmos is really a participatory universe in which all elements are interconnected and interdependent, functioning as a perfect whole which Albert Einstein termed this phenomenon "spooky action at a distance (Clegg 2006, 3)." It is noted in the interaction of two or more particles of energy which share a common origin will continue to interact with each other even though they are separated by great distances. They display an interconnectedness even though they appear separate. The point is this interaction is demonstrated instantaneously, faster than the speed of light which was thought to be impossible in his time. Is there a concept faster? Perhaps it is consciousness. The conscious response is as if space-time boundaries are non-existent. Objects of energy appear connected beyond the physical realm, and this sphere is the realm of consciousness. Since it is not physical electromagnetic energy, it is not bound by time's limits nor the speed of light.

Is this a valid concept? Yes. The human body has long been suspected of entanglement with the earth through biorhythms and circadian cycles. This is further implicated in the female menstrual cycle which is entangled with the moon's phases; and astrology, which for centuries has called the affairs of humanity to be interconnected beyond the physical realm to the planets, stars, and constellations. Entanglement occurs due to initial similar origin, indicating a single source of energy such as the Big Bang. Even though space forces a mental construct of unendingness and distance; everything is still touching, connected, entangled. Every action, thought, feeling, and emotion is so connected that it can affect the whole on many dimensions.

Albert Einstein described the observation in a letter to another scientist named Max Born in which he says,

> I cannot make a case for my attitude in physics which you would consider reasonable… I cannot seriously believe in [quantum theory] because the theory cannot be reconciled with the idea that physics should represent a reality in time and space, free from spooky actions at a distance (Clegg 2006, 3).

The German phrase *spukhafte fernwirkungen* is literally translated as "spooky or ghostly distant actions" found in *The Born Einstein Letters by Max Born* (Clegg 2006, 3). The word describing the observed action of entanglement entered the physics plane by Erwin Schrodinger in an article to the Cambridge Philosophical Society. Schrodinger whose thought processes were German used the German word *verschrankung* which has a richer meaning than the English idea of entanglement as out of control, messed up, or chaotic. The German meaning according to Clegg, is more balanced and structured "and is about enfolding and crossing over in an orderly manner (Clegg 2006, 3)." He goes on to explain the difference beautifully by describing a ball of yarn a kitten had been playing with as knotted and all tangled up but a carefully woven tapestry incorporating yarn and applying the German concept of *verschrankung* is a piece of art and something functional and beautiful (Clegg 2006, 3).

According to Talbot, many physicists attempted to debunk Aspect's finding and others were inspired to formulate other reasons. One of those was University of London physicist David Bohm, who believed Aspects findings demonstrated that objective reality does not exist and despite the appearance of solid objects before the eyes the universe is entirely holographic and this is the concept Talbot takes in his book *The Holographic Universe* in my opinion. A hologram seemingly duplicates the whole in all its parts and this amazing observation offers a new and profound way of looking at order from chaos. It portrays the process of dissection, the cutting open in order to look into, may not serve to unlock holographic principles. The holographic concepts of the cosmos strongly suggest this is not the best way to understand because when a hologram is deconstructed one only gets smaller wholes. This idea provided Bohm another avenue of understanding

Aspects findings. "Bohm believe the reason subatomic particles are able to remain in contact with one another regardless of the distance separating them is not because they are sending some sort of mysterious signal back and forth but because their separateness is an illusion. Bohm suggested that at some deeper level of reality such particles are not individual entities, but are actually extensions of the same fundamental something (Matai 2011)."

Bohm offers an amazing and clear analogy to his theory by considering an aquarium (Talbot 2006). In demonstration of his concept he says consider and aquarium in which you have a fish and you cannot look directly at the aquarium but your view is from two cameras mounted at ninety-degree angles from each other. As you watch the two monitors, being unaware of the number of fish in the aquarium you might assume the cameras are presenting to your senses two fish because of the cameras angles. But as you watch you become acutely aware of a certain relationship between "the two fish" you see on the monitors. You notice as you watch one turns and the other one on the second monitor makes a corresponding movement also offering the perception of communication between the two fish. Bohm concludes this is the action of the particles and entanglement demonstrated in Aspect's experiment; the distance or separation is an illusion.

Bohm explains we view objects such as subatomic particles as separate from one another as demonstrated from the aquarium because we see only a portion of their reality and as the fish being a single specimen so to the particles are not separate but are facets of a yet not understood concept of unity that is holographic and therefore indivisible. And due to this conclusion Bohm suggests "everything in physical reality is comprised of these forms or images the universe is itself a projection of a hologram (Talbot 2006)" further suggesting if the perceived separateness of subatomic particles is an illusion then on an amazingly deeper level of reality "all things in the universe are infinitely interconnected. The electrons in a carbon atom in the human brain are connected to the subatomic particles that comprise every salmon that swims, every heart that beats, and every star that shimmers in the sky. Everything interpenetrates everything" (Talbot 2006). The interpenetration described by Talbot is Perichoresis at its most intense meaning.

What is this ultimately suggesting? The cosmos is infinitely open and the quantum world presents unlimited possibilities in which all paths may be taken. In a quantum cosmos, nothing is predictable, or nothing is excluded allowing for the elements of myth to flourish. The quantum connection forces the observer to use terms such as mystery, wonder, awe, and magic in describing reality which is presented to the senses. O'Murchu points out "Life is not determined by blind external forces; it is affected by the quality of our respect for its inherent processes and our willingness to interact with and all life forms in a gentle, non-exploitive, cooperative manner (O'Murchu 2012)." He is simply saying life is not a cause and effect process but rather an interactive perichoretic dance with the Logos, the Breath of God, Tao, and other descriptors of the perennial concept of God's intrusion including the quantum unified field.

Unified Field – The Logos, Energy of the Cosmos

The Unified field is a theory that unites all fundamental forces and elementary particles into a single field and is the matrix of potential not bounded by time or space. It is an infinite non-space part of an electromagnetic world yet through quantum principles able to impact our material world. The unified field is the quantum hologram manifesting a field of influence in our physical realm through energy manipulation. When a magnet is cut in half, the original magnetic field is not divided with one part being the north pole and the other half the south. Each half rearranges within each part of the magnet possessing the north and south poles. Each part becomes a complete magnet unto itself surrounded by a complete magnetic field. Each half alone possesses a slightly weaker field but the sum of the two possess a slightly greater field than the original.

What is the origin of the Unified Field concepts? O'Murchu responds, "they seem to have emerged at a very early stage in evolution, perhaps within the first few milliseconds of the Big Bang. Their purpose seems to be primarily one of self-organization, potential sources of creativity. Mystically, we can envisage fields as the macrocosm that complements the microcosm of the wave particle duality. The latter is the smallest energy force we know; the field is the largest. Life needs both (O'Murchu 2004, 73)."

Is the Quantum Principle implying that human thought can determine, or at the least influence reality? Is thought not how God created according to the Genesis account? Quantum Physicists think so. In the early Twentieth Century, a research called "The Double Slit Experiment" observed that a determining factor of the behavior of energy as particles at the quantum level was affected by the awareness of the observer. Said another way, electrons under identical conditions would behave like particles (position) and at other random times act like waves (momentum). It seemed that what the observer expected to happen did happen as the quantum field seemingly obeyed the will of the observer. Is this telling humanity they are really creators and fully in charge of their own destinies? But the problem is this: the quantum level of reality is not a local singular occurrence in creation, it is not historical. It is omnipresent and this is the most significant aspect of the unified field itself. The consciousness of humanity; more so the consciousness of God is interacting and directing the quantum field at all times as the energy of our beliefs and intentions exert force into this field causing a disruption of a very beautiful dance step. The interpenetration of our thoughts, emotions, beliefs, and intentions are continuously effecting the quantum reality in and around us at each moment of our lives. In effect, and as the author says, "reality is flashing in and out of existence, hypothetically at Planck time which is 10^{44} times per second as explained by The Resonance Project biophysicist William Brown, every time our reality oscillates between form, and the pure energy state of the field, our awareness which is constant and doesn't flash in and out of existence informs the field what to reappear as when it makes its transition back to form at the quantum level (West 2014)." He goes on to explain "reality is flashing in and out of form. Our bodies are a holographic projection of our consciousness, and they are the sum total of our beliefs about ourselves. If we can change our beliefs about ourselves, and thus if we can change the energy that defines our human energy field, then we can change the energetic blueprint which our body aligns with as it re-materializes back into form 10^{44} times per second (West 2014)." This process takes advantage of the off cycle, the gap in our thoughts, where our beliefs no longer affect reality. It is at this point we are in tune with universal principles at which time our energies are at one, atoned, with those coming from the field of all potentiality which are those that promote a union with Life, Light and Love. As one connects to the infinite energy of Light, Life, and Love; the formless potentiality of Logos; the return is the reflection of the fulfilled state of the body. "The projection of your body can only be disrupted by a disturbance in your energy field – your consciousness – caused by unbalanced thoughts and emotions, and limiting beliefs (West 2014)." Your body is not the real you. Your body is merely a projection of what you believe yourself to be. The writer of this article says the ill effects in the body are a function of one's perception. He states, "you are holding disease, illness, pain, and injuries within your consciousness, and thus, they are imprinted in your energetic field, and only then do they proceed to manifest in your physiology (West 2014)."

In quantum concepts, matter only exits under observation. According to certain quantum physicists it requires the interference of an observer for the physical world to materialize, otherwise it is a non-local cloud of energy. In this vein of thought, the entire cosmos is a massive field of quantum energy under observation, a cloud of quantum energy that has collapsed into matter and remaining in the physical state indicates it remains under constant observation. Who is the Observer? Is it possible that God is not only Creator but also Prime Observer of the cosmos and not only sustaining it by His voice or word but also by his eye? Conceptually, in quantum thought, without the observation of the Creator the cosmos would exist as a non-material state, a cloud of quantum energy as potential awaiting to be viewed. Yet there is a secondary observer, which is us who also holds influence in the physical realm as we learn to call things that are not to be, speaking in the Creator's voice and call things into being.

The Unified Field theoretically contains all things, the totality of the cosmos, including past, present, and future. This vast amount of information is holographically encoded in the unified field so that all exists simultaneously and continuously enforcing the eternal present moment. Everything exists at once but we perceive the on/off moments which we partition into time, into a past, present, and future (West 2014). We consider motion as elapsed time because we perceive change as movement translates into time passing. The incremental energy fields of on/off and movement are a perceptive element of the holographic cosmos. It is this collapse of energy flashing in and out of existence as the consciousness of the observer effects the Unified Field causing our ideas of history; our past, present, and future to react to the observer.

As stated earlier, time is only marked by humanity therefore relative. Is time the effects of our perception of the Unified Field as we attempt to catalog its perceived movements? Time is a construct of man and does not naturally arise out of the cosmos. Time is the division of cycles marking the on/off rate of change as reality forms and then un-forms. If the cycles or gauges of time were absent, time could not be measured and would thus lose it effect on our perceived reality. Consider this observation by Deepak Chopra, in a lecture series with Wayne Dyer entitled "Living Beyond Miracles." They relate the story of a group of miners who experienced a cave in in Germany, trapping them underground for an extended period of time. They had no light and no way of judging the cycles of the universe, therefore no frame of reference for their perception. There were a total of seven men who were trapped underground, and only one had a watch. The man with the watch, wanting to ease the fear and worry of his friends, decided to call out that one hour had passed every time two hours had actually passed. On the seventh day they were rescued and all survived except the man with the watch. Because he took it upon himself to call out that one hour had passed when by his watch two hours had passed; he slowed down time for everyone causing them to alter perception of time. "He had them change their collective agreement as to what constituted time, it's an agreement. And then they aged accordingly and he couldn't fool himself because he had a watch (West 2014)."

Unified Field and Time Concepts

Time is seemingly entrapped in quantum entanglement or rather muted. Time is present enforcing limits for internal observers which see the parts, the dualistic pairs, and division of man; but is amazingly absent or mute for the external observers seeing the whole, the singularity, and the soul of being. Phil Davies says, "time is a product of the observer rather than an objective attribute of space (Mason 2010, 77)." The German Christian mystic poet, Angelus Silesius, wrote in the 17th century: "Time is of your own making, its clock ticks in your head, the moment you stop thought, time too stops dead. Do not compute eternity, as light year after year, one step across that line called time, eternity is here (Mason 2010, 78)."

Just as particles exist only when observed so too does time. 18th Century Anglican Bishop Berkeley indicated nothing is real "unless it exists in the mind of some observer, whether it is some finite spirit or the mind of God." His famous dictum is "to be is to be perceived" indicating objects exist only in perception rather than matter (Ward 2013). Nobel Laureate Eugene Wigner writes: "The very study of the external world led to the conclusion that the content of the consciousness is an ultimate reality (Wigner 2017)." This quantum physics principle that observance brings existence concludes that consciousness is the ultimate reality. A case in point is the analogy of color as objects do not emanate color but through observation color is perceived as a refracted wavelength of light from the object as the light is interpreted by the optic nerve and brain. Objects have properties that emanate the sensation of color and when observed, interpreted as color but the object does not have an intrinsic color element. Consciousness must exist for us to perceive physical reality. Color, taste, and smell only exist to an observer that has the propensity to detect this aspect of reality. It is exciting to consider the possibilities of quantum physics offers a deeper reality from a totally different venue of the power of conscious thought seen in the interconnectedness of quantum entanglement is more real that human perception.

Tied so uniquely to time is the concept of eternity and infinity. Considering the mathematical principle of the number line, Augsburger contends, "Infinity is not the end of a number line. It is a mathematical recognition of a never-ending line. Anything less than infinite, even slightly less, cannot arrive at infinity by going father on the number line. It is not there. Then, where is it? Infinity is an indication of eternal movement. It is, in a very real sense, a verb. It does not reside at any given location, yet it is everywhere and is ever moving (Augsburger 2013, 89-90)." Alarmingly, this is also true of eternity as it too is everywhere but when a measurement is attempted, it moves away or turns aside so no measurement is possible. It was once thought everything was infinitely divisible but not so when the quantum principle is involved as the object defines its divisibility. Money for example is not infinitely divisible. A dollar can be broken into four quarters, ten dimes, twenty nickels, or one hundred pennies; but not further divisibility exists as the penny is the smallest unit of currency at this time.

Some in Quantum Theory suggests there is no motion, nor time, but only the perception arising from our experiences as we relate to the unified field participating in the expansion and contraction of creation. Is there movement then, or change? Possibly not as in the infinite hologram all encoded information comes to light in us as we shift perspective. Lao Tzu said, "The Tao does not act yet it is the root of all action. The Tao does not move yet it is the source of all creation (Lao Tzu 2001, 48)." He poses equality with the Greek Logos which is also equated by this author with the Unified Field.

The wave particle duality seen in quantum physics does seem to parallel the creative process in amazing ways. Particles of light are not simply a solid object that passes through the air but are found to behave as a wave which can be scattered when an interference is introduced, it can be defused, bending through slits and can be refracted. The behavior of light as it is refracted is described in wavelengths of color at various oscillations and yet also behave as particles. We must remove from our concepts light being a small spherical solid object with boundaries as first described by Newton in the seventeenth century. It is realized to be more like clouds of energy, yet having a discoverable propensity when observed. Light does not disperse like clouds but maintains a unity. It is quantum physics which attempts to describe how light behaves as waves/clouds yet maintains contact and union with a single response as particles.

Is the process of defined movement hidden when the observer measures the atom's position; and conversely, is location hidden when the observer measures momentum? They are not masked in the usual sense of meaning as both measurable attributes of momentum and position are potentially present but are not present in actuality until a measurement is taken. How the observer choses to interfere will determine whether the wavelength (momentum) side of reality or the particle (location) aspect of reality manifests. The dual information is not lost but rather the observer shapes the present moment, energizing potential reality moving it to actuality. What is masked is still fully and potentially present. It was the EPR experiment which determined even though the momentum and position were simultaneously present in a potential state; neither was physically real (Wolf 1989, 140, 159).

The unified field is the union of all matter and it is the concept that points to a single source because all matter was once in contact in singularity. McTaggart says,

> Perhaps the most essential ingredient of this interconnected universe was a living consciousness that observed it. In classical physics, the experimenter was considered a separate incident, a silent observer behind glass, attempting to understand a universe that carried on, whether he or she was observing it or not. In quantum physics however, it was discovered, the state of all possibilities of any quantum particle collapsed into a set entity as soon as it was observed or a measurement taken. This astounding observation also had a shattering implication about the nature of reality. It suggested that the consciousness of the observer brought the observed object into being. Nothing in the universe existed as an actual thing independently of our perception of it. Every minute of every day we were creating our world (McTaggart 2002, 11).

Quantum Perichoretic Harmony

What is the unified field's purpose in the cosmos? Many ascertain its concepts are stored in the perennial philosophy described in all cultures to explain what was seen in the cosmos but not understood. The Western mindset seeks an explanation grounded in logic and reason while the Eastern view mainly endeavors to accept what is and integrate it into their lives. The ancient views described humanity as part of the All and in relation to it and identified it as the force that unites and permeates the entire cosmos. Gregg Braden says this unifying principle is "not out there somewhere [but] it is a part of ourselves as well as part of all that we perceive (Braden 2003)." Braden goes on to call the unified field the Quantum Hologram and adds it responds to our actions and thoughts allowing us to be a participant in the creation of the cosmos. Science explains this field is everywhere and exists in all times. It is an infinite quanta of energy present everywhere rather than being generated and migrating to another location. In his conclusion, he makes the statement that "except for the language, this field sounds very similar to what the ancients called God (Braden 2003)." It also describes the function of the Greek Logos, the Principle of the Egyptian Maat, the Chinese Tao, and others all correlate to the new scientific analysis of the unified field of quantum physics and in particular the principles of quantum entanglement. All describe a creative potential fully active in kinetic movement or agitation. The Unified Field in the context of physics describes a set of properties in a unique point in space and time and is the reactionary area between the primary forces whose theoretic ranges are infinite. It is not a set location but is a response to forces, energies, words, thoughts, and consciousness. Max Planck refers to the unified field as the matrix (Braden 2007, 56)." Edgar Mitchell, Astronaut in the Apollo 14 mission, calls it "nature's mind (Braden 2007, 55)." Stephen Hawking, astrophysicist, refers to the unified field as the "Mind of God (Braden 2003)."

All particles are moving and demonstrate the holographic concept of fractal and vibrational fields. The cosmos is a unified field playing a quantum perichoretic symphony. The key might be found in understanding the melody. This movement or vibration is inherent in each living cell too. This means each cell in the human body resonates this energy field. The movement or vibration of these particles, or actually everything in the cosmos is the particle exiting one location and entering another without the interference of space and time. Perhaps a more accurate account is the particles are flashing on and off in one locale. Swimme suggests they "surge into existence and just as suddenly dissolve from this location to become in another (Swimme 1996, 102)."

Clegg offers a brilliant yet simple description of a singularity through a balloon and a marker (Clegg 2012, 110). Partially blow up a balloon and using a Sharpie, make three or four marks on the balloon representing galaxies. Blow up the balloon a little more and note the marks and their distance from each other. Blow up the balloon yet again noting the change in distance. Recognize the spots are not moving on the balloon yet the distance is increasing. The space is expanding while the marks are in the same location on the balloon. Similarly, in the universe the space is expanding. No single galaxy can be the center of the universe. Let the air out of the balloon a little bit and imagine time moves backwards. The balloon ceases shrinking when it reaches its original size. The distance between the dots has gotten smaller yet remain the same place on the rubber of the balloon. As the balloon shrinks further to a dot, any mark on the balloon returns into that single one dot. In this sense the Big Bang occurred everywhere as all was in the single point. Where ever you are you can rightly claim to be the center of the Big Bang because the entire cosmos is the location of the beginning of everything. The Big Bang posits everything started out of nowhere and in no time—in a singularity. The singularity is not a point in space, nor a point in time.

Another example explaining the concept of the singularity is found in the movie Interstellar (Dolan 2015). In the movie, Dr. Romily postulates one needs to see inside a blackhole as this blackhole contains the singularity entombed in darkness and incalculable gravity. He compares the concept of the blackhole to an oyster and the pearl inside the oyster, the singularity, being held firm by forces and hidden in darkness behind the event horizon.

A singularity is a point of infinite gravity and density, a point of which nothing can be measured as the known laws of physics cease to function or exist. The singularity of all things is the Big Bang. Straight mathematical concepts speculate that a length can be subdivided into halves indefinitely but quantum concepts negate this idea. The length defined as Planck's Length is 10^{-33} centimeters is indivisible. How is this possible? Because it is beyond the dimensions of the subatomic particles that are dividing. The same is true of mass, energy, and time. The unit of time which cannot be reduced is 10^{-43} seconds. The quantum world has introduced humanity to the limits of reality; a boundary at which the subatomic particles cease to be objects and yet these elements possess no literal dimension. What holds these particles, the quanta in seemingly communication? Light. It is light which maintains the union of the atom and molecule forming material objects. In this essence, all forms of matter are made up of light. Light was the first vocal act of creation as light is the glue binding all together.

According to Talbot, Bohm's analysis of quantum ideologies led him to believe the deepest order of existence which births the physical world is the implicate (enfolded) order of quantum physics and he says that which the implicate produces at the human level of perception is the explicate (unfolded) order. Talbot says he uses these terms because he associates the orders of existence as the result of "countless enfoldings and unfoldings between the two orders (Talbot 2011, 46)."

Nachmonides, an ancient Jewish scholar of the 12th century, studied and authored an amazing commentary to Genesis ascertained the cosmos had ten dimensions and defined four as knowable while the other six were beyond the ability of humanity to grasp. Physicists today acknowledge we too live in ten dimensions and it is the three spatial dimensions with time that we can physically discern and measure. The other six are curled or enfolded in less than the indivisible Planck length of 10^{-33} centimeters and only can be acknowledged by indirect means.

There is a conjecture among philosophers and physicists that the original ten dimensions were the dwelling reality of humanity but endured a fracture based on the account of Genesis three (characterized as the fall) which essentially resulted in the division of the spiritual and physical worlds. The *Onkelos Translation* says in Genesis 1:31 the cosmos was experiencing "a unified order (Schroeder 2001, 33)." This concept does suggest the current entropy laws of physics, called the bondage of decay, might have been the effect of the fall of humanity and the loss of state of creation (Romans 8:21). But did entropy exist before Genesis three as the world was without form and void? Interestingly, the words for "evening" and "morning" might come into play. The laws of entropy imply the universe is winding down into more and more chaos or loss of order; but for this to be valid it had to have been wound up. Is the six days of creation really an infusion of the wind up as the terms in Genesis used are *erev* and *boker* which were translated as evening and morning but have a richer etymology. Erev carries the concept of dark, obscurity, and randomness. It is this darkness that is without form and void. It is from this concept that evening was derived; the period of the day when light is waning and we lose the ability to discern color, shapes and identities. Morning is the rising of light when things again are discernable and order and functionality begin to materialize.

Talbot says,

We too, have two very different aspects to our reality. We can view ourselves as physical bodies moving through space. Or we can view ourselves as a blur of interference patterns enfolding throughout the cosmic hologram. Bohm believes this second point of view might even be the more correct, for to think of ourselves as a holographic mind/brain looking at a holographic universe is again an abstraction, an attempt to separate two things that ultimately cannot be separated. What makes it difficult is that in this case we are not looking at the hologram. We are part of the hologram (Talbot 2011, 55).

I am a part, yet fully functional as the whole, therefore, I am the whole; yet differentiated.

Zero Point Field – Womb of Creativity

The zero point vacuum appears as nothing and is mathematically functioning as zero or an origination point. Assume a game of tug-o-war and both sides have equal strengths regardless of the number of players. With equal strengths, the rope remains in the same place—unmoving and mathematically movement equals zero—the strengths are balanced. In other words, the forces on the rope equal zero. Suppose you cannot see either team but only the center of the rope with the flag. You see nothing moving because we only perceive differences. We, if we did not know the game, would not be aware of the state of tension or potential energy stored within the rope by forces being applied by strengths we cannot see.

Similarly, the vacuum state of zero energy exists everywhere and if it remains in a state of zero sum, we do not perceive the stored energy. Movement is manifested when a change in equality (loss of balance) occurs. The rope, no longer in a state of being in balance, responds to the now unequal forces and shift in the direction of the stronger force. Potential energy becomes kinetic resulting in movement of the rope. The shift is an energy release in the vacuum and becomes visible. The energy released is wave or particle enforcing matter (Davidson 1989, 31-33).

What is this energy seen in the energy field, the sea of light, this string theory universe? Davidson defines this energy as:

> The dance of life and form. Energy is both the pattern and the thing itself. It is movement that makes up the illusory show of reality. It is vibration that makes every subatomic particle exist. It is the motion of the stars and galaxies. To the mind, it is causality and matter; to the soul it contains the essence of the Creator's love. Energy is the essence of our thoughts and our emotions, it is the fabric of our bodies. Energy is a snowflake, a flower, a leaf. It is the hazy calmness of a summers day, the power of the hurricane, the crush of a great ocean breaker. It is the gentle flame of a candle, the explosion of a supernova. It is both the information and content of the carrier wave (Davidson 1989, 44,45,47).

Manners adds, "The most important thing about energy is that there is nothing else. Within every particle of created matter there lies a distant echo of the formative and creative power of the primal energy of life" (Davidson 1989, 47). The Bible seemingly presents this force as the Logos with the base translation of word having lost its deeper etymology of thought or intent. The Indian mystics refer to this energy life force as *shabd* meaning sound, and the Vedas carry the same implication. In Hindi, the translation of John 1:1 says shabd was present with God. Native Americans call this force "Creation Song" (Davidson 1989, 77). It is a personal, relational primal force of Light, Life, and Love.

Zero-Point Field: The Matrix of Potential Energy

Brian Swimme, says the quantum matrix or the unified field does not have geometric form or describable shape but depicted mathematically as "quantum potential" and he chooses a personal and meaningful description which meshes with his cosmic concepts calling it the "all-nourishing abyss (Swimme 1997, 97-100)." This phrase is overflowing with meaning by exhibiting a dual process he calls the generative potentiality of the cosmos and the ability of infinite energy absorption (Swimme 1997, 100). His phraseology depicts the cosmos emerging from the all nourishing abyss not in the far distant past in time but in every present moment. He states; "the all nourishing abyss then is not a thing, nor a collection of things, not even, strictly speaking, a physical place, but rather a power that gives birth and that absorbs existence at a things annihilation (Swimme 1997, 100)." He says the "foundational reality of the universe is this unseen ocean of potentiality (Swimme 1997, 100)." Our Western religion concepts imagine "out of nothing" missing the amazing and mysterious potential from which God extracted creation, the singularity of all things. An awe inspiring image is possible when God is stated as the All in All, all things, in all places, and at all times—the Singularity.

The Zero-point field was considered dead space according to Newtonian physics which postulated all molecular movement ceased at zero degrees Kelvin (-273 degrees Celsius) and no energy could be measured. Instead of finding no energy as expected, Dr. Harold Puthoff discovered a "seething cauldron (Talbot 2006)" of energy destroying Newton's concept and this energy was given the name zero-point energy. Puthoff proved that a physical vacuum was not devoid of energy but instead of being an empty energy-less vacuum, it was a space filled with matter and not empty and chaotic as was originally conceived. This background energy field explains the quantum discovery of the unexplained movement of subatomic particles which could migrate between this unseen field and physical visual reality. This proved physical reality is not the only reality we have indicating our cosmos is never idle nor empty and motionless. It is interesting to note this energy is not powerless or useless. John Wheeler and Richard Feynman of Princeton University estimated that a single cup of this energy is sufficient to bring the earth's ocean to the boiling point temperature (Pilkington 2003). The constant motion of this energy from unseen to seen and back again and its ability to pass between realms is the dance of the cosmos, the effect of the Word of God; energy awaiting the word to become.

Metaphorically, the zero-point field can be described as a sea of light supporting all of creation. God may not be the zero-point field but perhaps it is the mechanism whereby man can get a glimpse of the Breath of God. Perhaps similar to the visible breath on cold mornings, energy to matter demonstrating the full impact of His words "Let there be…" could indicate the zero-point field might be the source of the light of creation accounts noted in many of the worlds creation myths. As the energy in this field is at the lowest state it is unobservable as we see things out of contrast and difference or through perceived movement. This energy field is essentially omnipresent permeating all things effectively causing us to be oblivious to it. Light that we see is above this energy level. The command "let there be light" takes on an amazing metaphysical dimension as the zero-point field, the sea of quantum light, is actually the sustainer of all that bombards our senses; all that we see, feel, hear, taste, and touch.

This matrix is the zero-point field projecting the holographic universe. This concept means the entirety of the universe, all that has ever existed or will exit, existed in one point. How can something that is technically infinitely small contain all the data, all the energy required to create our solar system with its sun and planets and life? The zero-point is essentially the origination point and is simultaneously the smallest and largest number. It is nothing yet contains everything. It is both without form and void yet full and functional. It is an undefined point in space in an undefined time that contains all that is with all that will be. It is the singularity of creation, the point of God's intent about to be projected by the Ruach of God.

As the zero-point contains all yet is nothing, according to Talbot it "contains every subatomic particle that has been or will be—every configuration of matter and energy that is possible from snowflakes to quasars to blue whales to gamma rays. It must be seen as a sort of cosmic storehouse of all that is (Talbot 2006)." Talbot adds, "although Bohm concedes that we have no way of knowing what else might lie hidden in the super hologram, he does venture to say that we have no reason to assume it does not contain more. Or as he's puts it, perhaps the super holographic level of reality is a mere stage beyond which lies an infinity of other development (Talbot 2006)." How can one say objects are made from no-thing? In the quantum world, objects are composed of molecules which consist of atoms being made of subatomic particles including protons, electrons, which are formed from even smaller subatomic particles such as quarks which came into existence out of nowhere; the Big Bang – the Zero Point, a singularity.

McTaggart explains the unified field is "a matrix or medium which connects two or more points in space, usually via a force, like gravity or electromagnetism. The field is considered that area of space where this charge and its effects can be detected. Simply put, a field is a region of influence (McTaggart 2002, 22)." McTaggart goes on to state, "the zero-point field is a repository of all fields and all ground energy states and all virtual particles – a field of fields (McTaggart 2002, 23)" implying an undeniable connectivity of every particle in creation and as this entanglement existed it was expressed in energy manifesting in the physical realm as light. Dr. Bernard Haisch has offered several possible connections between the creation and the zero-point field in which he refers to the zero-point field as a "sea of light (Haisch 2006, 70)." It is religion that insists this light is physical but there is another light expressed in theology and that is an inward light. This idea of the zero-point field as the sea of light takes on a whole and beautiful concept as the offering of a scientific basis for the metaphysical identification of the field being expressed in the Chinese cultures as the life force being qi and having been described as a type of life energy field. The book of Genesis offers its concept of the energy field when God said, "Let there be light and there was light" several days before the creation of the sun and stars.

The waves of energy that comprise the unified field allow the transmigration or exchange of informational form and these waves have an unlimited capacity for storage and retrieval. These subatomic waves are continuously imprinting and recording matter—the continuous creation and functioning as the forerunner containing all frequencies of waves. The zero-point field is then a mirror image of the cosmos as a recorder of everything that ever was and the wellspring of all that will be contained in the zero point of singularity. It is this vacuum of singularity that is the beginning and the end of everything in the cosmos. Does the Einstein equation "$E=mc^2$" indicate two components are required to produce energy?

In considering the quantum model where matter and light are charged particles of energy; the equation simply states "Energy = Energy" pointing to the concept that matter is illusory. It was Arthur C. Clarke who said the vacuum or "empty space is actually a cauldron of seething energies equal to the zero-point field (Clarke 1997, 258)" pointing to the without form and void of the Genesis account alluding to the zero-point field being chaos; the potential of all potentialities from which all of creation was called (McTaggart 2002, 33).

The Creative Vacuum of Life

The creative vacuum is the quantum state with the lowest possible energy level which contains no physical particles and is also called zero-point energy. It exists as a fullness of all possibilities rather than an emptiness and this background or base energy exists in every space in the cosmos. It is an energy field that contains all the "formative blueprints (O'Murchu 2004, 77)" or the cosmic blueprints which McTaggart says the zero-point field multitasks by retaining memories of history from past experiences and can govern patterns of future influence and is also able to receive influence, thereby impacting the future (McTaggart 2002, 90,96). Our mental concept of a vacuum is an empty and dead space yet it has been found to contain vibrations and movement awaiting expression. It is the now known properties of the creative vacuum, the reservoir of unlimited potential which serves to remind of an "ancient mystical conviction that creation is more like a great thought rather than a great machine (O'Murchu 2004, 77)." This points to a move away from Newtonian physics to that of the quantum model and in which O'Murchu links the Greek Logos or intent.

O'Murchu says "the world is the arena of divine disclosure (O'Murchu 2004, 83)" and goes on to say "the vastness of space is not just to accommodate the dance of life. It is an aspect of the dance itself, in fact, a very critical dimension. It is grossly misleading to suggest that it is empty. Its fullness is a reservoir of prolific energy which Davidson (1989) very rightly calls the creative vacuum (O'Murchu 2004, 111)." Max Planck, while giving a lecture in Florence Italy, said of himself;

> As a man who has devoted his whole life to the most clearheaded science, to the study of matter, I can tell you as the result of my research about the atoms, this much: there is no matter as such. All matter originates and exists only by force which brings the particles of an atom to vibrate and holds this most minute solar system of the atoms together... We must assume behind this force the existence of a conscious and intelligent Mind. This Mind is the matrix of all matter (Davidson 1989, 128).

Quantum concepts tell us this space vacuum is far from empty and inactive but is alive with potential. The vacuum exists and under certain conditions of matter and energy bring forth something from nothing. John Wheeler, American theoretical physicist, said, "no point is more central than this, that empty space is not empty. It is the seat of the most violent physics (Wheeler 2017)." A very astute Facebook post offered this assessment of the vacuum. This vacuum exists as the most centralized collection of energy in which potentialized energy awaits the call to become as the elusive Higgs boson, which has yet to be observed, energizes this zero-point field. It is the potentiality from nothingness and this nothingness exists everywhere as quantum concepts point to the matter-less aspect of the atom now stating it consists of very little matter yet abundant in space once thought to be dead space. It is from this empty space of boundless potential that we were called from. Brian Swimme enlivened this point when he enlarged the atom proportionally. He enlarged the atom to the size of Yankee Stadium noting it would mainly consist of empty space as the nucleus would be smaller than a baseball in center field. The electrons of the atom would resemble tiny gnats buzzing at an altitude higher than "any pop fly Babe Ruth ever hit." In the area between the baseball and the gnats is emptiness, nothing; causing Swimme to proclaim, "you are more emptiness that you are anything else." Catholic theologian and mystic Thomas Merton said "There is in all things an invisible fecundity, a dimmed light, a meek namelessness, a hidden wholeness. This mysterious unity and integrity is wisdom, the mother of us all' ("Mystical Order of the Gnostics' Facebook page, accessed June 25, 2017, https://www.facebook.com /groups/OrderoftheGnostics.).

Through the aspects of Quantum Perichoresis, several factors can now be developed through quantum theory and its amazing aspects in theology. The major offering is life is maintained by this amazing creative energy that is manifested in vibrational movement, cyclic rhythm, and fractal patterns. O'Murchu says "creation is sustained by a superhuman, pulsating restlessness, a type of resonance vibrating throughout time and eternity (O'Murchu 2004, 209)." This energy expresses the change from potential to kinetic as evolving life in relationship and harmony with the force that creates it. As this principle is expressed it does not negate the concept of an intimate creator. Secondly, as the concept of the hologram is applied, O'Murchu says "evolution is underpinned by a deep unfolding structure, characterized by design and purpose, necessitating an unceasing interplay of order and disorder, randomness and creativity (O'Murchu 2004, 210)." In this chain of thought and as the whole is greater than the sum of its parts is a statement of dynamic possibility; the quantum principle expresses non-duality forgoing the old paradigm of good versus evil. In this vein, creation is invited to participate in the becoming of the cosmos as redemption is not a necessity because there is no division or separation for the redemptive act to correct. As no redemption is needed there was no sin causing a perceived separation therefore nothing missing and nothing broken. It is those moments of sacred space and time we are invited to participate in understanding the mystery that is our journey of discovery. This journey is that of love enveloped by a myriad of possibilities even to the subatomic potential revealing a God who O'Murchu says is not "a passive, detached, external ruler, but a passionate, relational presence, in the creative, evolutionary process itself" (O'Murchu 2004, 214). Quantum Perichoresis offers a mysterious and magical God who has enfolded Himself in our evolution and unfolds within us offering enlightenment of our relational identity.

Quantum Physics and Unified Field Theory — Redefining God

Astrophysicist Bernard Haisch says there is an infinite consciousness "who has infinite potential, whose ideas become the laws of physics of our universe and others, and whose purpose in so doing is the transformation of potential into experience (Haisch 2006, xi)." If the idea of the unified field is an emanation of God, fully representing the Source of creation then we can deduce ideas of the Creator's character. In contemplating the unified field with our current understanding, we can deduce God cannot demand any action from us that will increase His happiness. This God cannot dislike nor hate anything that we do and are. He does not punish us because that would ultimately represent a form of self-punishment. God did not create a literal place called hell where He is not nor heaven where he only is. These concepts can potentially lead us to further corollaries such as this God experiences life, the flow from potential to actual through us. This God chooses relationship not servitude and worship should be from love not out of fear. The consequence of our actions can produce detrimental responses that we must pass through and in this aspect, one creates their own hell. Ultimately our consciousness will be united with the infinite consciousness of God resulting in heaven. This view instills the desire to live a life in relation to the creative intelligence, experiencing the mind of God which plans a journey of spiritual growth and peace in which nothing is missing nor nothing broken. Haisch states "Creation did not happen, it is (Haisch 2006, 22-23, 122)."

Why is it so difficult to experience the mystical relationship that seems to be observed and offered in quantum ideologies? It is because our views are entrenched in the Newtonian mindset which is categorized as mechanical, binary, independent, and completely isolated from reality. It is this view that portrays man as parts (body, soul, spirit) and act as distinct and separate. The alienation is complete and one fails to see an inherent interconnectedness which is offered by quantum physics resulting in a third prospect— that of functional harmony which is amazingly portrayed in music.

God Sings and the Cosmos Dances

Music has an unprecedented involvement in the human journey. Its inherent creative energy is utilized in many cultures as a sound or call to war and at the very opposite a call to rest and peace. The force of creation, depicted in the Biblical account as God spoke exemplifies the power of creation being in sound. Did God sing? It is not out of the realm of possibility as music is the power of sound and later became exemplified in the Hebrew word dabar but its Aramaic etymology did not stop at "word" but linguistically it represented an unrequited creative potential energy that exploded into manifested kinetic energy and the cosmos has been dancing ever since.

O'Murchu carries this idea deeper into the human journey as he notes "music, song, incantation, and droning all embody this primordial creative potential which animates the created order (O'Murchu 2004, 54)." O'Murchu addresses the possibility of echoes found in superstring theory when he quotes Brian Green who says, "the fundamental energy that enlivens everything in the universe may be compared to the vibrating energy that occurs when we move the bow over a musical string, the music being the 'voiced' language of silent energy (O'Murchu 2004, 54)." Swimme and Berry (1992) elicit the idea of "humanity's role as a sounding board for a universe that is essentially melodious in nature (O'Murchu 2004, 55)." God sings. O'Murchu goes on to extrapolate a potential dancing cosmos evoked by Pythagoras' Music of the Spheres or *Musica Universalis* being an ancient philosophical concept that regards proportions in the movements in the known celestial bodies at that time (the Sun, Moon, and planets) as musical forms. This music is not usually thought to be literally audible but a harmonic, mathematical, and religious concept. The cosmos dances as God sings. O'Murchu, adds through Davidson, that we are invited to dance "according to some higher strings (Davidson 1989, 402)." Is it possible that the Logos is melodious as it enlivens the cosmos and the animation we perceive is the responsive dance? "With the discovery of string theory, musical metaphors take on a startling reality, for the theory suggests that the microscopic landscape is suffused with tiny strings whose vibrational patterns orchestrate the evolution of the cosmos. The wind of change, according to superstring theory, gust through an aeolian universe (Greene 1999, 135)." O'Murchu therefore posits his first principle of Quantum Theology as he states:

> There is more to our world than what can be perceived by the human senses or envisaged by the human imagination. Life is sustained by creative energy, fundamentally (benign) in nature, with a tendency to manifest and express itself in movement, rhythm, and pattern. Creation is sustained by superhuman, pulsating restlessness, a type of resonance vibrating throughout time and eternity. (O'Murchu 1998, 55)

It is music which demonstrates the contrast of Newtonian duality and quantum harmony. A piano, made up of white and black keys each making a distinct sound but when played together they produce a chord of harmony. The harmonic chord forming the whole correlates with the mystical application in which alienation is negated. Harmony forms an energy filled connection manifesting non-duality and non-locality.

The quantum theory dictum which states the whole is greater than the sum of its parts has merit because life, according to the quantum world, is the product of a myriad of interactions and relationships. It does not truly operate in the realm of cause and effect of the Newtonian paradigm. Newtonian views the whole is complete because the parts function as designed. The Quantum view is weighted because the whole is contained in each part as a hologram. The holographic concept negates the previous laws of cause and effect as the quantum cosmos does not exist alone but is fully integrated, relational, and completely interdependent. The parts represent the whole and function on behalf of the whole. The cosmos can't dance in cause and effect.

Fractal Language and the Echoing Strings

The fractals of language are demonstrated in the etymological component of words; but more so in linguistics which explores not only depths and origin of meaning but also syntax (sentence formation) and pragmatics (language use). Augsburger declares "language is fractal. Each word in a sentence is in a sense redefined by the string of words surrounding it (Augsburger 2015, 405)." Greene says "the fundamental particles of the universe…including electrons, neutrinos, quarks, and so on – are the 'letters' of all matter (Greene 2003)." String Theory adds to each quantum particle a fractalized language—a micro loop or string that vibrates, oscillates, and dances. These echoing strings—the energy locus of the particle speaks, conveying the sound of music throughout all creation from the quantum level to the visible universe interacting, harmonizing, and projecting the symphony. The quantum concept of theology implies the creative potentiality resides within the cosmos and emerges responding to sound as letters and words. "The original power of creation is described in many religions as the power of sound, which in Judaism and Christianity we refer to as the Word. As already indicated, the Hebrew dabhar does not mean word as understood linguistically, but rather an irresistible created energy exploding into voluptuous and prodigious creativity (O'Murchu 2004, 54)."

Gerhard Von Rad, a German theologian and scholar, defines wisdom as found in Proverbs eight as the word behind all of creation, as the instrument which orders the primeval world, and as the mystery behind the creation of the world. The Hebrew concept of wisdom also focused on humanity as wisdom seeks to offer assistance to humanity. Von Rad explains "this mysterious order in the world not only addresses man; it also loves him (Fox 1983, 38)." Religion has traditionally made dabar to be the word from a stuffy God up there but Fox says "the true dabar of God is as much right brain (affection, play, and love) as it is left brain (verbal, truth oriented, cognitive). This is one more reason why to translate dabhar as 'word of God' today is destructive of the rich meanings behind God's creative energy (Fox 1983, 38)." The Hebrew intent of dabar is more than word, it also carries the concept of action that is the effect of the word. It contains energy that is creative and able to convert energy from potentiality to actuality.

How does string theory enter the cosmic ideal? Quantum Theology, according to O'Murchu "abhors the human tendency to attribute literal significance to the sacred writings of the various religions. It acknowledged that the sacred text of all the religions may be divinely inspired, but that inspiration has been, and continues to be, mediated through the human mind and imagination and is committed to human language that is always conditioned by the particular influences and nuances of specific cultures. Language is a human invention, a symbolic system that seeks to convey meaning in local cultural settings. It can never be absolutized to communicate the depth or totality of the divine intent (O'Murchu 2004, 57)."

This dance of energy and life is mimicked in the entire cosmic realm; from the creative vacuum that was once thought to be void space to the intrusion of divinity and humanity. As the participants are arrested by the rhythm and tempo of the music, the experience moves to union. It is at this point the parties merge into one and the sacred dance is enlivening. O'Murchu says "Energy is the substance of life, the unrelenting wellspring of pure possibility, escalating and undulating as in a great cosmic dance (O'Murchu 2004, 45)" and "There is motion, but they are ultimately no moving objects; there is activity, but there are no actors. There are no dancers; there is only the dance itself. To join in the dance, we need to shed a lot of fears and inhibitions – not a few of which are religious in nature. It is only by participating that we learn what the dance is all about. The day of the neutral observer is well-nigh over (O'Murchu 2004, 40)"!

Greene goes on to imply that from this one principle of everything at its most microscopic level consists of combinations of vibrating strands one extrapolates that string theory provides a single explanatory framework capable of encompassing all forces and all matter (Greene 2003). Augsburger continues in this vein of thought when he states "all the strings in the universe comprise a cosmic symphony. In this case, it is more than analogous to a symphony: it is the symphony (Augsburger 2015, 190)" and later noting the comment of one of his students who postulated the strings may be God's vocal echo from "Let there be... which was placed in past time when God never retracted the command to be. (Augsburger 2015, 226).

The implication of perichoretic movements between the components of creation offer metaphorically a new and vibrant theology in which the Creator and created are in union and are participants of a single vision. Quantum Perichoresis offers a movement, a synergy which views the divine unfolding inside the vault, the womb of creativity. Often, religion places this life energy as outside, or up there but O'Murchu places this creative potential squarely within creation not outside of it when he says "the creative energy that makes all things possible and keeps all things in being is within and not outside the cosmos. The notion of an external creator is a construct of the human mind, a projection initially adopted to assuage our fears of threat and possible annihilation. Creation is sustained from within, not from without (O'Murchu 2004, 65)."

While writing this last chapter I watched the movie *Interstellar* (Dolan 2014) for more than the second time; and like the Matrix already referenced in this book, it caused me to look deeper and to consider possibilities. In one thought provoking scene, they encounter the power of love. Cooper and Amelia Brand are returning to the ship after traveling though the worm hole and their ship-mate, Dr. Romily, has aged over 23 years to their actual time of a few hours. They begin to discuss their options as they question the relationship of gravity, space, and time. In deciding to forego theory and science, Brand expresses the power of the heart. She says love is not the invention of humanity and it has the capability to transcend time and proves her point by asking Cooper, do you love someone who has died? She says love could be an artifact of a higher dimension that is consciously unperceivable. She pounds her point home when she argues "Love is the one thing we are capable of perceiving that transcends the dimensions of time and space. Maybe we should trust that even though we can't understand it yet." By our current concepts God is love and therefore, Love is God. Is love an artifact of the unlimited dimensional God? Is love a yet unexplained dimension of the quantum enigma?

God sings and the beautiful potentiality of the "without form and void" vibrate in an amazing cosmic dance as God inhaled and expressed His heart-song "Let there be..." He sang those words of creation as the intent of His heart and were very lovingly expressed negating the harshness of creation instilled in the Western mindset which teaches a need of correction. The Singing Ruach initiated the dance. The space of potential which had been traditionally termed chaos was the matrix of potentiality which was far from the disorderly without form and void. It stood waiting, pulsing, and vibrating—alive yet undefined. It was the Ruach which converted the matrix of vibrational disharmonies into rhythm as waves of pre-sound effected these energies, setting them to their functional and beneficent state.

The ideas of quantum entanglement suggests creation is so interconnected even to the subatomic level that creational reality hangs on those words as potential energy became actualized. There is no God out there or up there; there is no separation. Listen to the music and enjoy the dance. In this dance, the body (creation) is not responding to the music but interpreting the rhythm, the quantum perichoretic union of the music, the song, and the dance making the entire cosmos participants, the singularity expanded and it is now.

Bibliography

Ambrose. Hexameron. 1961. *The Fathers of the Church. A New Translation. Vol 42.* Translated by John Savage. Internet Archive. Accessed June 2016. http://www.ia802702.us.archive.org. PDF.

Aristotle. 2015. Time is the Measure of Change. Aristotle's Physics (Book IV, part 10-13). Accessed May 2015. http://faculty.uca.edu/rnovy/Aristotle--Time%20is%20the%20Measure.htm

Armstrong, Karen. 2005. *A Short History of Myth.* New York: Canongate.

Armstrong, Karen. 2009. "Metaphysical Mistake." The Guardian. Accessed March 2016. https://www.theguardian.com/commentisfree/belief/2009/jul/12/religion-christianity-belief-science.

Armstrong, Karen. November 7, 2005. "Karen Armstrong: Myths and the Modern World." (Transcript). NPR Radio. Accessed January 2015. http://www.npr.org/templates/transcript/transcript.php?storyId=4992705.

Augsburger, S.F. 2015. *Slices of God: Strange, Dimensional, and Fractal Perspectives on God and the Cosmos.* Kentucky: Achronos Media.

Barancik, Jill et al. 2015. "Oprah and Author Richard Rohr: The Search for Our True Self." *Super Soul Sunday.* Oprah Winfrey Network. Los Angeles, CA: OWN. February 8, 2015.

Barrs, Jerram. 2009. "Echoes of Eden." CSLewis.com. Accessed April 2015. http://www.cslewis.com/echoes-of-eden/

Bell, Rob. 2011. *Love Wins: A Book About Heaven and Hell and the Fate of Every Person Who Ever Lived.* New York: HarperOne.

Blake, William, and Geoffrey Keyes. 1908. *The Marriage of Heaven and Hell.* The Poetic Works. Accessed November 2012. http://www.bartleby.com/235/253.htm.

Bonting, Sjoerd. 2005. *Creation and Double Chaos: Science and Theology in Discussion.* Minneapolis: Fortress Press.

Borg, Marcus. 1995. *Meeting Jesus Again for the Very First Time: The*

Historical Jesus, The Heart of Contemporary Faith. San Francisco: Harper.

Borg, Marcus., and N.T. Wright. 2007. *The Meaning of Jesus: Two Visions*. San Francisco: HarperSanFrancisco.

Boyarin, Daniel.2001. "The Gospel of the Memra: Jewish Binitarianism and the Prologue of John." The Harvard Theological Review, Vol. 94, no. 3, July 1, 2001. Accessed March 2013. http://www.nes.berkeley.edu/web_Boyarin/BoyarinArticles/108 %20Gospel%20of%20the%20Memra%20(2001).pdf.

Braden, Gregg. 2003. "Oneness and the Quantum Hologram." The Spirit of Ma'at, Earth Energies. Accessed March 2016. http://www.spiritofmaat.com/archive/jul3/braden.htm#top

Braden, Gregg. 2007. *The Divine Matrix Bridging Time, Space, Miracles, and Belief.* California: Hay House Inc.

Brown, Grady. 2002,2003. *The Dayspring Bible*. Brownsville, TX: Dayspring Bible Ministries, Inc.

Brown, William P. 1999. *The Ethos and the Cosmos: The Genesis of Moral Imagination in the Bible*. Michigan: Wm. B. Eerdmans Publishing Co.

Bruno, Giordano. 2016. AZQuotes.com, Accessed May 2016. Wind and Fly LTD, 2017. http://www.azquotes.com/quote/687599.

Bultmann, Rudolf. 1955. *Theology of the New Testament*. Translated by Kendrick Grobel. New York: Charles Scribner's Sons.

Caird, G. B. 1980. *The Language and Imagery of the Bible*. Philadelphia: Westminster Press.

Campbell, John Y. 1950. *A Theological World Book*. Edited by Alan Richardson. New York: Macmillan Co.

Campbell, Joseph. 1988. *The Power of Myth with Bill Moyers*. Edited by Betty Sue Flowers. New York: Double Day.

Campbell, Joseph. 2001. *Thou Art That, Transforming Religious Metaphor*. Edited by Eugene Kennedy, PhD. California: New World Library.

Campion, Nicholas. 2012. *Astrology and Cosmology in the World's Religions*. New York: University Press.

Clark, Robert. "The Christ Mind." http://www.thechristmind.org/. PDF.

Clarke, Arthur C. 1995. "The Colors of Infinity." 53:10. Posted by Russell A. https://www.youtube.com/watch?v=pJA8mayMKvY.

Clarke, Arthur C. 1997. *3001: The Final Odyssey*. New York: Harper Collins.

Clegg, Brian. 2006. *The God Effect: Quantum Entanglement, Science's Strangest Phenomenon*. New York: St Martin's Press.

Clegg, Brian. 2012. *The Universe Inside You: The Extreme Science of the Human Body*. New York: MJF Books.

Corley, Ed. 2013. "The Framework of the Inner Man." Maschil. Accessed November 2013. http://www.maschil.com/psalms/index.php/framework-of-the-inner-man.

Cox, Brian AZQuotes.com, Wind and Fly LTD, 2017. Accessed February 2015. http://www.azquotes.com/quote/461538.

Cousins, Ewert. 1992. *Christ of the 21st Century*. Massachusetts: Element, Inc.

Crabtree, Vexen. 1999. "The Illusion of Choice: Free Will and Determinism." The Human Truth Foundation. Accessed January 2014. http://www.humantruth.info/free_will.html.

Crossan, John Dominic and Richard G. Watts. 1996. *Who is Jesus? Answers to Your Questions about the Historical Jesus*. Kentucky: Westminster John Knox Press.

Crossway Bibles. 2007. ESV: Study Bible: English standard Version. Wheaton, Ill: Crossway Bibles.

Cullmann, Oscar. 1956. "Immortality of the Soul or Resurrection of the Dead?" Accessed May 2013. http://www.religion-online.org/showbook.asp?title=1115. PDF.

Cullmann, Oscar. 1962. *Christ and Time: The Primitive Christian Concept of Time and History*. London: SCM Press LTD. PDF.

Damascene, Hieromonk. 1999. *Christ The Eternal Tao*. California: St. Herman of Alaska Brotherhood.

Davidson, John. 1989. *The Secret Creative Vacuum: Man and the Energy Dance*. England: C.W. Daniel Company.

Davies, Paul. 1988. *The Cosmic Blueprint: New Discoveries in Nature's Creative Ability to Order the Universe*. New York: Orion Productions.

Davis, John Jefferson. 2002. *The Frontier of Science and Faith: Examining Questions from the Big Bang to the End of the Universe*. Downers Grove, IL: InterVarsity Press.

Eckhart, Meister. 2016. "The Logos Continuum: The Incarnation." Stoa del Sol. Accessed October 2016.

http://www.bizint.com/stoa_del_sol/logos/index.html

Eliade, Mircea. 1963. *Myth and Reality*. New York: Harper & Row.

Eliade, Mircea. 1987. *The Sacred and the Profane, The Nature of Religion*. New York: Harcourt Inc.

Eliade, Mircea. 1991. *The Myth of Eternal Return or Cosmos and History*. Princeton: Princeton University Press.

Encyclopedia Mythica from Encyclopedia Mythica Online. 2016. "Chaos." Accessed June 2016.

http://www.pantheon.org/articles/c/chaos.html.

Fagg, Lawrence W. 1985. *The Two Faces of Time*. Illinois: Theosophical Publishing House.

Feuillett, A, 1966. *Le Christ Sagesse De Dieu d'Apres Les Pauliniennes*. (Christ, the Wisdom of God According to the Pauline Epistles.) Paris: J. Gabalda et Cie.

Fideler, David. 1993. *Jesus Christ Sun of God: Ancient Cosmology and Early Symbolism*. Illinois: Quest Books.

Fillmore, Charles. 2014. The Metaphysical Bible Dictionary. Virginia: Wilderpubs2yahoo.com.

Foundation for Inner Peace. 1992. *A Course in Miracles: Combined Volume*. Section 27 "What is Death?" CA: Foundation for Inner Peace.

Fox, Matthew. 1983. *Original Blessing; A Primer in Creation Spirituality*. New Mexico: Bear and Company.

Freke, Timothy and Peter Gandy. 2000. *The Jesus Mysteries: Was the "Original Jesus" a Pagan God?* London: HarperCollins.

Fudge, Edward. 1982. *The Fire that Consumes: A Biblical and Historical Study of Final Punishment*. Fallbrook CA: Verdict Publications.

Gaiser, Frederick J. "Paul Ricoeur's Myth of Evil in Biblical Perspective." Word and World, Vol XIX, #4. Fall 1999. Accessed June 2013. http://wordandworld.luthersem.edu/content/pdfs/19-4_god_and_evil/19-4_gaiser.pdf

Gaskell, G. A.1981. *Dictionary of All Scriptures and Myths*. New Jersey: Gramercy Books.

Gibbon, Edward. 2014. A-Z Quotes. Accessed April 2014. Wind and Fly LTD. http://azquotes.com/quote/109405.

Graham, Lloyd M. 1975. *Deception & Myths of the Bible. Is the Holy Bible Holy?* New Jersey: Bell Publishing.

Graham, Ruth. 2010. Billy Graham Evangelistic Assoc. Fear Not Tomorrow, God is Already There." Accessed April 2016. http://www.billygraham.org.

Green, Clifford J., and Michael DeJonge. 2013. *The Bonhoeffer Reader*. Minnesota: Fortress Press.

Greene, Brian. 1999. *The Elegant Universe: Superstrings, Hidden Dimensions, and the Quest for the Ultimate Theory*. New York: W.W. Norton & Company.

Greene, Brian. 2003. "The Theory of Everything." Accessed November 2016. http://www.pbs.org/wgbh/nova/physics/theory-of-everything.html.

Gregory, Andrew. 2013. *Ancient Greek Cosmogony*. London, UK: Bloomburg Academic.

Gundry, Robert. 1976. *Soma in Biblical Theology with Emphasis on Pauline Anthropology*. Cambridge: Cambridge Universiy Press.

Gunkel, Hermann. 2006. *Creation and Chaos in the Primeval Era and the Eschaton, A Religio-Historical Study of Genesis 1 and Revelation 12*. Cambridge: Eerdmans.

Haisch, Bernard. 2006. *The God Theory: Universe's Zero-Point Fields, and What's Behind It All*. San Francisco: Weiser Books.

Hands, John. 2015. *Cosmosapiens: Human Evolution from the Origin of the Universe*. New York: Overlook Press.

Hawken, Paul. 2009. "You are Brilliant and the Earth is Hiring." Yes! Magazine. Accessed June 2015.

http://www.yesmagazine.org/issues/columns/you-are-brilliant-and-the-earth-is-hiring.

Hayes, Lynn. 2012. Lake DeGray Conference. April 2012.

Hedrick, Charles. 1999. *When History and Faith Collide: Studying Jesus*. Peabody, MA: Hendrickson Publishers.

Herschel, Abraham. 1999. *God in Search of Man: A Philosophy of Judaism*. Philadelphia: Jewish Pub. Soc. Of America.

Hick, John. 1976. *Death and Eternal Life*. New York: Harper& Row Publishers.

Hillar, Marian. 2012. Internet Encyclopedia of Philosophy. "Philo of Alexandria (c. 20 B.C.E. - 40 C.E.)." Accessed November 2012. http://www.iep.utm.edu.philo/.

Hillar, Marian 2012. *From Logos to Trinity: The Evolution of Religious Beliefs from Pythagoras to Tertullian*. Cambridge:Cambridge University Press.

Hillar, Marian. 2015. "Philo of Alexandria (c. 20 BCE - 40 CE)." Internet Encyclopedia of Philosophy. Accessed October 2015. hhtp://www.iep.utm.edu/Philo/#H11.

Hunt, Marquis. 2014. "The Heavens Declare." 4th Annual Journey Into the Christ Conference. October 25, 2014. Conway, AR.

International Standard Bible Encyclopedia Online. 2013. "Death". Accessed May 2013. http://www.internationalstandardbible.com/D/death.html.Edited by James Orr, published in 1939 by Wm. B. Eerdmans Publishing Co.

Jastrow, Robert. 1977. *Until the Sun Dies*. New York: NASA, Goddard Space Institute

Jetmundsen, Norman Jr. 2005. "The Subtle Power of God and God's Antidote." Knowing and Doing. Spring 2005. C.S. Lewis Institute. Accessed August 2013. http://www.cslewisinstitute.org/The_Subtle_Power_of_Evil_and_Gods_Antidote_FullArticle1.

Johnston, Charles. 1923. "The Logos Doctrine." Universal Theosophy. December 19, 2013. Accessed June 2016.

http://www.universaltheosophy.com/articles/johnston/the-logos-doctrine.

Kant, Immanuel. 1781. *Critique of Pure Reason. 1878 Ed*. Trans by J.M. D. Meiklejohn. London: Henry G. Bohn. 1962. http://philosophy.eserver.org/Kant/Critique-of-pure-reason.txt. PDF.

Kant, Immanuel. 1962. *The Mask of God: Oriental Mythology*. New York: Viking Press.

Kaplan, Aryeh. 1997. *Sefer Yetzirah: The Book of Creation*. San Francisco: Weiser Books.

Keck, Leander E. 1969. "New Testament Views of Death." In *Perspectives on Death*, edited by Liston O. Mills, 3-98. Nashville: Abigdon Press.

Keller, Catherine. 2003. *The Face of the Deep*. A Theology of Becoming. London: Routledge Publishing.

Keller, Catherine. 2008. *On the Mystery Discerning Divinity in Process*. Minneapolis: Fortress Press.

Keller, Timothy. 2008.*The Reason for God: Belief in an Age of Skepticism*. New York: Dutton.

Kelley, Carl Franklin. 1977. *Meister Eckhart on Divine Knowledge*. New Haven: Yale University Press.

Kepnes, Steven. 2004. "Adam/Eve: From Rabbinic to Scriptural Anthropology." The Journal of Scriptural Reasoning. Accessed August 2013. http://jsr.shanti.virginia.edu/back-issues/vol-4-no-2-october-2004-the-image-of-god/adameve-from-rabbinic-to-scriptural-anthropology.

Kister, Menehem. 2007. "Tohu wa Bohu, Primordial Elements and Creatio ex Nihilo." Jewish Studies Quarterly. Vol 14, 229-256. Acedemia.edu. PDF.

Knoch, A. E. 2013. "What is Death?" The Herald of God's Grace. Accessed May 2012. http://theheraldofgodsgrace.org/Knoch/whatisdeath.htm.

Knowles, Brian. 2014. "The Hebrew Mind vs The Western Mind." Godward.org. Accessed April 2014.

http://www.godward.org/hebrew%20roots/hebrew_mind_vs_th
e_western_mind.htm.

Kohler, Kaufmann. 2012. "Immortality of the Soul (Late Hebrew,
"hasharat ha-nefesh"; "ḥayye 'olam")." Jewish Encyclopedia.com.
Accessed on November 2012.
http://www.jewishencyclopedia.com/articles/8092-immortality-
of-the-soul.

Kuhn, Alvin Boyd. 2015. *Who is This King of Glory? A Critical Study in the
Christos Messiah Tradition.*
http://www.themasonictrowel.com/ebooks/christianity/Boyd_Ku
hn_-_Who_is_this_King_of_Glory.pdf. PDF.

Kuschner, Rabbi Lawrence. 2006. *Kabbalah A Love Story.* New York:
Broadway Books.

Ladd, George Eldon. 2015. "The Johannine Dualism." Accessed
November 2015.
https://www.monergism.com/thethreshold/articles/onsite/Ladd_
Johannine.html.

Lane, Dermont A. 1975. *The Reality of Jesus, An Essay in Christology.* New
York: Paulist Press.

Lao Tzu, Laozi. 2001. *Tao Te Ching: The New Translation from Tao Te Ching:
The Definitive Edition.* New York: Tarcher.

Lao Tzu, Laozi. *The Tao Te Ching.* Ch. 25. Accessed April 2016.
http://www.with.org/tao_te_ching_en.pdf

LaPan, Kathy. June 25, 2006. "Why Christianity is Exclusive: The Only
True Religion." London, United Kingdom: Battersea Town Hall.

Larson, Alfred Martin. 1977. *The Story of Christian Origins or The Sources
and Establishment of Western Religion.* Washington: J.J. Binns.

Law, Stephen. 2007. *Visual Reference Guides: Philosophy.* New York: Metro
Books

Levenson, Jon D. 1988. *Creation and the Persistence of Evil: The Jewish
Drama of Divine Omnipotence.* San Francisco. Harper & Row.

Lorenz, Edward. 1963. "Deterministic Non-Periodic Flow." Journal of the
Atmospheric Sciences. M.I.T. Vol 20, pg 141. Accessed December
2015. http://www.journals.ametsoc.org. PDF.

Lorenz, Hendrik, "Ancient Theories of Soul", The Stanford Encyclopedia of Philosophy (Summer 2009 Edition), Edward N. Zalta (ed.), URL = <https://plato.stanford.edu/archives/sum2009/entries/ancient-soul/>.

Lyons, Craig. 2013. "Egyptian Religion and its Relationship to Judaism and Christianity." Bet Emet Ministries. Accessed November 9, 2013. https://archive.org/details/BetEmetWebsitesInPdf.

Mack, Burton. 2015. *Who Wrote the New Testament? The Making of the Christian Myth*. San Francisco:HarperOne.

Mason, Phil. 2010. *Quantum Glory: The Science of Heaven Invading Earth*. Arizona: XP Publishing.

Matai, D.K. 2011. "The God Particle, Quantum Entanglement, and the Holographic Universe." Accessed May 2016. http://www.businessinsider.com/the-god-particle-quantum-entanglement-and-the-holographic-universe-2011-4.

May, Rollo R. 1991. *The Cry for Myth*. New York: W. W. Norton & Co.

Mayers, F. J. 1948. *The Unknown God, Ain Soph*. Birmingham: Thomas's Publishing. PDF.

McLaren, Brian. 2004. *A Generous Orthodoxy*. Grand Rapids: Zondervan Pub. House.

McLaren, Brian. 2010. *A New Kind of Christianity: Ten Questions That Are Transforming the Faith*. Location 1241. New York: HarperOne.

McTaggart, Lynne. 2002. *The Field. The Quest for the Secret Force of the Universe*. New York: Harper Collins Publishers.

Melville, Hermann. 1851. *Moby Dick*. Accessed January 2016. http://www.gutenburg.org.

Meme: "You're not just one piece of the cosmos..." Waking Life. Accessed 2016. https://onsizzle.com/i/youre-not-just-one-piece-of-the-cosmos-youre-the-8598992

Mitchell, Jonathan. 2014. Jonathan Mitchell New Testament. Accessed October 2014. http//www.jonathanmitchellnewtestament.com/nt-download-apps/nt-download.

Mitchell, Jonathan. 2014. Jonathan Mitchell New Testament. Accessed

October 2015.
http//www.jonathanmitchellnewtestament.com/nt-download-apps/nt-download.

Moltmann, Jurgen. 1995. *Jesus Christ for Today's World*. Minneapolis: Fortress Press.

Myers, Jim. 2013. "Ruach: Spirit or Wind or ???" Biblical Heritage Center. Accessed April 2013.
http://www.biblicalheritagecenter.org/Bible%20Studies/ruach.htm.

Neuendorf, Andrew. 2013. "What is Mythlogy? (Part 6)". Andrew Neuendorf. July 16, 2013.
https://andrewneuendorf.com/tag/joseph-campbell/.

Niditch, Susan. 1985. *Chaos to Cosmos: Studies in Biblical Patterns of Creation*. California: Scholars Press.

Nietzsche, Friedrich. 2013. AZQuotes.com, Wind and Fly LTD. Accessed August 3, 2013. http://www.azquotes.com/quote/347280.

Nietzche, Friedrich. N.d. Beyond Good and Evil (Aphorism 153).

Nolan, Christopher, Jonathan Nolan, Emma Thomas, Lynda Rosen Obst, Matthew McConaughey, Anne Hathaway, Jessica Chastain, et al. 2015. *Interstellar*. Video

Oldmeadow, Harry. 2003. *Frithjof Schuon and the Perennial Philosophy*. Indiana: World Wisdom Publishers.

O'Murchu, Diarmuid. 2004. *Quantum Theology Spiritual Implications of the New Physics*. New York: Crossword Pub Co.

O'Murchu, Diarmuid. 2012. "Writings Toward Reconciliation." BWBlog. January 7, 2012. Posted by B. P. Weaver. http://www.abraham-ishmael.blogspot.com/2012/01/the-psychological-role-says-that-when.html.

Pannenberg, Wolfhart. 2004. *Anthropology in Theological Perspective.* Translated by Matthew J. O'Connell. Kentucky: Westminster John Knox Press.

Pascual, Arturo Marcelo. 2010. *Scriptures Sacred Writings of the World's Religions*. CT: Konecky & Konecky.

Pelikan, Jaraslov. 1999. *Jesus Through the Centuries, His Place in the History of Culture*. New Haven, CT: Yale University Press.

Pember G. H. 1971. *Earth's Earliest Ages. A Study of Vital Questions*. New Jersey: Fleming H. Revell Company.

Peters, Ted. 2000. *God--The World's Future: Systematic Theology for a New Era*. Minneapolis: Augsburg Fortress Press.

Peterson, Eugene H. 2002. *The Message: The Bible in Contemporary Language*. Colorado Springs: NavPress. Print.

Pilkington, Mark. July 17, 2003. Zero Point Energy. The Guardian.com. Accessed March 2017. www.theguardian.com/education/2003/jul/17/research.highered ucation.

Planck, Max. 1932. *Where is Science Going?* New York: W.W. Norton Company, Inc.

Ricoeur, Paul. 1967. *The Symbolism of Evil.* Boston: Beacon Press.

Robinson, H. Wheeler. 1934. *The Christian Doctrine of Man*. Edinburgh: T & T Clark.

Robinson, John A. T. 1963. *Honest to God*. London: SCM Press LTD.

Rosado, Caleb. 2000. "What is Spirituality? Memetics, Quantum Mechanics, and the Spiral of Spirituality." Accessed April 2017. http://www.rosado.net/pdf/What_Is_Spirituality_.pdf.

Ross, Kelly L. 2002. "Myth, Religion, and Philosophy." Accessed March 2014. http://www.friesian.com/myth.htm.

Rotherham, Joseph Bryant. 1994. *Rotherham's Emphasized Bible*. Grand Rapids, MI: Kregel Publications

Rowling, J. K. 2004. Edinburgh Book Festival. Gutenberg.org. Accessed 2016. http://self.gutenberg.org/articles/eng/Abracadabra.

Sacred Texts. 2014. ben Jochai, Rabbi Simeon. The Book of Light. Ben Jochai, Rabbi Simeon. Accessed July 2014. http://www.sacred-texts.com/jud/zdm/zdm010.htm

Sagan, Carl. 2015. Good Reads. Accessed January 2016. http://www.goodreads.com/quotes/604655/cosmos-is-a-greek-word-for-the-order-of-the-universe.

Sanford, John. 1994. *Mystical Christianity: A Psychological Commentary on the Gospel of John*. New York: Crossroad Publishing Co.

Schroeder, Gerald L. 2001. *The Hidden Face of God: How Science Reveals the Ultimate Truth.* New York: Free Press.

Schucman, Helen Dr. 1992. *A Course in Miracles.* California: Foundation for Inner Peace.

Sire, James. 2009. *The Universe Next Door: A Basic World View Catalog.* Downers Grove IL: InterVarsity Press.

Smoley, Richard. 2002. *Inner Christianity: A Guide to the Esoteric Tradition.* Boston MA: Shambhala.

Smolin, Lee. 1997. *The Life of the Cosmos.* New York: Oxford Univ. Press.

Spong, Bishop Shelby. 2000. *A New Christianity for A New World: Why Traditional Faith is Dying and What Should Take its Place.* San Francisco: Harper San Francisco.

Spong, Bishop Shelby. 2001. *Resurrection Myth or Reality.* New York: Harper Collins World.

Spong, John Shelby. June 15, 2005. "Q&A On Biblical Criticism, Weekly Mailing." JohnShelbySpong.com Accessed March 2013. RSS. http://www.johnshelbyspong.com.

Starr, Karen. 2016. Karen Starr's Facebook page, accessed November 29, 2016. https://www.facebook.com/profile.php?id=100005463275914.

Stace, W. T. 1934. "A Critical History of Greek Philosophy." Internet Archive. Accessed June 2013. http://www.archive.org/details/acriticalhistory33411gut. PDF.

Stewart, R. J. 1989. *The Elements of Creation Myth.* Shaftesbury (Dorset): Element.

Super Soul Sunday. "Oprah and *The Shack* Author William Paul Young on the Lies He Says We Believe." Season 8 Episode 801. July 9, 2017. http://www.oprah.com/app/super-soul-sunday.html.

Swimme, Brian. 1996. *The Hidden Heart of the Cosmos, Humanity and the New Story.* New York: Orbis Books.

Symons, Barbara. 2013. *Escaping Christianity: Finding Christ.* Barbara Symons.

Talbot, Michael. 2011.*The Holographic Universe.* New York: Harper Perennial.

Talbot, Michael. 2006. "The Holographic Universe. Does Objectivity Really Exist?" Accessed May 2016. http://www.rense.com/general69/holoff.htm.

The Babylonian Talmud. The Talmud. Accessed March 2012.http://www.sacred-texts.com/jud/talmud.htm. Rabbi Shemuel ben Nachmani, as quoted in the Talmudic tractate Berakhot.

The Hexaemeron. 2016. Accessed January 2016. http://www.elpenor.org/basil/hexaemeron.asp?pg=15.

The Interpreter's Dictionary of the Bible. 1952. Edited by George A. Butterick. Tennessee: Abingdon Press. https://ia800406.us.archive.org/30/items/interpretersbibl028041mbp/interpretersbibl028041mbp.pdf

The Original Aramaic New Testament in Plain English with Psalms & Proverbs (8th Ed). Accessed March 2014. http://biblehub.com/aramaic-plain-english/psalms/33.htm.

The Voice. 2011. Thomas Nelson. Bible Gateway. Accessed 2013. https://www.biblegateway.com/passage/?search=psalm+19&version=VOICE.

The Ways of Hermes. New Translations of The Corpus Hermeticum and The Definitions of Hermes Trismegistus to Asclepius. Translated by Clement Salaman, et al. Vermont: Inner Traditions.

This Day in History. 2009. "Earthquake Causes Fluvial Tsunami in Mississippi." Accessed September 2016. http://www.history.com/this-day-in-history/earthquake-causes-fluvial-tsunami-in-mississippi.

Thompson, Robert V. 2017. "Christ Not a Person." SBNR.com. Accessed July 2017. http//www.sbnr.org/Christ-of-the-21st-century-a-power-not-a-person.html. Review of Christ of the 21st Century by Ewert H. Cousins. Mass: Element, Inc.

Tolle, Eckhart. 1999. The Power of Now. A Guide to Spiritual Enlightenment. California: New World Library

Tolle, Eckhart. 2005. A New Earth Awakening to Your Life's Purpose. New York: Penguin Group.

Tolle, Eckhart. 2016. Symphony of Love. Accessed February 2016. http://lovequotes.symphonyoflove.net/eckhart-tolle-love-quotes-and-sayings.html

Trismegistus, Hermes. 2015. The Corpus Hermeticum. Translated by Marsillo Ficino. Sacred Texts. Accessed October 2015. http://www.sacred-texts.com/chr/herm.

Trismegistus, Hermes. 2013. The Emerald Tablet of Hermes Trismegistus. New York: Merchant Books. Digitized Book 2013.

Tsumura, David. 1989. *The Earth and the Waters in Genesis 1 & 2: A Linguistic Investigation*. England: Sheffield Academic Press. PDF.

Vail, Eric M. 2009. "Using 'Chaos' in Articulating the Relationship of God and Creation in God's Creative Activity." PhD diss., Marquette University. Http://www.epublications.marquette.edu/dissertation_mu5.

Vine, W. E. 1985. *An Expository Dictionary of Biblical Words*. Nashville: Nelson.

Wachowski, Andy, Larry Wachowski. 1999. The Matrix. Burbank, CA: Warner Home Video.

Walton, John. 2009. *The Lost World of Genesis One. Ancient Cosmology and the Origins Debate*. Madison, WI: Intervarsity Press.

Ward, Keith. 2013. *Pascal's Fire. Scientific Faith and Religious Understanding*. London, UK: Oneworld Publications. https://books.google.com/books?isbn=1780744587.

Warren, Janet. 2011. "Chaos and Chaos-Complexity Theory: Understanding Evil Forces with Insights from Contemporary Science and Linguistics." American Scientific Affiliation. Vol 63, No 4, 12-2011. Accessed December 2015. http://www.asa3.org/asa/pscf/2011/pscf-12-warren. PDF.

Waskow, Arthur Rabbi. 2004. "Why Yah/Yhwh." The Shalom Center. Accessed August 2014. https://theshalomcenter.org/content/why-yahyhwh

Watts, Alan B. 1968. *Myth and Ritual in Christianity*. Boston: Beacon Press.

Watts, Alan B. Alan Watts Quote. A-Z Quotes. Accessed June 2014. Wind and Fly Ltd. Http://www.azquotes.com/quote/308447.

Weinert, Friedel. 2013. *The March of Time: Evolving Conceptions of Time in the Light of Scientific Discoveries*. New York: Springer--Verlab Berlin Heidelberg.

Weiss, Harald. 2003. "The Golden Mean as Clock Cycle of Brain Waves." Chaos, Solitons, and Fractals. March 12, 2003. http://www.v-weiss.de/chaossolitonsfractals.pdf.

West, Brandon. 2014. "Is Anything Really Moving? The Unified Field and the Illusion of Time." Accessed April 2016. http://www.wakingtimes.com/2014/04/21/unified-field-illusion-time-understanding-source-creation.

West, Robert W. 2011. "A Resurrection to Immortality: The Resurrection, Our Only Hope of Life after Death." Accessed on July 2012. https://www.sats.edu.za/userfiles/A-Resurrection-To-Immortality.pdf.

Wheeler, John. 2017. Strange Wondrous.net. Accessed May 2017. http//www.strangewondrous.net/browse/author/w/wheeler+john/start=21.

Wigner, Eugene. "Information Philosopher." Accessed May 13, 2017. http://www.informationphilosopher.com/solutions/scientists/wigner.

Wikipedia contributors, "Maya (illusion)," *Wikipedia, The Free Encyclopedia,* https://en.wikipedia.org/w/index.php?title=Maya_(illusion)&oldid=804007978 (accessed April 12, 2015).

Wikipedia contributors, "Religion and Mythology," *Wikipedia, The Free Encyclopedia.* https://en.wikipedia.org/w/index.php?title=Religion_and_mythology&oldid=807802118 (accessed April 2015).

Wolf, Fred Alan. 1989. *Taking the Quantum Leap*. New York: Harper & Row.

Wong, John B. 2002. *Christian Wholism: Theological and Ethical Implications in the Post-Modern World*. Landam, MD: University Press of America.

World Wisdom. 2015. "The Central Idea of the Perennial Philosophy." A

Definition of Perennial Philosophy. Accessed March 2015. http://www.worldwisdom.com/public/slideshows/view.aspx?Sli deShowID=41&SlideDetailID=373.

Wright, N. T. 1980. "Foreword." Foreword. In book *The Language and Imagery of the Bible* by G. B. Caird. xxii. Philadelphia: Westminster Press.

Young, William P. 2007. *The Shack: Where Tragedy Confronts Eternity.* Newbury Park, CA: Windblown Media.

Zeyl, Donald. 2013. The Stanford Encyclopedia of Philosophy (Spring 2013 Ed.). "Plato's Timaeus." Edited by Edward N. Zalta. Accessed November 2013. http://plato.stanford.edu/archives/spring 2013/entries/plato-timaeus/>.

ABOUT THE AUTHOR

Michael Clegg has been involved with Biblical and Religious studies since his early teens. He, being a passionate reader, chose to read the books you were warned not to read. Those texts usually offered a different way of understanding God and the ideas of the Sacred. *The Cosmogonical Cipher* may well be one of those books also.

He holds a BS in Biology and a BA in Theology. He works in the healthcare industry in the clinical laboratory.

49590619R10197

Made in the USA
Middletown, DE
20 June 2019